Praise for *The Art of Managing Professional Services*

"Maureen Broderick offers a comprehensive and insightful look at the professional service discipline by zeroing in on one key question: 'What do the best firms do?'"
—**Jim Quigley**, CEO, Deloitte Touche Tohmatsu Limited

"Leading and managing professional service firms is more art than science. It is an arena where judgment, intuition, energy, a thick skin, and keeping balance at all times are critical factors for success—particularly given the unusually high intellect, super-sized egos, and mobility of those whom you lead, most often at their discretion. Of all the books I have read on the professional service industry, Maureen Broderick has best captured the very essence of those best practices which have enabled some of the industry's most successful firms to prosper and grow."
—**Joe Griesedieck**, Vice Chairman, Korn/Ferry International

"This book provides invaluable insight into what makes professional service firms successful. It will change every person into a better leader. Plus it provides real-life examples that are fun to read."
—**Ed Nusbaum**, CEO, Grant Thornton International Ltd.

"By uncovering the various paths to success that these diverse professional service firms have taken, the reader develops his or her own ideas on how to navigate the professional service terrain. *The Art of Managing Professional Services* is a valuable source for these insights into firm strategies."
—**Evan Chesler**, Presiding Partner, Cravath, Swaine & Moore

"This is a book about entrepreneurial leadership…looking under the hood of the 'best in class' professional service firms' vision and culture. The book captures what makes service organizations tick as successful global leaders. The takeaways are fantastic!"
—**Andy Cohen**, Co-CEO, Gensler

"Edelman enhanced its quality program to help manage the company's rapid diversification and globalization. Maureen Broderick's insights into building high-performance firms would have made our transition smoother and faster."
—**Richard Edelman**, President and CEO, Edelman

"Broderick's research has revealed the views and practices of some of the world's top professional firms, presented in an easily absorbed style. Very informative."
—**David Maister**, author of *Managing the Professional Service Firm* and *Strategy and the Fat Smoker*

"Maureen Broderick's book, *The Art of Managing Professional Services*, provides a valuable contribution to the very limited body of knowledge on managing professional service firms. These firms are simply very different than other corporate structures, and successfully managing them requires a very different approach. Maureen's insights from her research and interviews provide a very useful understanding of the subtleties of managing these institutions."
—**Bob Dell**, Chairman and Managing Partner, Latham & Watkins

"Maureen Broderick distills the art of firm management into clear, concise practices through candid insight and perspective from leaders of the world's most prestigious firms. Every professional service partner—and aspiring partner—should read this book."

—**Paul Laudicina**, Managing Officer and Chairman of the Board, A.T. Kearney

"High praise for Maureen Broderick and *The Art of Managing Professional Services*. Maureen has bridged from the principles to the pragmatic in exploring the key drivers of firm success. In so doing, her analysis reflects the lessons of many—both in successes and failures—and presents a thorough compendium for today's and tomorrow's leaders. This analysis gives leaders a leg up in competing on the global landscape."

—**James Turley**, Chairman and CEO, Ernst & Young

"Broderick delivers more valuable insights per page than any business book that I have read in recent memory."

—**Geoff Smart**, Chairman & CEO of ghSMART and coauthor of *The New York Times* bestseller *Who: The A Method for Hiring*

"I wish I had had Maureen Broderick's new book when I cofounded Peppercom 15 years ago. It's quite simply the best 'how to' book on the subject of managing a professional service firm I've ever read and should be mandatory reading for the leaders of today and tomorrow."

—**Steve Cody**, Co-Founder and Managing Partner, Peppercom

"In contrast to manufacturing companies which are identified by their output, professional service firms are defined by their essence—their leadership, culture, and values. Maureen Broderick brings shape and clarity to the vital, but abstract, essence of professional service firms, and she insightfully captures what makes them successful."

—**Ralph Shrader**, Chairman and Chief Executive Officer, Booz Allen Hamilton

"Too many business books take 300 pages to do no more than espouse one or two theories. This work is not like that. There is a lot here, and I think anyone involved in the management of a professional service firm will find real value here."

—**David Childs**, Global Managing Partner, Clifford Chance

"By their very nature, professional service firms must excel at employee and client engagement—the best ones always have; it is their lifeblood. In today's hyper-competitive business world, for any business of any type to win, engagement is more important than ever. Broderick's book is filled with best practices that will help all kinds of companies—whether they are professional service firms or not—meet the challenges of doing business in the 21st century and come out on top."

—**Ray Kotcher**, Senior Partner and Chief Executive Officer, Ketchum

The Art of Managing Professional Services

Insights from Leaders of the
World's Top Firms

Maureen Broderick

Vice President, Publisher: Tim Moore
Associate Publisher and Director of Marketing: Amy Neidlinger
Wharton Editor: Steve Kobrin
Executive Editor: Jeanne Glasser
Editorial Assistant: Pamela Boland
Operations Manager: Gina Kanouse
Senior Marketing Manager: Julie Phifer
Publicity Manager: Laura Czaja
Assistant Marketing Manager: Megan Colvin
Cover Designer: Chuti Prasertsith
Managing Editor: Kristy Hart
Project Editor: Anne Goebel
Copy Editor: Gayle Johnson
Proofreader: Williams Woods Publishing Services
Indexer: Rebecca Salerno
Compositor: Mary Sudul
Manufacturing Buyer: Dan Uhrig

© 2011 by Maureen Broderick
Publishing as Wharton School Publishing
Upper Saddle River, New Jersey 07458

Wharton School Publishing offers excellent discounts on this book when ordered in quantity for bulk purchases or special sales. For more information, please contact U.S. Corporate and Government Sales, 1-800-382-3419, corpsales@pearsontechgroup.com. For sales outside the U.S., please contact International Sales at international@pearson.com.

Printed in the United States of America

First Printing November 2010

ISBN-10 0-13-704252-3
ISBN-13 978-0-13-704252-4

Pearson Education LTD.
Pearson Education Australia PTY, Limited.
Pearson Education Singapore, Pte. Ltd.
Pearson Education Asia, Ltd.
Pearson Education Canada, Ltd.
Pearson Educación de Mexico, S.A. de C.V.
Pearson Education—Japan
Pearson Education Malaysia, Pte. Ltd.

Library of Congress Cataloging-in-Publication Data:

Broderick, Maureen, 1949-
  The art of managing professional services : insights from leaders of the world's top firms / Maureen Broderick.
    p. cm.
  ISBN-13: 978-0-13-704252-4 (hardback : alk. paper)
  ISBN-10: 0-13-704252-3
  1. Professional employees. 2. Personnel management. I. Title.
  HD8038.A1B758 2011
  658--dc22
                          2010024569

This book is dedicated to my husband David and my children, Emily, Daniel, and Bridget. Thank you for your love and support.

Contents

Lessons from Leaders

Foreword

by Jay Lorsch

Successfully managing a professional service firm is indeed an art—as the title of this book suggests—as well as a science.

In the 15 years that I have chaired Harvard Business School's continuing education program, "Leading Professional Services," I have had the pleasure of meeting thousands of senior leaders of professional service firms of all sizes and sectors and across geographies. During these many years of teaching, writing, and consulting on firm management, I have developed a great deal of respect for this fascinating industry with its unique structure and governance style, highly talented professionals, and passionate focus on client service.

As Maureen Broderick states in her book, leading a professional service firm is not a job for the faint of heart. Keeping a firm of independently minded, highly intelligent professionals united and focused on firm goals and strategy requires a delicate balance between structure and autonomy and a unique leadership style.

A handful of levers are critical to building and managing a prosperous professional service firm: talent acquisition, development, and retention; client and services management; strategic thinking; infrastructure design and governance style; equity and compensation; and financial planning and oversight. To work effectively, all of these important management areas of focus must be aligned with the firm's vision, values, and culture which ultimately form the core around which all decisions are measured.

But alignment around vision and values, even for the best-run firms, is not easy in a professional service firm with many owners, diverse practices and services, and sometimes multiple geographies. The environment in which firms operate is fluid and dynamic. Clients and professionals move in and out of the organization, service needs and preferences change, new competitors enter the market, and the economy fluctuates—sometimes violently, as we have certainly witnessed in the first decade of this century. All of these events can trigger the need for organizational adjustments and sometimes fundamental restructuring. As Tom Tierney and I described in our 2002 book, *Aligning the Stars*, staying on course and in alignment in the midst of change is a tough job for firm leaders.

The Art of Managing Professional Services presents a framework for professional service management that addresses the top areas of focus that firm leaders must monitor to build and maintain a strong organization. The book distills insights, practices, and recommendations from leaders of some of the best-run firms in the business. While there are unfortunately no "one-size-fits-all" best practices or processes for managing a successful firm, you will take away some tangible ideas to adopt and incorporate into your own unique business and culture.

Broderick and her research team have done an excellent job of capturing both the philosophy and the nuts and bolts of professional service firm management. This book is an important contribution to the industry and will undoubtedly remain on all of our shelves as a continuous reference and guide.

Jay Lorsch is the program chair of Harvard Business School's professional service programs and is widely recognized as one of the world's leading authorities on professional services. He is the author of more than a dozen books, including Aligning the Stars: How to Succeed When Professionals Drive Results *(with Thomas J. Tierney, former head of Bain, Harvard Business School Press, 2002). As a consultant, he has worked with some of the world's leading companies and financial institutions, including many global professional service firms.*

Acknowledgments

Most major research-based books take years to develop and write, but thanks to my highly skilled, all-women core team, we were able to turn this book around in 16 months, undoubtedly a record somewhere.

The anchors of our team are my colleagues, Carol McAvoy and Laura Scheflow, without whom this study and book would not have been conceived, let alone completed. Together, the three of us conducted over 130 in-depth interviews with professional service firm leaders around the globe—sometimes on major holidays and sometimes in the middle of the night. All of these interviews had to be captured, processed, and sorted by topic and segment before we could even begin to think about the arduous task of synthesizing and analyzing the hundreds of hours of interview content and 1,000-plus pages of data. The three of us spent many months discussing and prioritizing content and outlining each chapter. Both of them have read and edited every word more times than they would like to remember. Together, Carol and Laura contributed more than 5,000 hours of their time to this project while continuing to manage our ongoing client assignments.

The third member of our team is my wonderful assistant, Lynn Purcell, who provided countless hours of support by scheduling and rescheduling interviews, repeatedly typing and editing the 60,000-plus words in the book, designing every chart and graph, and performing support functions too numerous to mention.

The actual writing of this book was a daunting task, and I am forever grateful to our talented business writer and colleague, Karin Abarbanel, who provided copywriting, editorial, and moral support throughout the project.

Special thanks go to our intrepid salesperson, Dianne Turner, who called and persuaded many of our 130 interviewees to participate in the study; our faithful University of California, Berkeley intern, Karolina Tekiela, who entered massive numbers of transcripts into our survey database; and to our honorary team member, Fred

Conta, Broderick & Company CFO, who provided behind-the-scenes support and encouragement.

We were very fortunate to receive early guidance from a group of senior industry leaders who critiqued our research topics and questions and served as the initial "test runs" for our interviews. Our advisory panel included Bill Achtmeyer, Chairman and Managing Partner, The Parthenon Group; Bruce Boulware, retired Chief Operating Officer, O'Melveny & Myers; David Dotlich, Founder and Chairman, Pivot Leadership; Mike Elzey, Senior Vice President, Black & Veatch Management Consulting; Karole Lloyd, Vice Chair and Managing Partner of the Southeast of the U.S. Ernst & Young firm; Phil Rohrbaugh, Vice Chair of the U.S. firm and Managing Partner, Chicago Office, KPMG; Geoff Smart, Chairman and CEO, ghSMART; and Reggie Van Lee, Executive Vice President, Booz Allen Hamilton. Special thanks to Jay Lorsch, Program Chair for Harvard Business School's executive education programs for professional service firms, who wrote the Foreword to this book.

As my official first outsider reader, Nancy Siegel, former management consultant and law firm executive director, invested many hours reading chapter drafts and offering excellent suggestions on content and structure as did Mike Denkensohn, Executive Director, Seward & Kissel; Jim Lang, Chairman, MedPanel, and former President of CERA and SDG; and Paul Reilly, CEO, Raymond James.

We are particularly indebted to those firms and their leaders who, in addition to participating in our interviews, agreed to be featured in the Lessons from Leaders included throughout the book: Paul Laudicina and Doug MacDonald from A.T. Kearney; Russ Hagey, Steven Tallman, and Wendy Miller from Bain & Company; Mike Elzey from Black & Veatch Management Consulting; Tom Stewart from Booz & Company; Ralph Shrader, Reggie Van Lee, and Marie Lerch from Booz Allen Hamilton; Rick Powell from Burson-Marsteller; David Childs and Amanda Burton from Clifford Chance; Evan Chesler and Deborah Farone from Cravath, Swaine & Moore; Lem Lasher from CSC; Jim Quigley, Jerry Leamon, Giam Swiegers, John Kerr, Cathy Benko, and John Hagel from Deloitte; Ron Ewing and Leslie Keelty from Dewberry; Richard Edelman and Janice Rotchstein from Edelman; Damien O'Brien from Egon Zehnder

International; Jim Turley, Mark Gaumond, Karole Lloyd, Steve Almassy, and David O'Brien from the Ernst & Young organization; Donna Murphy from Euro RSCG Life; Alan Jenkins from Eversheds; Andy Cohen from Gensler; Geoff Smart and Ron Zoibi from ghSMART; Brad Robbins from Hildebrandt Baker Robbins; Ed Nusbaum from Grant Thornton International Ltd., and Brad Wilson and Tamara Smith from Grant Thornton's U.S. member firm; Matt Levin from Hewitt; Joe Griesedieck and Linda Hyman from Korn/Ferry International; Tim Flynn, Phil Rohrbaugh, and Pat Dolan from KPMG; Bob Dell, LeeAnn Black, and Despina Kartson from Latham & Watkins; Marcia Silverman from Ogilvy Public Relations Worldwide; A.B. Culvahouse and Bruce Boulware from O'Melveny & Myers; Steve Cody from Peppercom; Bill Hermann and Chris McCoy from Plante & Moran; Eric Friedman and Sally Feldman from Skadden, Arps; and Andrew Grech from Slater & Gordon.

In addition to these firms and participants, we would like to thank all the firm leaders who spent several hours of their very busy time on the phone with us, sharing their insights on the art of professional service management. They include David Morley from Allen & Overy; Mike Goss from Bain Capital; Steve Harty from BBH; Steve Gunby and Dave Fondiller from The Boston Consulting Group; Allen Friedman and Thomas Mackiewicz from Celerant Consulting; Tom Finegan from Clarkston Consulting; Donna Imperato from Cohn & Wolfe; James Burrows from Charles River Associates; Rafael Fontana from Cuatrecasas, Gonçalves Pereira; Frank Burch and Jay Jeffcoat from DLA Piper; Brett Marschke from Duff & Phelps; Dan Merlino from ECG Management Consultants; Peter Devlin from Fish & Richardson; Ted Burke from Freshfields; Dave Senay from Fleishman-Hillard; Rich Silverstein from Goodby, Silverstein; Clark Manus from Heller Manus Architects; Brad Hildebrandt from Hildebrandt Baker Robbins; Colin Hill and Richard Hickson from Hill & Associates; Craig Beale from HKS; Clark Davis from HOK; Scott Adelson and Scott Beiser from Houlihan Lokey; Roger Banks from Incite; Michael Broshar from Invision; Michael Lotito from Jackson Lewis; Lauralee Martin from Jones Lang LaSalle; Ray Kotcher from Ketchum; Allen Adamson from Landor Associates; Carter Brown from Major, Lindsey & Africa; Jim McTaggart from Marakon; Kathleen Reichert from Mayer Brown; Brett Gosper from

McCann Worldgroup; Rajat Gupta from McKinsey; Jim Lang from MedPanel; Bradley Mallory from Michael Baker Corporation; Joe Fuller from Monitor Group; Don Rushing from Morrison & Foerster; Bill Nichols from NBBJ; Carla Hendra from Ogilvy & Mather; Stephen Rhinesmith from Oliver Wyman; Ralph Baxter from Orrick; David McGrane from Ozone Advertising; Bill Achtmeyer from The Parthenon Group; Ben Fisher from Perkins+Will; Andrew Duff from Piper Jaffray; David Dotlich from Pivot Leadership; Dennis Nally, Sheldon Laube, Keith Wishon, and Mitra Best from PwC; Paul Reilly from Raymond James; Mike Denkensohn from Seward & Kissel; Carl Roehling from SmithGroup; Milo Riverso from STV; Bob Gomes from Stantec; Rodge Cohen and Sergio Galvis from Sullivan & Cromwell; Amy Freedman from Thomas Weisel Partners; Rick Dreher and Ulrike Harrison from Wipfli; and Peter Stringham from Young & Rubicam Brands.

I would also like to thank Tony Angel, Peter Horowitz, Bill Pace, Chris Pierce-Cook, and Chris Williams for sharing their professional service firm management expertise.

Special thanks to my very professional agent Leanne Sindell who guided me through this journey and to my invaluable legal advisor Ellen Stiefler for her expert counsel.

Finally, I am deeply thankful for my great good fortune to have met and married David Thompson. He has been my best friend and my base for over thirty years. And I can't imagine life without my three wonderful children, Emily, Daniel, and Bridget, who have taught me to have faith, laugh, and "chill."

About the Author

Maureen Broderick, founder and CEO of Broderick & Company, has spent 30 years directing strategic market development programs for many of the world's leading professional service firms. She held in-house marketing director positions with Price Waterhouse, Booz Allen Hamilton, Brobeck, Phleger & Harrison, and SRI International before launching her own professional service industry consulting firm in 1996. For more information about Maureen Broderick, go to www.broderickco.com.

Introduction

The influence and clout of the professional service industry are immense. It would be difficult to find a business, government, or nonprofit organization that doesn't rely to some extent on a mix of external professional service providers. Behind every successful global company you will undoubtedly find a team of outside experts who all play a role—sometimes a pivotal one—in supporting that company throughout its history.

With 2010 revenues estimated at close to $2 trillion and a conservative average annual growth rate of 10 percent over the past three decades, the industry is one of the fastest-growing sectors in the world. Accounting, advertising, architecture, consulting, engineering, executive search, financial services, law, marketing, public relations, real estate, research, staffing, and a host of other knowledge-based workers who provide advice and support to businesses are included under the enormous professional service umbrella. The industry employs roughly 20 million people who work in over one million individual firms that range in size from one-person businesses to the Big Four global accountancies that collectively employ over 500,000 professionals.

Yet, despite its enormous size and influence, the professional service industry remains largely invisible to most people. Most professional service firms are privately held businesses, managed for the benefit of their partner-owners. They prefer to work behind the scenes and let their clients take credit for their work. The industry has never been subjected to the same level of scrutiny facing most other sectors. Wall Street analysts don't follow them, business reporters typically don't write about them, and the sector has never been included in any major market research studies by popular business gurus. Only rarely does a professional service provider make the headlines, as was the case with now-defunct accounting firm Arthur Andersen and the Enron debacle.

This almost-clandestine nature of the industry is unfortunate for two reasons. First, professionals in the industry have very few places where they can turn for advice and best practices on how to run their business. Segment- and region-specific trade groups gather and share financial benchmarks and management tips and tools from their memberships, but only a few academic institutions, such as the Harvard Business School, Oxford University's Saïd Business School, and the Cass Business School, City University London, have provided a forum for industry leaders across segments and geographies to study and share ideas.

Second, the general business world can learn a lot from professional services. Ten years ago Peter Drucker predicted that leadership in the world economic scene would shift to the countries and industries that have most successfully deployed knowledge workers. Professional services are, of course, the quintessential knowledge-based businesses. Most business and management gurus spent a good portion of the 20th century improving the systemization and productivity of manual labor. In contrast, professional service firms have been perfecting a business model that attracts, nurtures, and retains the best and brightest knowledge workers. Plus, as the old-fashioned mass-marketing and sales transaction models of the last century are replaced by customer-focused product development and relationship-based selling, who better to turn to than the masters of customization and client relationships? Professional service firms, with their talent savvy, fluid service structures, and relationship management know-how, are in many ways the model for the company of the future.

There are several compelling reasons why everyone in professional services and in the general business world should read this book:

- *A comprehensive study of the industry.* Based on more than 130 in-depth interviews with leaders of professional service firms across seven major segments, this book offers an in-depth, behind-the-scenes look at this major global sector.

- *Management insights from the best in the business.* The lineup of firms and professionals who participated in the study reads like a "who's who" of professional services. The Broderick research team spent hundreds of hours with the senior leadership of these impressive businesses, all of whom were extremely candid and generous with their time and insights.
- *Tangible, practical takeaways.* So many business books admire the problems without offering any practical, concrete solutions. This book includes 40 featured "Lessons from Leaders" detailing management practices developed and successfully deployed in some of the world's most respected professional service firms. Firm leaders can shop through these practices and select programs, or components of programs, to tailor and adapt to their organizations.

The Research

Since our goal was to learn from the best, it was important that the firms we interviewed met three basic criteria. First, they needed to be acknowledged and respected by their peers. Because of our many years of work in the industry, we knew which firms were the leaders in each segment. But we confirmed our choices by reviewing the top-rated firms as defined by measures such as top revenue, most prestigious, and best place to work. These organizations were cited by trade associations, independent rating companies, and publications such as *Vault*, *Fortune*, and *BusinessWeek*.

The lineup of firms studied represents many of the top brand names in professional services, as shown in Exhibit I.1. Of the segments studied, consulting is the largest and most amorphous and represents the greatest percentage of interviews, as shown in Exhibit I.2. The consulting umbrella includes numerous subsegments, from the broad category of management consulting to narrower functional areas of focus such as human resources, operations, IT, marketing, business advisory services, and strategy. It also includes firms that focus exclusively on a single industry.

EXHIBIT I.1   Participating Firms

ACCOUNTING
Deloitte
Ernst & Young
Grant Thornton
KPMG
Plante & Moran
PwC
Wipfli

**ADVERTISING/PR/
RESEARCH**
BBH
Burson-Marsteller
Cohn & Wolfe
Edelman
Euro RSCG Life
Fleishman-Hillard
Goodby, Silverstein
Incite
Ketchum
Landor Associates
McCann Worldgroup
MedPanel
Ogilvy & Mather
Ogilvy Public Relations
    Worldwide
Ozone Advertising
Peppercom
Young & Rubicam Brands

**ARCHITECTURE/
ENGINEERING**
Black & Veatch
Dewberry
Gensler
Heller Manus Architects
HKS
HOK
Invision
Michael Baker Corporation
NBBJ
Perkins+Will
SmithGroup
Stantec
STV

CONSULTING
A.T. Kearney
Bain & Company
Booz & Company
Booz Allen Hamilton
The Boston Consulting
    Group
Celerant Consulting
Clarkston Consulting
Charles River Associates
CSC
ECG Management
    Consultants
ghSMART
Hewitt Associates
Hildebrandt Baker Robbins
Hill & Associates
Jones Lang LaSalle
Marakon
McKinsey & Company
Monitor Group
Oliver Wyman
The Parthenon Group
Pivot Leadership

EXECUTIVE SEARCH
Egon Zehnder
    International
Korn/Ferry International
Major, Lindsey & Africa

FINANCIAL SERVICES
Bain Capital
Duff & Phelps
Houlihan Lokey
Piper Jaffray
Raymond James
Thomas Weisel Partners

LAW
Allen & Overy
Clifford Chance
Cravath, Swaine & Moore
Cuatrecasas, Gonçalves
    Pereira
DLA Piper
Eversheds
Fish & Richardson
Freshfields
Jackson Lewis
Latham & Watkins
Mayer Brown
Morrison & Foerster
O'Melveny & Myers
Orrick
Seward & Kissel
Skadden, Arps
Slater & Gordon
Sullivan & Cromwell

EXHIBIT I.2 Interviewees by segment

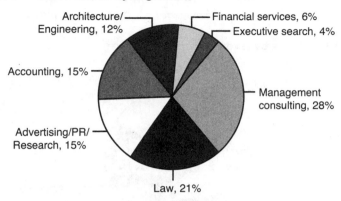

Architecture/ Engineering, 12%

Financial services, 6%

Executive search, 4%

Accounting, 15%

Management consulting, 28%

Advertising/PR/ Research, 15%

Law, 21%

Second, the firms interviewed had to be in business for a decent length of time—in fact, the older the better. We wanted to study firms that had survived a downturn or two, and, even more impressive, had survived beyond their founding fathers. As shown in Exhibit I.3, 84 percent of our responding firms are more than 50 years old, and 28 percent are more than 100—certainly a decent survival rate for any business.

EXHIBIT I.3 Length of time in business

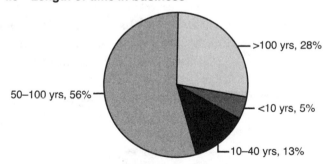

>100 yrs, 28%

50–100 yrs, 56%

<10 yrs, 5%

10–40 yrs, 13%

Finally, the firms studied had to be financially successful. Most professional service firms are privately held businesses, so financial data is not readily available. Although all of our interviewees volunteered their top-line revenue numbers, we do not know, nor did we ask, for bottom-line profitability numbers or percentages. We viewed compliance with our first two criteria as evidence of financial stability. The top-brand firms in the business typically translate into the highest revenue generators. As a result, many of the firms we studied fall into the top revenue brackets in the industry. However, we also spoke to a selection of superbly managed small businesses that range in size from $5 million to $100 million in revenue, as shown in Exhibit I.4.

EXHIBIT I.4   Firms by revenue

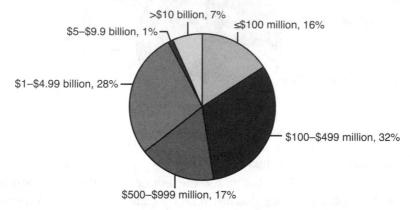

We interviewed the leaders of each organization, which included the chairmen, CEOs, and managing partners, as well as a mix of COOs; regional, service, or industry leaders; and nonbillable department heads in finance, marketing, and talent management. Typically, the chairman, CEO, or managing partner was the first in his or her organization to be interviewed, followed by others in the firm who were recommended for follow-up discussions. Sixty-two percent of our interviewees were the top leaders of their organization—chairman, CEO, or managing partner—as shown in Exhibit I.5.

EXHIBIT I.5   Interviewees by title

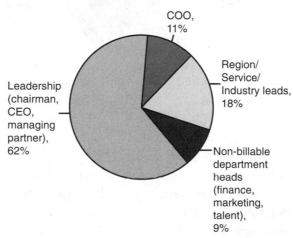

Chapter Guide

This book discusses some of the keys to firm management that emerged from our interviews. Chapter 1 presents an overview of industry characteristics, both good and not so good, and introduces the Broderick PSF Leadership Model which introduces the ten areas of focus for professional service firm leadership that formed the basis of our research. Chapters 2 through 10 discuss each area of focus in the model and present profiles of best practices uncovered during the course of our interviews. Chapter 11 explores the elusive subject of leadership. It features insights and musings from our interviewees on what it takes to be a successful leader of "incredibly smart and independent people" in the challenging and demanding world of professional services.

If you're a professional in the industry, you will enjoy reading the direct quotes from your colleagues on various aspects of the business. On a practical note, you will take away many good ideas and practices to incorporate into your organization. Most professionals tend to benchmark themselves with other firms within their individual segments. You will be surprised and pleased to find that many excellent ideas and best practices can be learned from a broader cross-segment. Advertising and public relations firms are superb at client account management, engineering and accounting firms are rigorous at strategic planning, consulting firms have some excellent training and mentoring programs, and law firms can teach us a great deal about successful teaming.

If you're not in the professional service industry, you will gain insight into the inner workings of some very successful firms, many of which you have probably worked with during the course of your business career. Hopefully you will discover some practices to apply to your own company. There is much to explore!

1

Professional Services

Characteristics, challenges, and leadership model

"The fundamentals of the professional service business are brutally simple; it's about talent, it's about clients, and it's about teaming to bring it all together to create and deliver value."

—Jim Quigley, CEO, Deloitte
Touche Tohmatsu Limited

"Those corporations that get out ahead of the curve and take a page out of the playbook of successful professional service firms are more likely to be successful themselves."

—Paul Laudicina, Managing Officer and
Chairman of the Board, A.T. Kearney

Operating a professional service firm is very different from running a product-based business. Infrastructures, governance, talent management, compensation, and profitability vary significantly from traditional corporate environments. Firm leaders will tell you that managing a successful professional service organization is a challenging business that requires a delicate balance between structure and autonomy and a unique leadership style. Not to mention the enormous challenge of managing an organization of extremely smart, highly autonomous, and somewhat quirky professionals. It's definitely not a job for the faint of heart.

Common Characteristics of Successful Firms

During the course of our research, we identified several characteristics shared by the world's top professional service firms that offer some important clues about what works and what doesn't in a knowledge-focused business. Some are common traits typically found in most successful businesses, and others are unique to professional services. Collectively they tell an interesting story about the nuances of managing a professional service organization:

- *Values and culture are inviolate.* The leaders of the professional service firms we interviewed were passionate about their firms' values and culture. Values are the bedrock of the organization—the rules that govern behavior toward each other, clients, and the communities in which they serve. In successful firms, adherence to the values is cultivated and rewarded; failure to comply can result in expulsion. The organizations we studied devote an enormous amount of time and resources to embedding their values and reinforcing their culture. In fact, the leaders we interviewed agree that the preservation and nurturing of their firm's values and culture is their number one job.

- *Everything revolves around the client.* Clients are the dominant force, the *raison d'être* in professional services. Everything is driven by client service—vision, values, and culture; infrastructure and governance; equity and compensation; talent management; service development; brand, marketing, and sales. You live or die in a professional service firm by your ability to acquire, serve, and retain clients.

- *They respect and invest in their people.* You might expect that professional service firms would be good at talent management. After all, people are the product. Without committed, highly skilled people, there is nothing to sell. Some impressive best practices are discussed in Chapter 3, "People," but perhaps the most important lesson is that people are treated with respect. Their opinions are valued, they are trusted to interact with clients early on in their careers, and their contributions are expected and rewarded. The successful firms invest significantly in training and mentoring their professionals. Professionals are given a great deal of freedom—as long as they adhere to the values—and often are limited only by their ability and willingness to perform. People at the best professional service firms feel special and privileged.

- *They operate in fluid, flexible teams.* Professionals move in and out of client and project teams, report simultaneously to multiple team leaders, and must learn to be proficient in a host of skill areas. They are constantly stimulated and challenged by a variety of mentors and team leaders and are exposed to a wide breadth of clients and businesses. As a result, the people in professional service firms are extremely flexible and adaptive. They thrive on the diversity and variety of their work. It's one of the reasons why so many top business school graduates—65 percent according to a Harvard statistic—join professional service firms. It is an exciting place for a bright person to work.

- *Organizational structures are extremely simple.* Even the global, multibillion-dollar professional service organizations we studied are essentially lean, flat organizations with a few leaders at the top and minimal administrative layers. In professional services, autonomy and entrepreneurship are encouraged and valued. Most professionals aspire to practice their skills and work with their clients, not lead the organization. Too much bureaucracy drives them crazy. In fact, if the firm's structure becomes too cumbersome and rigid, more often than not people will simply ignore or bypass it.

- *The senior team owns the business.* In a partnership model, a group of professionals are invited through a rigorous selection process to buy into the firm and become owners of the business. Not all professional service firms are partnerships; in fact, many are corporations, and although most are privately held, a few are publicly traded. What is interesting is that no matter the structure, the senior leaders are treated as owners. Professional service firms have created an environment in which the senior team is empowered and committed to making their firm successful. Becoming a "partner" is considered an honor, awarded after years of challenging work, long hours, and intense training. It is a serious commitment, not only financially, but also emotionally.

- *Everyone serves.* "I serve at the pleasure of my partners." "My job is to be a custodian of our values and culture." "You know I don't get paid any extra to do this job—I do it because I love this place." Most of the leaders we spoke with in our study grew up in their organizations, and all are highly skilled and respected in their areas of expertise. All have managed some of their firm's most valued client relationships and have generated significant revenue over time. Many leaders continue to either actively manage or are heavily involved in client work. Unless you are in the industry, you probably can't name many professional service firm leaders. They largely work behind the scenes. Yet many of them have been at the helm of their organization for years—some for decades. They are, in fact, the epitome of business author Jim Collins' Level 5 leaders, described in his book *Good to Great*. Not only do leaders serve their partners and their organizations—everyone serves. Go to any website or pick up any professional service firm brochure, and you will undoubtedly see this word repeatedly. Professionals serve their clients, their communities, and each other. It is an ingrained mind-set within the industry.

- *They stick to their knitting.* Diversification is not an important concept in professional services. While many professional service firms offer a mix of service offerings and often tout multiple areas of expertise, they never venture too far from their roots. The Big Four accounting and consulting firms that work hard to distinguish between their audit, tax, and consulting services still remain firmly under the general advisory services umbrella. Even the major industry segment roll-ups of WPP, Publicis, Interpublic, and Omnicom stick to the related worlds of advertising, public relations, and market research. Many product-based businesses, particularly in the technology sector, have created consulting services or solutions businesses to extend their offerings and interactions with current customers, elevate their relationships to the C-suite executives, and capture the higher margins that services typically provide. In contrast, professional service firms have chosen not to venture into the product world, preferring to remain close to their core competencies.

- *It's about the work more than the money.* Profit is not the primary driver in professional services. People typically enter the business because they really like what they do and often have spent many years studying and training to perfect their skills. They typically don't join the industry to start their own firm or build a giant business. They want to do what they have spent years learning to do—practice the law, design and build a bridge, launch a global ad campaign, or solve a complex business problem.

It's Not All Good News

Of course, not all professional service firms are successful or wonderful places. Similar to other businesses, the vast majority of firms do not survive beyond their founders, growth is challenging, and some are just plain unpleasant and dysfunctional places to work. And just as the broader business world definitely could learn some lessons from professional services, the industry likewise needs to learn a thing or two from its clients. Some of the most notable lessons we observed in our research revolve around innovation, long-term strategic planning and investment, process efficiency, and marketing—or, more precisely, the lack thereof:

- *Change is slow.* The professional service industry is slow to evolve. Although service offerings have changed over time to adapt to changing client needs, competition has intensified—as one interviewee complained, "It's just not as gentlemanly as it used to be"—and mergers and acquisitions have altered the landscape for many segments. Technology has made managing the business and serving clients more efficient. Occasionally an event or disruption occurs in the market—such as the Sarbanes-Oxley Act in the accounting world, the rise of digital media in the advertising business, and the banking crisis for financial services—that forces firms to make some significant changes to what they do and how they do it. But basically the underlying structures and business models have not changed much in the past century.

- *Professional service firms are shortsighted.* Unlike product-based businesses, which have concrete deliverables, predictable production and sales cycles, and standard performance metrics, professional services is oriented toward the short term. Work traditionally is project-based and typically short-lived; clients come and go, making the sales pipeline unpredictable; and most professionals rarely stay in one firm for their entire career. Keeping busy short-term-oriented professionals focused on the big picture and a long-term strategy is a challenge to firm leaders. Plus, in a partnership structure, most of the firm's annual profits are distributed to the firm owners every year. Firm leaders lament the fact that it is often difficult to find funding for long-term strategic investment in new ideas and projects, because this involves reallocating partner earnings.

- *Process improvement is low on the agenda.* In general, process efficiency and improvement have not been a top management focus for professional service firms. Particularly in the bill-by-the-hour segments, there is little incentive to improve the underlying process of how work gets done. There is a general belief in the industry that each assignment is unique and therefore few processes can be made routine. Independent professionals like to run their own show and are resistant to the concept of standardization. Firms that offer more repeatable solutions, such as in the outsourcing and systems integration businesses, are much further down the path of understanding and managing their cost structures and revenue drivers.

- *Marketing and sales are evolving.* Marketing and sales, with a few notable exceptions, are relatively unsophisticated to nonexistent in professional services. The concept of brand is understood and carefully protected in the successful firms we studied, but most do not know how to strategically target and expand their markets or systematically sell their services and manage pipelines. For many professionals, marketing and sales are still mysterious and somewhat distasteful activities.

- *Diversity is just a concept.* As in most of the corporate world, diversity has not reached the upper ranks of professional service firms. Of our more than 130 interviewees, only four women and one non-Caucasian male held the top positions in their organizations. Green shoots of diversity programs surfaced throughout our interviews, and quite a few firms have invested time and resources to attract and retain women and minorities. But the truth is, it is primarily a white male world in the leadership ranks, and it will be quite some time before this fact changes significantly.

The Broderick PSF Leadership Model

We identified ten management areas of focus that we hypothesized were at the top of the leadership agenda in professional services. We started with the traditional McKinsey 7-S Framework for organizational structure, shown in Exhibit 1.1, as the foundation of our study. We planned to develop the questions around each of the seven variables in the model. But based on discussions with our research advisory panel and the initial group of interviewees, we redesigned the framework to reflect several important areas of focus that are both critical and unique to professional service firm management.

EXHIBIT 1.1   The McKinsey 7-S Framework ©

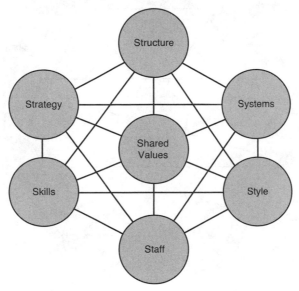

In the end, we expanded the variables from seven to ten, kept some of the S's, and added some P's and one F to create the Broderick PSF Leadership Model, shown in Exhibit 1.2. We determined that the original atom figure of the McKinsey model was the best way to visually depict the importance of organizational interdependence and the need for alignment around each of the ten variables. As in the McKinsey model, our research validated that shared values, along with a shared vision and culture, are the nucleus of every successful professional service firm.

EXHIBIT 1.2   The Broderick PSF Leadership Model ©

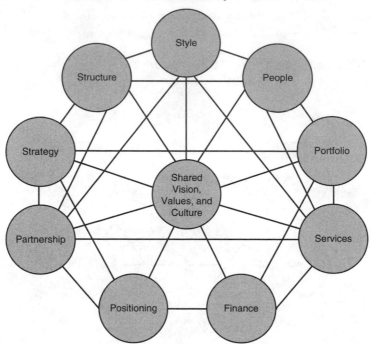

To keep the firm operating at maximum strength, leadership must constantly monitor and tinker with each of these critical pieces of the organizational puzzle. But even the best firms in the business can find themselves out of alignment at certain periods in their life cycle. And virtually all of the leaders interviewed admitted that many areas of their organization need attention and improvement. The key is maintaining a vigilant focus on the firm's vision, values, and culture—the anchor and core of every successful professional service firm.

2

Shared Vision, Values, and Culture

Building, communicating, and maintaining

"For a professional service firm, vision, values, and culture are really 99 percent of the equation."

—Damien O'Brien, CEO, Egon Zehnder International

"We place a lot of weight on shaping, nurturing, and enforcing our values and culture."

—Bob Dell, Chairman and Managing Partner, Latham & Watkins

"If you don't get this stuff right, you might as well forget the rest of it. You are going to be just another organization."

—Peter Stringham, CEO, Young & Rubicam Brands

In a profession that sells a promise of performance versus a tangible product or service, a firm's vision, values, and culture lie at the heart of that promise. Collectively, they form the core around which its business is built. The most successful professional service firms treat this interconnected trio as priceless strategic assets and powerful growth drivers. Who you are and what you value and seek to preserve as an organization affects every aspect of your firm's performance and growth: how your firm is structured; how it governs and shares profits; how it recruits, trains, and manages people; and, ultimately, how it positions and brands itself in the marketplace.

During my more than 30 years in professional services, I have been fortunate to work in-house for a wide range of leading organizations, from Price Waterhouse and Booz Allen Hamilton to the law firm Brobeck, Phleger & Harrison and the research institute SRI International. In addition, for the past 15 years, my firm, Broderick & Company, has consulted with well over a hundred professional service firms of all shapes and sizes across the industry. No two of these firms have been exactly alike. Price Waterhouse, for example, was professional and white shoe; Booz Allen, eclectic and inquisitive; Brobeck, entrepreneurial and aggressive.

Each firm that I've belonged to or consulted for has had a distinct look and feel, personality, and work ethic—its own signature style and organizational DNA. And like the interwoven strands of DNA, each organization has been shaped by a myriad of factors: internally by its history, the type of people it hires, and how it acculturates them, and externally by how it interacts with clients and the markets it serves. Taken together, all these factors create a unique and potent mix or, as Tom Finegan, CEO of Clarkston Consulting, described it, "that secret sauce that defines the firm."

In our research we set out to determine how this secret sauce is created. Why are some firms wonderful to work in and others uncomfortable and discordant? How are firms' visions, values, and cultures established? How are they nurtured and embedded within an organization? Even tougher, how do you change a firm's vision, values, and culture when, for whatever reason, a new direction is in order?

Most of the leaders we spoke with defined vision in aspirational terms. In general, they viewed vision as a somewhat vague destination that they continually strive for but, in fact, never really achieve or even expect to reach. Michael Lotito, Senior Partner at law firm Jackson Lewis, summed up this attitude when he referred to vision as "that North Star thing."

In contrast, we found a tremendous amount of interest and passion around the issues of value and culture. The leaders we spoke with expressed great energy and enthusiasm in describing how these factors play out in their firms. In fact, a remarkable 99 percent of those interviewed said that the combination of vision, values, and culture is the most important area of focus for firm leadership, placing it at the top of our rating chart (see Exhibit 2.1).

EXHIBIT 2.1 Vision, values, and culture ranked first in order of importance

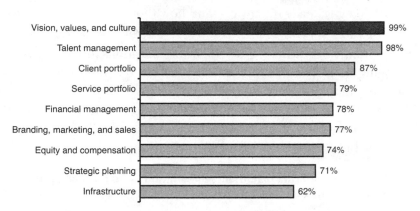

We asked our interviewees to distinguish between the terms vision, values, and culture and to discuss their collective impact from a management perspective. Steve Cody, Managing Partner and Cofounder of public relations agency Peppercom, probably best summed up the prevailing views on this theme when he observed, "Vision is where we are headed. Values are the behaviors we hold important, and culture is the feel, the energy, the buzz, the society within the organization."

As this comment suggests, values are the bedrock of an organization, the rules that govern behavior toward each other, the clients, and the communities in which they serve. Many believe that values are the moral compass that guides an organization through tough times when it faces difficult decisions and conflicting priorities. Culture is viewed as the invisible glue that holds everything together— the collectively accepted modes of behavior and unspoken rules that shape a firm's working environment and operating style. Culture is dynamic—it dictates how things get done within a firm and how its values are put into everyday practice. Culture and values bind a firm together in service to its clients and its vision.

Professional service firms all solve problems. That's why it's often difficult to differentiate in a given segment based on what you do. How you do business based on who you are and what you value is what differentiates one firm from another, regardless of industry segment. In successful firms, vision, values, and culture entwine and enrich each other. And these firms are successful precisely because they work constantly to make sure that the people who represent them in the marketplace understand what they need to do and why they're doing it in a certain way—and how their contributions reflect the values and support their firm's vision as a whole.

Overall, interviewees gave their organizations high marks for managing their firm's vision, values, and culture. Almost 85 percent said they do an excellent or very good job, as shown in Exhibit 2.2. However, there was widespread agreement that managing vision, values, and culture is a demanding job that absorbs significant energy at all levels, but particularly at the top.

EXHIBIT 2.2   Most firms give themselves high marks for managing vision, values, and culture

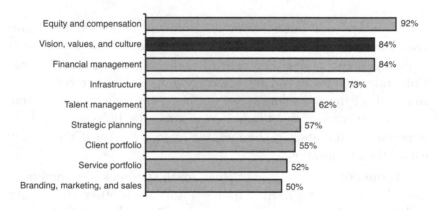

Equity and compensation	92%
Vision, values, and culture	84%
Financial management	84%
Infrastructure	73%
Talent management	62%
Strategic planning	57%
Client portfolio	55%
Service portfolio	52%
Branding, marketing, and sales	50%

Five Essentials of Vision, Values, and Culture

"The challenge is for leadership to constantly monitor adherence to values and maintain a nurturing, rewarding culture. Never lose focus; always evaluate any initiative or decision in terms of alignment with values."

"We don't invest a whole lot in pithy vision statements about being the best at this or that. We concentrate a lot more on the core values and culture of the firm, which is really, really important every day."

Interestingly, although all organizations have distinct DNA, the firms that we studied have amazingly similar core values—even to the point of using the exact same words on their value statements (see Exhibit 2.3). The top values mentioned—integrity, collaboration, client focus, professionalism, and respect—speak to a collective passion for and dedication to their respective professions, colleagues, and clients. Achieving a high degree of professionalism, quality, and excellence in their work is the primary motivator for most professionals.

Exhibit 2.3   Professional service firms share similar values

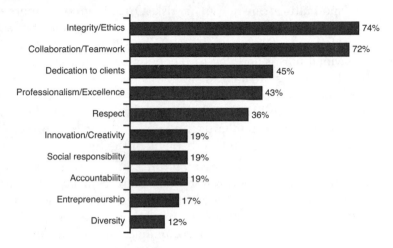

It's easy to say that collaboration and teamwork are important, but it's quite another thing to truly live by and enforce these values. The ability to embed and preserve values over time is one of the distinguishing characteristics of a successful firm. During our interviews, we found that leading firms share five qualities when it comes to reinforcing their values and expectations:

1. *Commit the time and resources to identifying core principles and drivers.* In a nutshell, successful firms have clearly defined visions, well-articulated values, and shared ways of behaving that bind their professionals across geographies and disciplines. Such clarity is no accident, but the product of commitment at all levels. Agreeing on vision and values is a highly collaborative, inclusive process; all partners typically weigh in. Vision and values are periodically reviewed and updated to reflect changes in firm dynamics and to reinvigorate the firm's commitment to its direction and ethos.

2. *Align strategy with vision and values.* In the top firms, all major decisions around structure, governance, compensation, talent, services, and clients are aligned with the firm's vision and values. Strategic planning—both long-term and annual—is viewed as the execution tool that drives the firm toward its vision and aspirational goals. The close linkage among vision,

values, and strategic planning ensures that the firm "walks the talk" and remains true to its core principles, however they are defined—even under enormous external pressure.

3. *Ensure that expansion doesn't destroy or dilute values and culture.* As firms grow larger and more globally complex, core values and culture can be put at risk. Organic growth, mergers and acquisitions, new service offerings, and surges in staff size can all test a firm's organizational resiliency and affect its behavioral norms and day-to-day operating environment. The best firms ensure that expansion has a positive rather than negative impact on core drivers. They use teaming, training, and mentoring to infuse cultural norms and values, promote consistent client service standards, and embed their core principles and behavioral expectations throughout the firm.

4. *Cultivate and reinforce their culture.* Successful PSFs recognize the importance of values and culture in attracting and retaining talented performers, and they invest significant time and money in recruiting and training their professionals. Savvy firms invest substantially in communication to inculcate and reinforce their values at every stage of professional development, from entry-level orientations to events that bring together partners from around the world for face-to-face meetings designed to reenergize core values.

5. *Monitor and measure adherence to values and cultural drivers.* In successful firms, adherence to values is firmly rooted and rewarded; failure to embrace them can lead to expulsion. Performance criteria clearly establish expectations around values, and professionals are evaluated and compensated based on performance against goals.

Embedding Values and Culture

"Culture doesn't just happen; it has to be crafted. It's not something that is serendipitous."

"Every time we make a decision about who we hire, we're making a decision about our culture."

"Many people think of culture as a soft thing. I see it as a very hard, strategic asset."

We asked our interviewees how they embed their firm's values and proactively manage their culture. Although it was clear that most of the firms studied have spent time developing and documenting their values, we wanted to see if the firms really live their values on a daily basis—which values are just etched on crystal desk cubes or framed and hung in the reception area, and which ones are really part of the fabric of the organization.

In fact, we found that most of the organizations we studied spend impressive amounts of time, money, and resources embedding their values and reinforcing their cultures using a variety of channels, tools, policies, and procedures. It is a constant, repetitive process to inculcate the values and culture—"the water dripping on stone approach," as one CEO put it. The instilling process typically begins with recruiting and is reaffirmed formally and informally through orientation and ongoing training, teaming, meetings and events, and prolific communications. Adherence to values and culture is often publicly rewarded and celebrated, while failure to follow the rules is critiqued and punished. And yes, some firms do have their values emblazoned on cubes and walls and "in thirty to forty languages on our screensavers." But for most, such public displays are just the beginning. It's not about showcasing core values and culture. It's about making them work.

The Reinforcement of Values and Culture Begins with Recruiting

For many firms, the process begins with recruiting. Getting the right people on board who are a fit with the firm's style and culture and who will uphold and exemplify its values is extremely important. Several firms described the rigorous screening processes they have in place to make certain that they make the right choices. This means finding people who are the right fit not just in terms of their skills and expertise, but because they are attracted by the firm's values and cultural dynamic. Firms that seek a strong meshing of talent with their institutional persona invest heavily in the recruiting process. Some fly candidates around the firm for twenty to thirty interviews. Candidates may talk to partners in multiple geographies to make certain that everyone feels that the candidates are in sync with the firm's culture. Of course, not all firms can fly people around the world. Still, the underlying message is clear: the best firms see potential conflicts in the areas of culture and/or values as deal breakers when it comes to new talent.

Telling the Firm's Story Reinforces the Culture

For many firms, immersion in values and culture starts the first day on the job and never stops. Many leaders believe that telling their firms' stories is an important part of orientation and the ongoing training process. Orientation programs often incorporate presentations and discussions of the firm's history, philosophy, and values as well as information on process and procedure. Colorful tales of legendary partners, breakthrough case studies, and company survival strategies all add spice and flavor to the firms' programs as they welcome new hires on board.

To celebrate its 60th anniversary, for example, the law firm Skadden, Arps produced a video for internal consumption that portrayed its heritage and many achievements. David Ogilvy, founder of advertising firm Ogilvy & Mather, wrote several books outlining his philosophy on running a successful advertising agency. His colorful stories and advice, "Only hire people you want to vacation with" and "Encourage innovation; change is our lifeblood, stagnation the death knell," which live on the Ogilvy website, have become an important part of the agency's legacy and lore. They are well documented and incorporated into the orientation process and the firm's ongoing life. Similarly, brand and design firm Landor has invested in The Embark Program, an online onboarding tool for new recruits. It begins with a history of Landor and the philosophies of the firm's founder, Walter Landor. Management consulting firm Bain & Company has launched a new heritage website called One Bain that codifies the stories that define the firm's history and success. The site contains over 200 videos that link to a specific firm value, a period of history, or a particular client success story.

Teams Teach You How to Live and Work in the Firm

Professionals in PSFs live and work in teams. The team environment is where firm values and culture are reinforced on a daily basis. A client team typically consists of a vertical slice of professionals in the firm—a senior partner, junior partners, and associates. Each team has a combination of people with various levels of firm knowledge, from those with many years of experience to new hires. Technical skills as well as firm values and culture are taught and experienced firsthand in this apprenticeship environment. Interviewees agree that a team-oriented setting is an ideal way to demonstrate what it means to live in the firm (see "Teaming at Cravath").

Many of the leaders we interviewed spoke with fondness and nostalgia of the mentors from whom they "learned the ropes" in their early days. Gifted mentors who showcase their talents in a team setting make their firm's values come alive and have a powerful and long-lasting impact on the future leaders who learn by watching them in action. These guides are valued not only for their expertise and experience, but also for their ability to put their firm's values to work in service of clients—and for the respect and attention they show their teammates.

Constant Communication Is Critical

For many of the firms studied, communication—constant and varied—is one of the critical tools used to instill values and reinforce culture. Face-to-face meetings are extremely important for both large and small firms. Offices, regions, practices, associates, and partners hold regularly scheduled meetings which are supplemented with periodic all-hands-on-deck meetings which can be face-to-face for small firms and held by webcast for large firms. In fact, most firms bring their partners together at least annually in multiday retreats to bond, plan, and renew their sense of commitment to the organization. In good times these retreats can be lavish. Interestingly, we found that the majority of firms did not cancel their partner get-togethers during the 2008–2010 economic crisis, preferring instead to scale them back. Interviewees emphasized that such events are critical to the firm's ongoing success. As one CEO explains, "A partnership is very tribal, and we need our ceremonies to solidify our pledge to the community."

Social media capabilities play an important role in communication. Many firms incorporate an assortment of vehicles into their regular communication channels of meetings, podcasts, webcasts, and e-mail. Several firms have specially designed programs to ignite the troops, share new ideas, and solicit input on key issues and potential improvements. Management consulting firm Booz Allen Hamilton hosts a monthly webinar for senior associates and partners called

Teaming at Cravath

Two-hundred-year-old New York-based law firm Cravath, Swaine & Moore has consistently ranked as one of the most prestigious U.S. law firms on Vault's Annual Top 100 Law Firms list. According to Presiding Partner Evan Chesler, Cravath's values have remained solidly intact throughout the firm's history. Chesler, who started with the firm as a summer associate in 1974, says the organization's culture and values have been passed from attorney to attorney over the years through a philosophy of "learning by living and doing."

New recruits are absorbed into the environment by a process referred to as the Cravath System. The system is designed to provide a training ground for attorneys to develop substantive technical and client relationship skills, and become immersed in the firm's values and traditions by doing hands-on work on client engagement teams. "As a young lawyer," Chesler explains, "I learned how to do things the right way, and I mean right in the sense of doing the right thing ethically and morally as a lawyer, by working closely with and for people dedicated to the firm's principles."

All associates of the firm are organized into teams led by a partner. When a new associate joins the firm, that person chooses to participate in one of four departments: corporate, litigation, tax and trusts, and estates. Within the selected department, each associate is assigned to work with a partner or small group of partners. After an appropriate interval—12 to 18 months—the associate rotates to work with a different team and partner. Associates continue to rotate throughout their tenure so that by the time they are eligible for partner they are immersed in all facets of the department's practice.

The teams are small—usually from 3 to 12 people, depending on the matter—and typically are composed of a mix of seniority levels, from peers to senior partners. The close-knit, fast-paced team environment provides a day-to-day indoctrination into the firm's values and ethics for conducting business. As Chesler explains, "You're all working in close quarters, and you're dealing with situations that put the firm's values under a spotlight. For example, what do you do about sharing the work responsibility but not taking credit for the work of others? What do you do about telling people the truth even when the truth hurts? Those are part of the value system that drives this place."

The teams provide the structure through which the firm conducts performance evaluations and ultimately selects new partners. To encourage and support their professional development, Cravath associates receive formal reviews from the partners with whom they work, typically at the midpoint and conclusion of their rotations, as well as real-time feedback on a regular basis.

In addition to providing apprenticeship-based training in its team settings, the Cravath System incorporates a formal classroom-driven program taught exclusively by the firm's partners. As Chesler sums up, "The whole infrastructure of the way we train our people, the way we socialize them with the values of the institution, the way we evaluate their performance and ultimately select the partners who join us, is all centered on the Cravath System."

Booz Allen Voice in which senior leaders cover a variety of topics. Advertising agency Ogilvy & Mather has a blog where any employee can ask questions and make comments. Management consulting firm McKinsey & Company holds a global annual Values Day when everyone in each geography gathers to discuss the firm's values. All professionals have a chance to express their opinion on whether McKinsey is living by its values and to offer suggestions on how to improve. According to Rajat Gupta, former Managing Director, "It's the one day of the year where everyone comes together to better understand and recommit to our values. It is very well planned and has existed for at least 20 years."

Many firm leaders—over half of whom continue to manage client work—spend a significant amount of time on the road, visiting offices, meeting with other firm leaders and professionals, and visiting clients. People don't collaborate with people they don't trust, and people don't trust people they don't know, which is why leading firms invest much time and money in helping people get to know each other across practices and borders.

Celebrate and Reward Good Behavior

Many firms have effectively utilized award programs to reinforce values and culture, inspire behavior, solve problems, and drive innovation. The rewards involved can be monetary, but most often they take the form of recognition and visibility with peers and leadership. Ernst & Young receives thousands of nominations for its Chairman's Values Award, from which ten professionals are selected to join the global management group at an annual celebratory dinner in their honor. Law firm Morrison & Foerster presents the Raven Award, named in memory of one of the firm's longtime leaders, to partners who best exemplify the firm's values through their practice and behavior. Public relations firm Cohn & Wolfe has several awards that focus on different aspects of its values, such as creativity, social responsibility, and corporate citizenship.

Making Values Stick

Our research proved that most of the firms studied have an abundance of tools, processes, and procedures to communicate and instill their values and culture. But we still wanted to know which firms actually enforce their values—and how they do it.

Will firms really fire a heavy revenue-generating professional if he or she doesn't uphold their values? Are performance evaluations and, ultimately, compensation affected if values are violated? The answer was most often yes, but not always. Some leaders assert that they are very willing to make the financial sacrifice to maintain the culture and have a zero-tolerance rule when it comes to violating values. These leaders claim that asking high-level performers to leave because they didn't adhere to the firm's values can have a remarkably positive impact on their organization. All agree that it is easier to take this step when you are a big-revenue firm with lots of rainmakers and when economic conditions are stable. It is a harder move for smaller firms to make, particularly in a down market. Still, as one senior leader said, "Excusing a prominent partner from doing the kinds of things that are consistent with the firm's values erodes the confidence that there really is a set of values that is important."

Several notable examples of performance agreements and performance evaluation processes reinforce and enforce values. The Ernst & Young organization has a code of conduct underpinning its values that EY personnel worldwide are required to acknowledge each year; partner-rank professionals sign annual certificates of compliance and their performance reviews are linked to compliance with the value statement. At consulting firm ghSMART, Chairman and CEO Geoff Smart hires based on the firm's eight values, develops operating plans based on those values, and measures both the firm overall and each individual against these values multiple times a year. (See "Recruiting at ghSMART" in Chapter 3, "People.") At consulting firm Booz Allen Hamilton, accountability and performance against values and key performance objectives are well entrenched and enforced. Booz Allen has incorporated the firm's ten core values into the performance evaluations of every employee, and it rigorously measures everyone against each value (see "Booz Allen Hamilton Core Values").

Many of the firms interviewed evaluated performance on values through employee engagement or annual trust surveys. Audit, tax, and advisory firm KPMG, for example, has created what it calls an Employer of Choice survey that is designed to encourage employees to reflect on what they value in their work environment and how their professional experience might be improved.

Booz Allen Hamilton Core Values

While most professional service firms have a values statement, strategy and technology consulting firm Booz Allen Hamilton has been especially successful in culturally embedding its values by tying them to professional performance. As Chairman and CEO Ralph Shrader observes, "We have something with teeth in it. People know our values are the rules we aspire to live by—not just words on a piece of paper."

According to Shrader, the firm's ten core values, established in 2000 prior to the separation of the firm's commercial and government businesses, formed the basis for its evolution from an individualistic, superstar model to an egalitarian culture that's built around sharing and teamwork. Values at Booz Allen range from Client Service (making the client's mission a priority), Excellence (developing high-quality intellectual capital), and Teamwork (sharing knowledge, skills, success, and failure)—to Diversity (maintaining an inclusive work environment) and Integrity (requiring and modeling ethical behavior).

The firm makes certain that everyone is aligned with the company's mission, culture, and values on a practical, day-to-day basis. The ten core values are listed on the first page of every employee's annual assessment form. Each of the core values is defined by an explicit set of criteria for measuring an employee's performance in demonstrating that value. In the case of the teamwork value, for example, the criteria are interacting collaboratively; sharing knowledge, skills, success, and failure; sharing vision and common objectives; and resolving conflicts professionally.

Professionals are evaluated based on whether they fully exhibit the core values, are not quite there, or have issues with any of them. To be in good standing, an employee must receive a "fully exhibits" rating for each core value. If professionals fall short in areas such as teamwork, remedial actions are outlined and they receive a post-review checkup in six months. However, if there are issues in areas reflecting ethical behavior, such as the core value of integrity, the firm issues a warning and termination may result.

"When it comes to embedding values, we have found that walking the talk at every level, from support staff to CEO, is critical," says Shrader. "Putting our values at the core of our career development strategy has made them a living, breathing part of everyday behavior and performance."

Revitalizing Vision, Values, and Culture

"Even great cultures and values need revitalization and modernization."

Most successful professional service firms continue to embody the spirit of their original founders. However, the world does change, and many firms periodically review and fine-tune their vision, values, and culture. The goal is to ensure that their core principles and operating style continue to reflect both the evolution of their partnerships and changing client needs. In many cases, this refreshment process in and of itself is seen as a powerful way to revitalize partner commitment and attract new talent.

Such renewal initiatives usually are driven by some inflection point within the firm or a disruption or change in the competitive landscape or in the marketplace. Traditional ways of working may become obsolete, and significant changes to governance, services, and culture are required to ensure continued viability. Intense mergers and acquisitions (M&A) activity over a prolonged period may result in cultural misalignments that require radical adjustment. Or, as frequently happens, growth surges and the drive to globalize may strain and dilute a firm's existing culture.

A change in leadership often triggers an effort to reflect and refresh. When Mark Penn, the new CEO at public relations agency Burson-Marsteller, came on board in 2006, he launched a process to modernize the firm. As Richard Powell, Global COO, tells it, "Mark focused on saying, 'OK, we know what's the best of the old Burson, but what do we have to do to make it relevant in the 21st century?'" The firm, according to Powell, ended up combining the new with the best of the old.

For public relations firm Edelman and law firm Latham & Watkins, the growing impact of globalization drove the refresh discussion. According to Latham & Watkins' Chairman and Managing Partner Bob Dell, in 1999–2000, the firm partners had to decide to "face the fork in the road"—to either solidify and reconfirm its vision to be the best law firm in the U.S., or to shift to a global perspective. During about the same time period, Edelman set out to expand its U.S.-centric focus to incorporate a worldwide perspective (see "Edelman Revisits Vision and Values").

Edelman Revisits Vision and Values

In 2000, public relations firm Edelman decided as a company to revisit its mission, vision, and values. A number of factors drove the decision to commit management's energy and resources to a comprehensive review and refreshing. Daniel Edelman, the firm's founder, had led the family-owned business for 45 years before being succeeded by his son, Richard Edelman, in 1997. Richard had made significant changes, particularly in growing the firm from a U.S. organization to a true global company, and the firm now wanted to transition from being a marketing PR firm to a more broad-based communications firm. As Edelman described -the situation, "We wanted to retain the culture and values of the original firm while making certain that our values remained relevant around the world. In essence, we wanted the firm's vision to be a statement of continuity, but with evolution."

As a first step, the executive committee met with an outside advisor to discuss their thoughts on the firm's vision, mission, and values; develop a straw-man vision to test with firm professionals; and map out the steps to manage the renewal initiative. The firm adopted a very collaborative and inclusive process to gather and assess firmwide views and opinions on the prospective vision. Edelman established an international task force of people from around the globe to lead one-on-one discussions with all senior managers. Each office held a half-day session with staff at all levels asking: How do you relate to the vision? How do you think our clients will relate to it? Is it culturally adaptable? Everyone in the firm was able to participate in a focus group interview and review the vision, mission, and values statements. Based on the feedback, Edelman's senior management distilled what they felt was a true representation of the culture.

According to Janice Rotchstein, Chief Quality Officer, "When we presented the new vision at the global leadership meeting, everyone agreed that it was absolutely right on. This is who we are, this is our vision, this is our mission, and these are our values. That told us we had done everything right and had listened well."

Firm leaders agree that launching and sustaining the initiative was as vital to the process as developing the new vision statement.

Edelman developed an intensive internal communications program to communicate and instill the vision, which subsequently won a Public Relations Society of America award for employee communications.

The Enron scandal and the subsequent dismantling of Arthur Andersen were a catalyst for tremendous introspection and reevaluation within the accounting profession. It was an extremely turbulent time. The Big Four and others in the industry were forced simultaneously to examine their fundamental business goals, scramble to acquire pieces of Andersen's global business, and absorb former Andersen partners into their firms.

Executive search firm Egon Zehnder International faced three significant disruptions when it launched a firm-wide evaluation in 2001. Egon Zehnder, the firm's founder, had recently retired after 36 years. Two of the firm's major competitors went public, which changed the dynamics around equity and compensation. And, the Internet was rapidly becoming an important tool and competitive advantage in the recruiting business. As CEO Damien O'Brien recalled, "The firm was unsettled, and there was a concern that the leadership had their head in the sand and hadn't really acknowledged that the world was changing so dramatically."

Driven by the same evolving industry dynamics in the executive search business, Korn/Ferry International began a multiple-year journey to broaden its business from an exclusive focus on search work to a more full-service talent management organization. The process involved systemic change to much of the firm's core structures and a shift in values and culture (see "Korn/Ferry Changes Its Vision and Culture").

Whatever the trigger, the process that firms undertake to revisit their fundamentals is typically intense, involving the entire firm and an enormous amount of management time. Collaboration and consensus are important components, and many leaders agree that the process of coming together to establish or reaffirm the vision and values is often as important as the result. It is an opportunity to unite and focus the organization on a common path.

Korn/Ferry Changes Its Vision and Culture

Over the past decade, executive recruiting and talent management firm Korn/Ferry International has undergone a fundamental strategic and cultural shift. In 1999, the firm went public for the second time in its 40-year history in the midst of the technology boom. The firm leaders at the time were looking to diversify and differentiate the business, and used the IPO as a means to fund the transformation. In 2001, the firm recruited Paul Reilly, former CEO of KPMG International, to lead the change. Under Reilly's guidance, the leadership mapped out a vision and plan to evolve the firm from its flagship search business to a broader talent management practice that supports the "lifecycle of a leader" from acquisition to evolution, development, retention, and compensation.

According to Linda Hyman, Senior Vice President of Global Human Resources, who played a key role in the firm's evolution, there are several key activities that firms should undertake when considering a major transformation:

- *Recruit the right team.* Reilly brought in a senior team of industry leaders to manage the transition, including seven former CEOs of search firms and a CFO, Gary Burnison from KPMG, who became CEO when Reilly left in 2009.

- *Validate the vision.* The firm commissioned a study to gather input from professionals inside the firm and from the market to validate the concept of diversification and test the need for a variety of human capital based services.

- *Acquire systematically.* When it was clear that the market would support an expansion, the leadership team developed an acquisition strategy to broaden the firm's capability in each of the target service areas. Over a 10-year period, the firm added 15 businesses to the organization.

- *Plan the culture shift.* Korn/Ferry's business had historically been focused almost exclusively on recruiting capabilities. As the firm added new service areas, it needed to evolve its culture of collegiality and teamwork, and apply it toward broader talent management solutions, while also maintaining its strong focus on the firm's successful flagship recruiting focus. As Hyman explains, "With our new compliment of diversified services, we needed to go to the client as a team and share relationships to grow the business, which at the time was a new concept to most firm professionals." For the firm to truly unlock the full potential of its transformational strategy, each of its colleagues needed to understand the vision and embrace a consistent go-to-market approach, representing a differentiated business. As a result, the core business has been expanded with broader, more consultative solutions and intellectual property—and nearly 26 percent of the business now comes from outside the legacy executive recruitment business.

Shifting the culture to support the strategic change is not a linear process and can take years to gel. "It is a classic organizational change process that takes planning, communication, and patience," said former Korn/Ferry CEO Reilly. "The first step is laying out the vision and plan, and then steadfastly moving the ship forward with empathy and understanding. Change in professional services is a process, not an event."

Such renewal efforts are both invigorating and uncomfortable. At their most effective, they can push a firm to new levels of performance and client service. Although each firm has its own signature operating style, an initiative to revisit a firm's core values and path typically includes five major components, as shown in Exhibit 2.4:

- *Solicit feedback.* In general, a renewal program is kicked off by taking the firm's organizational temperature—soliciting internal views on what works and what doesn't. Every aspect of an organization, from values and operating style to branding and marketplace perceptions, may be scrutinized. A vision-and-values inventory in some form is frequently conducted to uncover aspirational goals that partners would like to see the firm embrace. Such goals might include creating a more positive work environment, taking on new types of clients or assignments, building a global brand, or sharing intellectual capital more effectively. Some firms expand this feedback process to include selected clients.

- *Envision success.* This often involves taking a blue-sky approach to reimagining a firm's vision, values, and culture. What aspirational goals and challenges would excite and energize the partnership at this point in time? What values would provide a moral compass to help the firm navigate successfully and thrive while meeting emerging client needs? What innovative tools would the firm have to integrate into its arsenal to radically improve operating efficiency and boost service performance? What changes in its work environment would foster greater partner satisfaction and collegiality—and attract fresh, committed talent? Creating a values statement that reflects widely embraced answers to questions like these can provide a rallying point for employees at all levels and a helpful touchstone when the transformation process encounters obstacles, as it inevitably will.

- *Scope the required changes.* Once the review process is completed, a small group of partners—or several subgroups—is mobilized to analyze partner suggestions and evaluate the degree and nature of the adjustments called for. Ultimately, the goal is to come up with a recommended slate of specific, practical improvements that can be made and tools that can be leveraged to achieve the desired results. Recommendations may vary from slight adjustments to values and culture such as committing to codifying and sharing knowledge more effectively or expanding community service activities, for example, to major organizational restructuring.

- *Map an action strategy.* Using the results of the scoping process as guidelines, the partnership team spearheading the renewal effort maps out the action steps required to make recommended changes a reality. To be effective, the strategy must include assigned responsibilities and accountability for each task, significant milestones, and a process to track, measure, and reward achievements.

- *Promote buy-in.* Once a potential renewal program has been mapped out, the next step generally involves taking it on the road to showcase it in face-to-face meetings and solicit a second round of feedback from partners. This helps ensure that the partnership as a whole feels that its responses and suggestions have been integrated into the action plan. It also sets the stage for buy-in around the renewal strategy and the investments required to push it forward.

EXHIBIT 2.4   Steps to renewing vision, values, and culture

Solicit feedback	Envision success	Scope the required changes	Map an action strategy	Promote buy-in
Formally gather input using a variety of means including focus groups, opinion surveys, brown-bag sessions, and web-based polling	Take a blue sky approach to reimagining the firm's vision, values, and culture	Mobilize a small group to analyze and evaluate feedback	Map action steps, including both internal and external changes	Involve firm leaders in communicating planned changes through a program of face-to-face meetings
Inventory vision and values to uncover aspirational goals	Identify tools to support the new culture	Review recommendations	Create timeline, budget, accountability, and metrics	Adjust plan as necessary
Include client input if appropriate	Identify changes needed in the work environment	Agree on a slate of specific practical improvements		Submit to vote of partnership if required
	Create a new values statement			Using change management techniques, roll out renewal plan

Culture change is rooted in changes in behavior. To encourage the new behaviors you want, be sure that your rewards-and-recognition system reinforces them at all levels. Reassuring everyone that their contributions count invites them to think of themselves as creative change agents who matter. Treat change as the key to driving and heightening performance—and as a journey rather than a destination. People must have a clear understanding of why change is required, what success will look like once transformation occurs, how it can potentially benefit them, and what is expected of them along the way. Vague, ambiguous mandates for change result in vague, ambiguous responses.

CHAPTER SUMMARY

Shared Vision, Values, and Culture

- Overwhelmingly, vision, values, and culture rank as the top priorities on management's agenda. Leaders across all industry segments see their role as guardians and exemplars of their firms' core principles as critical.

- The best-run firms reinforce the importance of vision, values, and culture by taking five critical steps:

    1. Commit time and resources.

    2. Align strategy with vision and values.

    3. Ensure that expansion doesn't destroy or dilute values and culture.

    4. Cultivate and reinforce their culture.

    5. Monitor and measure adherence to values and cultural drivers.

- Embedding values and cultural norms is seen as an ongoing process that begins with recruiting, takes root in a team setting, and must be supported by creative and constant communication.

- Refreshing a firm's vision, values, and culture can have an energizing and mobilizing effect. This process has five basic steps, as shown in Exhibit 2.4.

3

People

Recruiting, training, and evaluation

"Creating an environment where people with very different backgrounds and skills feel that they can have a successful career is essential."
—Dennis Nally, Global Chairman, PwC

"I don't think you can manage talent. I think you can nurture it, you can encourage it, and you can facilitate it."
—Lem Lasher, President, Global Business Solutions Group and Chief Innovation Officer, CSC

"Do people drive the business to success, or does the business drive satisfied, high-performing people? I have yet to determine which comes first—and it doesn't really matter."
—Ray Kotcher, Senior Partner and CEO, Ketchum

Turn to any segment of the professional service industry and you'll find one constant: the relentless search for outstanding talent. It's axiomatic that without highly skilled and motivated performers, service firms have nothing to sell. The best PSFs achieve and maintain their competitive edge by attracting and retaining the most gifted people, who then attract and retain good clients with interesting work, which, in a virtuous circle, attracts the most qualified candidates.

PSF leaders are vitally aware of the critical value of recruiting, retaining, and developing talent. Talent management ran virtually neck-and-neck with vision, values, and culture for star billing as the most important top management issue. While vision, values, and culture was rated by 99 percent of respondents as their top priority, talent management placed a close second, with 98 percent of those interviewed ranking it as a critical issue for their firms (see Exhibit 3.1).

EXHIBIT 3.1   Talent management tied as the top area of importance

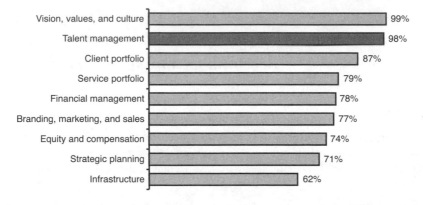

How well do firms perceive themselves performing in the intensely competitive talent sweepstakes? Overall, the professional service firms studied consider themselves relatively adept at finding and cultivating good talent. Sixty-two percent of the leaders interviewed gave themselves high marks in the talent management area, as shown in Exhibit 3.2.

EXHIBIT 3.2   Over half rated themselves highly on talent management

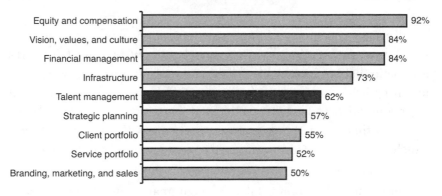

Close to half of those surveyed indicated that they have developed a formal firm-wide process for managing all aspects of their talent base, from recruitment through outplacement, as shown in Exhibit 3.3.

EXHIBIT 3.3   Talent management ranges from opportunistic to strategic

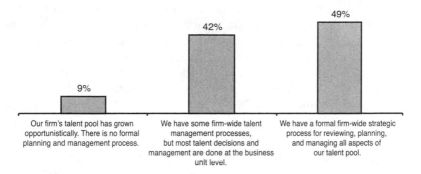

9%	42%	49%
Our firm's talent pool has grown opportunistically. There is no formal planning and management process.	We have some firm-wide talent management processes, but most talent decisions and management are done at the business unit level.	We have a formal firm-wide strategic process for reviewing, planning, and managing all aspects of our talent pool.

Seven Essentials of Talent Management

"It's the care and feeding of our professionals that makes the whole organization work. It's how they're recruited, trained, and nurtured along their career path. That's where retention comes from."

"Our biggest impediment to growth is finding the right talent."

"I would rate us as a shoemaker on talent management. We don't do a damn thing."

"The phrase talent management is misleading; successful firms manage assets and manage budgets, but they cultivate talent."

When it comes to effective execution of the talent equation, the best-run firms share seven noteworthy characteristics. Specifically, these organizations do the following:

1. *Adopt a stewardship mindset.* Creating an environment where people are respected and nurtured is a distinguishing feature of the most successful PSFs. It is a stewardship mindset—a belief that the firm has a responsibility to develop its people versus a "we own them" organizational mentality. It is a philosophical choice that has a fundamental impact on how the firm does business. As Jim Turley, Chairman and CEO of Ernst & Young Global, says about his organization's people-first focus, "It means that when we're making decisions around strategies, structure, compensation— you name it—we think at the outset about how it's going to impact our people."

2. *Devote professional time and resources.* For the top firms, participating in talent management is everyone's job—from first-year recruits to the most senior partners. Professionals at all levels are engaged to support recruiting, training, and mentoring activities. Internal educational programs include classes on people management and development skills as well as "train the trainer" programs to incorporate professionals into the firm's training curriculum. In some firms it is considered an honor to be asked to lead a recruitment drive or develop and teach a new training curriculum.

3. *Recruit the right people from the start.* How many times and by how many management gurus have business people been told the importance of hiring the right people and eliminating the wrong ones? It was a mantra for Jack Welch at General Electric, and it is a strongly held belief and practice for many of the firms included in our study. Astute PSFs spend a great deal of time analyzing, profiling, and recruiting the people who are a good fit—both culturally and technically—for their organizations. Hiring decisions are collaborative efforts where many professionals interview and weigh in on potential candidates.

4. *Carefully plan and manage careers.* For most PSFs, professionals must march steadily up the seniority ladder. Performance expectations are clearly mapped and communicated for each career phase. Progress is closely monitored through both formal performance evaluation programs and informally through continuous feedback and guidance from partners and mentors. Those who do not meet expectations are routinely counseled out of the firm.

5. *Invest in training.* Smart, ambitious knowledge workers, like volunteer armies, are notoriously mobile and inclined to vote with their feet, which makes retention a perennial challenge. Training is an effective tool to keep professionals who inherently love to learn engaged and onboard. It is also a powerful vehicle to continuously upgrade and enhance the organization's skill level and capabilities. The best firms invest time and resources to provide continuous learning opportunities for both professionals and staff.

6. *Make talent management an accountable responsibility.* For the best-run firms, participation in talent management is not only encouraged, it is expected, monitored, and reported in performance evaluations. For many, it is one of several criteria used to determine annual compensation for partners and all levels of professionals.

7. *Commit to diversity.* Virtually all the executives we interviewed expressed a commitment to building a diversified workforce and opening the road to partnership to talented individuals of all backgrounds. Most of the firms studied have launched programs to recruit and retain a more diversified professional workforce.

Recruiting: Refreshing the Ranks

"We're trying to do a better job of linking targeted selection of talent back to our strategic initiatives."

"We finally have companywide recruiting coordination. But we're not as fluid and strategic as I'd like to be. That's my confession."

Culture, type of business, and market position play pivotal roles in determining recruiting strategy. As we have discussed, the best firms are meticulous at selecting people who will fit into the culture and adhere to the values. Potential candidates are well vetted and well informed of the firm's services, work, and professional ethics so that no one is surprised when a new hire comes onboard.

Who and how you recruit varies depending on the business. Segments such as accounting, engineering, advertising, and public relations tend to hire a high percentage of people right out of undergraduate school and grow and develop them internally. Consulting, executive recruiting, and law firms, on the other hand, are looking for more experienced professionals with advanced degrees or work experience. Lateral hiring from competitive firms is prevalent across segments and is seen as a way to increase expertise, shorten the learning and training curve, and potentially attract new clients who may follow a professional from firm to firm. Law firms often recruit an entire practice group of both partners and associates from another firm to jump-start their business and add or supplement a service offering to their portfolio of capabilities.

Brand strength and reputation play important roles in who firms recruit—and how and where they find candidates. Large, well-established firms benefit from high brand visibility, whereas niche firms vying for the same talent pool must fight harder for recognition.

To compete, smaller firms must aggressively differentiate their brands by promoting attributes such as market responsiveness, entrepreneurial drive, close client relationships, collegiality, and flexible lifestyle options to attract candidates. Even well established firms find that working against type can be an effective branding strategy when it comes to recruiting. Skadden, Arps, for example, a highly regarded and extremely profitable law firm, has bypassed a white-shoe image in favor of a bolder, less conformist persona. (See "Brand Management at Skadden, Arps" in Chapter 7, "Positioning," for details.)

When it comes to the business of finding new talent, leading firms collectively identify and court candidates via a fairly standard set of recruiting channels, ranging from on-campus interviews and internships to alumni networks. Most firms employ multiple channels, although the resources invested in each vary by firm. Overall, PSFs rely on six sources for tapping new talent:

1. **On-campus recruiting**—For the firms that prefer to find and acculturate promising performers early in their careers, on-campus recruiting remains a widely used channel for new hires. Most PSFs target their on-campus recruiting dollars and resources, limiting their scope to schools that have a track record of producing candidates who best fit the firm's desired profile. As social mores and expectations change, firms are evolving their recruiting approach. Enticing the Generation Y segment to join a professional service firm requires completely different tactics from Generation X recruiting. The firms that do this best spend time strategizing and planning the message and approach to effectively appeal to this age group; develop multitouch marketing campaigns that incorporate social media, campus events, and well-orchestrated office visits; and train and deploy their young professionals to play ambassador and advocate roles in the recruitment process.

   Edelman enhanced its on-campus approach with an innovative recruiting initiative focused on professors rather than students. Capitalizing on the surge in social networking, the firm hosted a Social Media Summit at Georgetown University. It attracted more than 100 professors from both the United States and Europe, some of whom were offered scholarships to participate. The Summit gave the educators who attended an insider's look at cutting-edge research on social media as a public relations tool, introduced them to

Edelman professionals, and showcased the firm as a career option for their students.

2. **Internships**—Many firms use internships to forge ongoing relationships with promising candidates. Bringing potential hires onboard for intensive semester or summer programs, generally during their sophomore and junior years, is used as a vetting and recruiting mechanism. Over time, many internship programs have evolved from loosely structured activities into formal, project-based assignments that give interns insider experience and insight into a firm's culture, work demands, and expectations.

Ernst & Young hosts a summer leadership program for college sophomores that offers an appealing mix of project work, leadership training, access to partners, and community service. The firm stays connected with top performers who attended its leadership program and hosts an event-filled weekend that culminates in job offers. Deloitte Australia forges links to selected college campuses through a program called the Deloitte Innovation Challenge. Students participate in the firm's Innovation Academy, which exposes them to project work, offers hands-on coaching opportunities with firm professionals, and encourages them to develop creative solutions to industry issues.

3. **Social media**—In their efforts to recruit digital-savvy young candidates, firms across the industry are beginning to exploit the interconnectivity offered by social media sites where they feature video profiles, business briefs, and bios of top performers. Advertising and public relations firms, which have integrated social networking media tools into mainstream client work, are particularly adept at harnessing this resource, as are some architecture firms. For example, architecture firm HOK's HOKlife.com showcases the personalities and varied interests of the many creative professionals across HOK's offices, providing a powerful recruiting tool and a lively communication channel inside and outside the organization.

4. **Internal incentive programs**—Firms across industry segments depend on current staff members to spot and recommend rising stars who they feel will add value and fit in culturally. Some use cash bonuses and/or other enticements to encourage referrals by staff members. Many firms actively encourage their partner corps to consistently and aggressively monitor their contacts, both professional and personal, for potential new hires and reward their efforts in performance reviews and compensation.

5. **Alumni networks**—Former employees are powerful new business and recruiting sources. Firms are reaching out in a variety of ways to keep their alums involved via dedicated websites, local and regional events, online and print newsletters, and webinars. PwC maintains a program called Alumni Key that actively tracks alumni and connects them to the broad PwC community with regular networking events, newsletters, technical training, and career guidance. McKinsey is legendary in the industry for its strong ties to alumni, many of whom become senior leaders of the world's leading corporations and remain loyal advocates of the firm.

6. **External recruiters**—In some instances where a specialized skill set, specific industry expertise, or geographic locale comes into play, PSFs turn to recruiting firms, many of which have special practices focused on talent acquisition for professional services.

Interviewing and Selection: Choosing the Best Candidates

When it comes to candidate selection and closing the deal, firms pursue a range of strategies. Some depend on their HR teams to find and screen candidates; others give office and practice leaders wide latitude in finding, wooing, and winning promising candidates. For most of the firms studied, recruiting is serious business, and the senior partners are intimately involved at every stage of the process.

As Michael Goss, COO and CFO of investment firm Bain Capital, observes, "It's just part of the culture that recruiting drives everything." Bain Capital's senior partners are involved in screening the most promising candidates, even for entry-level analyst positions. During the peak recruiting period, the firm sets aside several days for the partners to devote to interviewing.

The best interview and selection approach involves a multistep process (see "Recruiting at ghSMART"). It begins with a thoughtful formal analysis and profiling of the tasks for the specific position or professional level to be filled; the technical skills and experience requirements to do the job; and the personality characteristics that best fit the firm and the role, such as leadership, communication, people development, and integrity. An interview team is then identified and meets before the interviews begin to agree on the profile and goals and areas to probe in the interview. Each interviewer follows prescribed interview techniques taught to him or her in internal training programs, fills out an interview summary form, and discusses his or her insights and recommendations with the group before a hire decision is finalized.

Some firms have developed interview methods tailored to their business style and service mix to help narrow the selection process. For example, one of Bain Capital's prime interviewing techniques is to present individual candidates with on-the-spot case studies that require them to quickly and incisively analyze investment problems and offer solutions. Consulting firm Monitor has developed a tailored interview technique designed to spotlight performance in a group setting. Instead of conducting interviews with individual candidates, the firm brings together groups of candidates applying for the same job to assess in real time how they interact with their peers in a problem-solving situation. Monitor executives overseeing the sessions evaluate individual candidates on a number of fronts: Are they good listeners? Are they good at drawing out others? Can they build on someone else's idea? Can they take the lead in pulling the group back from an unproductive line of attack?

Mapping a Career Path

The career development process varies significantly across firms and, like everything else in professional services, is driven by values and culture. At one end of the spectrum are the "sink or swim" firms. After the recruiting process is completed and new hires are onboard, these firms see little or no need to spend dollars on development. Instead, they expect professionals to proactively manage their own careers with minimal support. Their message: we hire smart, aggressive people, and we expect them to go out and get what they need to fulfill their potential. At the other end of the spectrum are the firms that take the nurturing and development of their people—both the professionals and staff—very seriously. These are the firms that consistently recruit the top students in the class or the best industry and service experts in their fields. These are also the businesses with the

Recruiting at ghSMART

ghSMART Chairman and CEO Geoff Smart, author of the best-selling book *Who: The A Method for Hiring*, says that "Great things or bad things flow downstream from who you hire—strategy, process design, leadership, innovation, financial decisions, legal decisions—everything."

Smart applies that philosophy to his own firm. Always rigorous in recruiting, the firm redesigned its recruiting approach in 2002 after a hiring mistake highlighted the need to codify and practice a more disciplined approach. According to Smart, the program has four key elements:

1. **Scorecard**—Smart and his team created a scorecard based on eight specific criteria that described the mission, outcomes, and competencies that the firm was looking for.

2. **Source**—A significant change the firm made was to shift the candidate base from being 75 percent recruiter-fed to 75 percent internal-referral-fed. Not only did the cost-per-hire decrease by 50 percent, but the results, Smart says, were four times better. Everyone in the firm is deeply invested in finding and hiring the best people. To maintain that investment, Smart offers a $100,000 "referral bounty" paid over nine years, as long as both the referring and referred employee are still at the firm.

3. **Select**—After an initial screening by the firm's head of recruiting, on average, one out of every 50 candidates advances to a three-step interviewing process. First, a ghSMART consultant conducts a 45-minute phone interview, during which candidates are asked to provide performance ratings from their last five supervisors. Those who survive move on to two five-hour in-person interviews, with Smart himself conducting the second interview. Finally, successful candidates participate in five scorecard-focused hour-long interviews with members of the recruiting team, all practicing consultants. Smart outsources background checks to complete the picture.

4. **Sell**—Having zeroed in on the best of the best, Smart closes the loop with a carefully crafted offer based on the "five Fs of selling: fit, family, fortune, freedom, and fun," which Smart says are the top five ways to seal the deal. The result? Seventy

percent of those who receive an offer accept. Along with the offer, candidates receive a detailed five-to-ten-page feedback report leading to an action plan for building on their strengths and improving on risk areas. The firm also debriefs failed candidates.

In addition to significantly reduced cost-per-hire and time-per-hire—the whole process, from phone interview to hire, is approximately three months—the firm has seen improved closure, growth, and retention rates. The firm spends 2 percent of its revenue on out-of-pocket recruiting expenses. The head of recruiting dedicates about 15 percent of his time to recruiting, and an HR coordinator devotes approximately 30 percent.

Smart's advice to those considering redesigning and reinvigorating their recruiting program: "Start with the end-state in mind, articulate your criteria, and know your metrics. Don't make tweaks; make a wholesale change."

highest retention rate of top performers and the highest scores on all the "Best Places to Work" charts.

The best firms don't leave career development to chance. They carefully map the competencies and performance expectations for each career stage across a variety of dimensions. These range from hard skills such as technical expertise, knowledge of firm service methodologies, and project management capabilities to softer skills that tie to firm values such as people development, team leadership, respect, and professionalism. In these firms, performance requirements are clearly communicated, and formal training, mentoring, and performance evaluation procedures are in place to guide and support everyone along the path.

Booz Allen Hamilton is one firm that has committed extensive resources to creating a multilevel career development framework which consistently wins high marks internally and a raft of external awards for its development approach. Top management believes this strategy is a major factor in the firm's high levels of employee satisfaction and retention (see "Career Development at Booz Allen Hamilton").

Career Development at Booz Allen Hamilton

Under the guidance of Chairman and CEO Ralph Shrader, strategy and technology consulting firm Booz Allen Hamilton has made a major commitment to the career development of employees at all levels. The result is a highly regarded program that has won the firm widespread recognition and garnered numerous awards as one of the "100 Best Companies to Work For." The key components of the firm's career development process are the Employee Development Framework and the Performance Management Cycle which together define and support career progression for every stage of development:

- **Employee Development Framework**—The firm has established very specific core competencies—both skills and behaviors—for each career level. Senior associates, for example, must build and exhibit capabilities in areas such as leadership, people development, client and market development, quality of work, and business management. Specific activities to build each of these capabilities are detailed for each category and are clearly articulated to every professional.

  To support professional achievement of core competencies, the firm has created a multifaceted development framework which provides guidance and tools for all staff. The program includes five specific learning opportunities: 1) on-the-job activities; 2) classroom training in areas such as leadership, business management, and client/market development; 3) self-paced courses, including 2,000 on-demand e-learning programs; 4) career relationships within the firm; and 5) external learning opportunities, such as MBA, MA/MS, and certificate programs offered by leading universities.

- **Performance Management Process**—The firm has developed an integrated performance management and development program that is an ongoing process of defining goals, setting expectations, expanding abilities, and measuring the real progress made during the 12-month evaluation period. There are two key components of the program:

  1. **Performance and Development Plan (PDP)**—Each employee creates and updates his PDP to set expectations, encourage continuous learning, and support the ongoing review and formal evaluation of achievements and results.

> The PDP provides employees and leaders with a struc-
> tured framework to identify goals and expectations, plan
> ongoing growth and development, and, most importantly,
> it serves as a guide to help individuals succeed.
>
> 2. **Competency Assessment**—Managers or third-party
>   reviewers conduct an annual key competency assessment
>   with 360-degree feedback from managers, peers, cus-
>   tomers, and colleagues. After the competency assess-
>   ment, the manager and reviewer provide direct feedback
>   to the individual and identify key developmental actions
>   that flow into the development section of the employee's
>   PDP for the coming year.
>
> The ingredients required for career progression at Booz Allen
> Hamilton are clearly defined. As Shrader says, "There's no mystery
> about what it takes to succeed at the firm." By combining high
> expectations, a well-charted career path, and a rich array of devel-
> opment tools, the firm has earned a global reputation for excep-
> tional standards of performance and professional integrity.

Training: Fostering Connectedness and Commitment

*"Everybody is so focused on driving the business and driving their clients'
business that we don't put as much focus and emphasis on training as we
should. I think it's endemic to the industry."*

*"Electronic training has its place in terms of cost-effectiveness and flexibility.
But the opportunity to get people in a room to share experiences, discuss
problems, and learn from each other is highly valued."*

When it comes to training initiatives that fuel employee satisfaction and boost retention rates, the reviews on performance were
somewhat mixed. Several executives candidly admitted that their
firms have lost key people who might have stayed onboard if they had
received better training and mentoring.

Although training programs are costly in terms of both time and
money, replacing seasoned performers is even more so. In an industry

where trust and interpersonal contact are essential to new business development, repeat business, and enduring client relationships, retaining gifted employees at all levels is the bedrock of growth and profitability.

Interestingly, the firms that excel in training are not exclusively the usual big-firm high-revenue suspects. In fact, several small firms in our study had excellent training programs. Although the magnitude of the training budget definitely impacts the programs' scope, good training options are available for all budget sizes. The larger deep-pocket firms have departments dedicated to developing and executing comprehensive, multichannel, university-like programs tailored to all stages of career progression through the organization (see "Latham & Watkins Multistage Career Training"). Smaller firms utilize a combination of face-to-face knowledge-sharing sessions taught by in-house professionals, online courses, and mentoring. The bottom line is that a core set of training tools are employed by firms across all industry segments:

- **Online instruction**—Like their counterparts in other industries, professional service firms have enthusiastically embraced the flexibility and rich array of resources available online. Efficient and cost-effective, virtual training is a very popular part of the mix at PSFs of all sizes. As firms grow more global and diverse, most interviewees expect this training tool to become even more ubiquitous.

- **Company universities**—A sizable number of firms have opted to deliver customized content and targeted instruction via their own universities. Deloitte U.S., Ernst & Young, Burson-Marsteller, Hewitt, Ogilvy & Mather, Peppercom, STV, Wipfli, and Young & Rubicam Brands have all embraced this approach.

  Deloitte U.S. Vice Chairman and Chief Talent Officer Cathy Benko believes there are strong, ongoing benefits to personalized, onsite programs, particularly for a far-flung global enterprise. Deloitte is making its largest ever investment in its people with the construction of Deloitte University, a state-of-the-art facility for learning and leadership development set to open near Dallas in 2011. Deloitte estimates that 40 percent of its people's formal learning will occur at the new facility, focusing on complex skill-building and supplementing other learning offerings delivered virtually and/or locally. It will also serve as a locus for

Latham & Watkins Multistage Career Training

Founded in 1934, Latham & Watkins, with over 2,000 attorneys in 30 offices around the world, is one of the world's premier business law firms. According to Latham Chairman and Managing Partner Bob Dell, the firm made a strategic decision in 1998 to invest heavily in formal training in addition to the on-the-job training that had historically occurred. Dell launched a new committee called Training and Career Enhancement (TACE) and appointed a team of respected partners from around the firm to design and oversee the development of the firm's program. Today, TACE offers a comprehensive development program for attorneys that includes multiple career-stage academies, a broad-based series of live and video-based monthly training conferences, annual hands-on workshops, and a firmwide associate mentoring program.

- **The Academies**—The program features multiday training sessions customized for each stage of career development. The Summer Academy introduces potential new recruits to the firm's values and cultures. The First Year Academy for new associates blends orientation, acculturation, and substantive training. The Third Year Academy provides the critical training needed to successfully transition from a junior to mid-level associate. The Fifth Year Academy focuses on an associate's career development and progression to a senior associate and includes training on both substantive skills and business development. The New Partner Academy introduces Latham's new partners to the firm's decision-making processes and operating systems and structures.

- **Formal training curricula**—The TACE Committee provides a host of training programs to all attorneys as well as staff throughout the year, which include live presentations and firmwide videoconferences. Most programs are posted to the firm's online training library so that professionals can review them at their convenience. The programs are organized and presented monthly through four formal curricula:

    1. The Core Curriculum is designed to introduce the newest attorneys to the nuts and bolts of key practice groups. It also offers focused training on essential junior-associate skills such as legal research and writing.

2.   The Interdisciplinary Curriculum includes courses on timely legal developments of interest to all lawyers across the firm's five departments.

3 & 4. The Advanced Transactional and Controversy Curriculum are two separate course tracks (transactional and litigation) designed to provide in-depth training on essential practical skills and current legal developments.

- **Hands-on training programs**—The firm dedicates significant resources to multiday hands-on programs such as deposition training and trial advocacy, where Latham partners act as faculty and provide real-time instruction, critiques, and demonstrations.

- **Mentoring**—Every first-year associate and new lateral associate is matched with a senior associate or partner mentor who is available to answer questions about the firm, provide career guidance, or act as a confidential advisor.

The firm invests heavily in training and dedicates thousands of attorney hours every year to developing, improving, and implementing these programs. "We believe it's well worth the investment," says Dell. "It has significantly strengthened the quality and consistency of our services. Our partners in any office around the globe have complete confidence that attorneys they enlist on a project from another office meet the firm's high standards. It also is a big plus from a recruitment standpoint."

Deloitte professionals from around the world, and there are plans to install similar facilities in Europe and Asia in the future.

In contrast, Edelman University (Edel U) operates almost entirely virtually. Its online database encompasses both local curricula created by the firm's various offices and globally generated content. During twice-a-month firmwide sessions, Edelman's senior professionals profile innovative case studies and discuss new initiatives and service offerings. These sessions are interactive and combine video streaming and online Q&A capabilities.

- **Teaming with academia**—Instead of creating homegrown programs, some firms turn to leading academic institutions to provide customized or advanced training tailored to their needs. DLA Piper, for example, offers a weeklong immersion program at Harvard Business School for 50 of its partners every year. Architecture and engineering firm Dewberry created a cooperative arrangement with George Mason University that offers both participants significant benefits. Through this initiative, George Mason offers a master's of engineering program at the firm's corporate center in Virginia, and Dewberry senior executives serve as visiting professors in some of George Mason's upper-level courses. These courses are also offered as a distance learning option to all Dewberry employees.

International communications firm Fleishman-Hillard invests heavily in career development; in 2008 alone, the firm provided almost 40,000 hours of training to its employees. Along with an external alliance with Babson College, the firm's practice groups conduct a wide-ranging series of webinars where executives share "tales from the front"—a steady stream of case histories on high-profile projects that are distributed via the firm's intranet. The firm's president and CEO, David Senay, also posts an internal blog to help employees stay up to date on major engagements and industry issues.

- **One-on-one coaching**—To supplement internal training and mentoring initiatives, some firms engage external coaches to work with top performers. These programs are viewed as valuable perks for both up-and-coming professionals and firm partners and can be a very effective tool to hone future leaders (see "Training at Bain & Company").

Mentoring: Providing Personal and Professional Support

Mentoring would seem to be the ideal training technique in an apprenticeship-driven professional service setting—and a substantial number of firms use this approach as one of the tools in their training arsenal. In theory, having someone help new hires and up-and-coming professionals navigate an organization and develop professionally makes great sense. Even so, many of our interviewees talked openly about the difficulties inherent in fostering these kinds of intensive professional relationships. As a number of executives noted, unless mentoring is embedded in a firm's culture and performance evaluation

Training at Bain & Company

Bain & Company, one of the world's leading business and strategy consulting firms, consistently tops the lists of the most coveted places to work. The firm's training program, ranked number one by Vault.com, is a crucial factor in Bain's ability to recruit and retain some of the most talented consultants around the globe. "Training is at the core of who we are and what we do at Bain," says Russ Hagey, Worldwide Chief Talent Officer and 25-year Bain veteran. "It's one of our core mission-critical investments year-in and year-out."

The firm's talent management philosophy focuses on recruiting very bright, highly motivated, and "fun" people; getting them up to speed quickly through an on-the-job, team-based, apprenticeship model; and supplementing hands-on learning with a formal training, mentoring, and coaching program:

- **Formal training**—Bain offers a continuous learning program of training sessions held regularly in locations around the world combined with local in-office sessions. Bain consultants follow a six-step career progression from associate consultant through partner. Every 12 to 18 months, consultants and partners at each level attend training sessions appropriate to their career stage. Sessions are from 3 to 10 days in length and afford participants the opportunity to meet and work with their colleagues from Bain offices around the world. Consultants at each career level attend at least two formal training sessions before moving to the next level. Each office offers individual training modules every 3 to 4 months tailored to individual needs for each career stage.

  The curriculum spans all aspects of skills that consultants need to grow into leaders of teams and agents of change in organizations. "We teach around a set of core skills, analytic tools, and points of view and then layer in soft skills including client, people, and team management," says Hagey. Curriculum is developed internally by partners in collaboration with Hagey's staff of training professionals. Programs are reviewed and refreshed every 2 years, based on feedback from trainers, participants, and offices. Ninety-five percent of training is conducted by Bain partners and experienced managers, who compete for the honor of teaching at the global training programs. Trainers are nominated by local offices and selected on the basis of skills and mindset, and then put through additional train-the-trainer programs. In any given year, 20 to 30 percent of partners and 10 to 15 percent of managers serve as trainers.

Formal training sessions are supplemented through the Bain Virtual University (BVU), an online repository of tools and templates, video-based training, and interactive quizzes and modules. BVU holds more than 500 training modules for consultants to access for refresher and independently driven training. Hagey reports an excess of 50 hits per consultant per month on BVU.

- **Mentoring and coaching**—Formal and informal mentoring play an important role in Bain's apprenticeship and continuous learning approach to training. Partners are expected to be active coaches and mentors for those on their case teams. Consultants and associate consultants are assigned managers or partners as mentors who are responsible for guiding their professional development and delivering formal performance appraisals twice per year. Partners are matched with more senior partners or third-party coaches for individualized coaching and mentoring. The firm ties rewards and incentives to good people management, coaching, and mentoring performance.

Hagey cites powerful benefits to the firm's training programs: Both trainers and trainees establish valuable ties and friendships that keep them at Bain and facilitate cooperation on client engagements, and the programs are an important way to embed the firm's culture and values consistently across offices and countries. As Hagey sums up, "Our training programs incorporate a heavy dose of what we characterize as Bain DNA—the cultural spark and energy that attracts people to our firm."

system, the everyday pressures of client work and billability can make these programs difficult to maintain.

Informal mentoring—where a professional finds and bonds with a partner who takes the employee under his or her wing—is very effective. In fact, many of the leaders we interviewed discussed the enormous benefit of having strong mentors throughout their careers. But not everyone can find and harness a gifted advisor, which is why many firms have tried to formalize the process. The PSFs that have strong mentoring programs work hard to keep them alive and effective. They usually involve assigning a mentor to a mentee, prescribed meetings and events to build and maintain the relationship, and a reporting element where both mentor and mentee discuss and evaluate results. Partners and senior professionals who are given a mentor role often participate in train-the-trainer programs to better understand and execute their responsibilities, and their performance as a mentor is considered in their evaluations and compensation.

Several firms have effectively combined senior mentors with peer-level teammates who introduce young professionals into the firm. Advertising firm Euro RSCG Life has developed a buddy system and mentoring strategy that provides extensive support, not just for new hires, but for senior executives as well. As Worldwide Managing Partner Donna Murphy describes it, "We want to acclimate people to our culture so they feel at home." When a new employee starts, he or she is assigned a buddy—a go-to person, almost like a big sister or brother when you join a sorority or fraternity—to teach him or her the ropes. For mid-level employees, the firm put in place a carefully planned mentoring strategy. The firm conducts a training program for buddies and mentors, who meet quarterly to discuss issues and exchange ideas. The firm also offers a formal mentoring program for its mid-level and above professionals, including the entire senior leadership team, who are assigned both mentors and coaches.

Skadden, Arps has developed a strong mentorship program. Summer associates are assigned an associate officemate who acts as a buddy, an associate liaison, and a partner liaison. In all, three people are looking out for each new hire to ensure that the person is engaged and exposed to projects in his or her areas of interest. Within practice teams, senior associates partner with junior associates. Skadden also provides ongoing coaching and mentoring to new partners to ease their transition.

Accounting firm Plante & Moran is another firm that has developed a unique and highly effective mentoring program. Top management believes that the multifaceted support system it has created is a pivotal factor in its exceptionally high retention rate (see "Plante & Moran's Team-Based Mentoring").

Plante & Moran's Team-Based Mentoring

In 2010, public accounting and business advisory firm Plante & Moran was named as one of the "100 Best Companies to Work For" by *Fortune* magazine—the firm's 12th consecutive year on this prestigious list. Frank Moran, one of Plante & Moran's founding partners, believed deeply that a strong and enduring culture was critical to the firm's long-term growth and viability. By the mid-1950s, when the firm was about 30 years old, he articulated the philosophy that mentoring and nurturing the next generation of firm leaders was a core responsibility of all members of the firm. This vision gave rise to a unique system of mentoring that the firm calls the team and buddy system. Every professional—from the entry-level staff accountant to the firm managing partner—is supported by a team of at least two people who guide and support their career development.

Everyone who joins the firm is assigned a team partner who is directly responsible for that person's career development. As young professionals take on various assignments working for multiple partners, their project performance evaluations are routed to the team partner. Team partners work with these young professionals to interpret the evaluations, build tailored professional development plans, and monitor progress. "The team partner," notes Partner and Human Resource Director Chris McCoy, "ensures that each young professional gets a diverse experience, learns our performance management system, and builds skills as they move from job to job."

Each new staff member is also assigned a "buddy," a nonpartner professional several years senior. The buddy serves as a guide to the culture, making sure newly hired professionals are learning the procedures and building networks within the firm. Buddies sit in with the team partner on performance evaluations and career planning sessions, which are held formally twice per year. Entry-level staffers are quickly integrated into the culture, while buddies begin to learn the art and science of mentoring and managing. "Looking back on my career, some of the best opportunities I had were when I was a buddy for a young staff person," notes McCoy, "I got to sit in the room and see how partners develop and challenge people. I learned from watching those partners develop others."

The partner and buddy form the young professional's team during his first years at the firm. As professionals mature and move into more specialized roles, the buddy is replaced by an advisory team—a more senior partner, and another professional, most likely within the same industry group. The process is necessarily fluid. "You can't assign mentorship," says McCoy. "You assign some of these career development responsibilities, and you hope it clicks. If it doesn't, we'll make a change." The firm reassesses, reevaluates, and changes the team partner assignments as needed.

The program represents a significant investment in professional time. Each partner spends at least 20 hours a year with each of his or her staff members, plus at least as much time behind the scenes. Depending on their roles, partners mentor between 6 and 12 professionals annually. "In a business where time is what you sell, the challenge is the constant balance of investing time with staff and investing time with clients," says McCoy. It takes a sustained commitment from firm leadership, a willingness to revamp rewards and measures, and the fortitude to stay with the program in the face of profitability pressures.

Some firms are seeking to capitalize on an increasingly tech-savvy workforce by encouraging reverse mentoring—a partnership in which younger employees coach more seasoned players on the ins and outs of social media networking or digital tools. Such arrangements can also enrich young coaches by giving them exposure to experienced professionals.

Performance Evaluations: Frequent and Thorough Feedback

"I think one of the reasons people leave is that they don't know where they stand; they feel like they're almost abandoned—that we're working them to death, but they don't feel any sense of clarity around the direction of their career."

Ambitious, hard-driving professionals crave feedback and recognition from their superiors, peers, and clients. This is true at all levels, from the most junior associate to the most senior partner. Particularly in the PSF apprentice-based business model, it is critical that professionals are constantly learning and striving to master and upgrade their skills. Doing this effectively requires a combination of formal and informal training, coaching and mentoring, and performance feedback. It is easier to pay attention to professional development in a small firm where junior professionals have a high degree of access to team leaders and partners. It is much more difficult to do so in a large, highly leveraged firm where the ratio of partner to associates can be as high as 1:20 to 1:40 in some areas.

As with training, good performance-review programs are not solely the purview of large, well-funded firms. Again, we found some excellent processes in the small firms we studied. The best-run programs share two common characteristics: they encourage a culture of continuous learning and sharing, and they incorporate formal performance reviews, often throughout the year. As with mentoring, it is tough to get very busy partners who must find, sell, and do client work, manage and grow their practices, and sometimes participate in firm governance, to take time to teach and give feedback to the junior team. All of us in the business have undoubtedly had to work with at least one gruff, overextended partner where "no news is good news" was the best you could hope for in terms of direction. The key, according to many firm leaders, is to create a culture where sharing and providing direction are valued, expectations are clearly defined, and good talent-development efforts are recognized and rewarded via the compensation system. In the best-run organizations, feedback is given continuously and supportively as a normal course of action—after a client meeting or presentation, for example, when events are fresh and the teaching opportunity is high.

The most effective programs supplement annual performance reviews with more frequent, less formal appraisals mid-year, quarterly, even monthly, as well as after each engagement. At ghSMART, consultants are evaluated in formal written quarterly dashboard reviews conducted with the firm's CFO as well as annually by the partners. Skadden, Arps does quarterly "flash" or short-form reviews as well as "deep dive" reviews—one-on-one sessions with a partner with input from others—annually for senior attorneys and semiannually for junior attorneys.

Timing for annual reviews varied across firms, with most opting to review everyone at the same time. Some firms evaluate professionals on their anniversary dates to break up the burden on the senior people; however, several leaders say that anniversary reviews make it difficult to look holistically at the talent base.

Diversity Looms Large—and Will Continue to Pose a Major Challenge

"We're trying to weave diversity into our strategy. The challenge is that the legacy of the industry is white men. That's not reflective of the talent pool, and it's not reflective of our client base."

Like the rest of the corporate world, service businesses are struggling to build and maintain a diverse workforce. Despite earnest efforts, the upper ranks of the majority of professional service firms continue to be filled largely by white males. As our survey progressed, it became clear that quite a few firms are beginning to show some success in attracting and retaining women and minorities.

Deloitte's diversity model, for example, allows gifted performers exceptional flexibility in charting their individual career paths and accommodating work/life concerns. The global organization has a number of initiatives focused on building and mentoring a diverse workforce, including an award-winning program for developing women leaders. Latham has also demonstrated a strong commitment to broadening its employee base through a variety of programs and initiatives including its Women Enriching Business (WEB) Initiative (a program designed to promote women in business by creating broader networks and productive business relationships, and by investing in the long-term success of women); an active Diversity Hiring Sub-Committee devoted to diversity outreach efforts; a firmwide mentoring program; associate-driven grassroots initiatives focused on supporting retention and promotion of attorneys with diverse backgrounds; diversity weekends; and hosted networking events. Investment firm Piper Jaffray is broadening its talent pool by moving beyond its traditional networks when recruiting both entry-level and industry hires. The firm works with professional recruiters to cast a wider search net and attract candidates with more diverse backgrounds, experience, and knowledge.

More and more firms realize that business-as-usual recruiting strategies won't give them access to broader talent pools—or meet shifting client needs. As clients grow more global, they are demanding fresh perspectives and service teams that reflect the diversity of their far-flung customer bases. According to a number of respondents, client and government pressures on service firms to diversify are intensifying. PSFs may be responding unevenly, but they *are* responding. As one executive summed up his firm's response to diversity, "We're very focused on it, but it's a weakness. That's something we're very cognizant of. We talk about it all the time—and we're working on it."

CHAPTER SUMMARY

People

- Close to 100 percent of the firm leaders interviewed place talent management at the top of the list of executive priorities.
- The best-run firms share seven noteworthy characteristics. These enterprises do the following:
    1. Adopt a stewardship mind-set
    2. Devote professional time and resources
    3. Recruit the right people from the start
    4. Carefully plan and manage careers
    5. Invest in training
    6. Make talent management an accountable responsibility
    7. Commit to diversity
- Culture, type of business, and brand strength play pivotal roles in determining recruiting strategy. All firms rely on a combination of sources for tapping new talent: on-campus recruiting, internships, social media, internal incentive programs, alumni networks, and external recruiters.

- The best interview and selection approaches involve a multi-step process:
    1. A formal analysis and profiling of the tasks, skills, and personality characteristics that best fit the firm and the role
    2. Identification of and pre-interview planning with an interviewee team
    3. Prescribed interview techniques and reporting procedures
    4. Discussion and agreement before the hire decision is formalized
- The best firms carefully map the competencies and performance expectations for each career stage; clearly communicate these to professionals; and have formal training, mentoring, and performance review procedures in place to guide and support professionals.
- Firms incorporate a core set of tools into their training programs: online instruction, company universities, teaming with academia, and one-on-one coaching.
- A successful mentoring program is formally planned and managed and includes an assignment of a mentor and a mentee, prescribed meetings and events to build and maintain the relationships, and a reporting element to evaluate results.
- Firms with the most effective performance-evaluation processes share two common characteristics: They encourage a culture of continuous learning and sharing, and they incorporate multiple performance reviews throughout the year.
- Despite major efforts and initiatives, diversity remains a challenge.

4

Portfolio

Strategy, client mix, and relationship management

"Client relationship management is critical. You can take nothing for granted. It's just like building a relationship with your spouse or your friends—you have to work at it."

—Ralph Baxter, Chairman and CEO, Orrick

"If you're serving the wrong clients, you don't have a chance for success."

—Bill Hermann, Former Managing Partner, Plante & Moran

"If you truly understand your clients, and you truly understand your mix within an industry or geography, you can more effectively manage the profitability of your portfolio."

—Rike Harrison, Chief Growth Officer, Wipfli

For PSFs, the client base, in effect, defines the business. Clients represent much more than a revenue stream: They are the magnet that attracts other desirable clients as well as top professionals to the firm. They help shape a firm's brand and have a powerful influence on its reputation and standing in the marketplace.

Clearly, our interviewees agreed that building and maintaining a strong client base is a top priority. Eighty-seven percent said that client portfolio strategy and management is a critical area of focus for firm leaders, placing it third in importance rating behind vision, values, and culture and talent management, as shown in Exhibit 4.1.

EXHIBIT 4.1 Client strategy and management ranks third in importance on leadership agendas

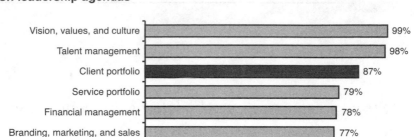

Vision, values, and culture	99%
Talent management	98%
Client portfolio	87%
Service portfolio	79%
Financial management	78%
Branding, marketing, and sales	77%
Equity and compensation	74%
Strategic planning	71%
Infrastructure	62%

Fifty-five percent of respondents gave themselves a top grade on performance in this area, as shown in Exhibit 4.2. However, most indicated that they are best at individual client management—their weakness is in overall portfolio management and measurement.

EXHIBIT 4.2 Half rate themselves highly on client portfolio management

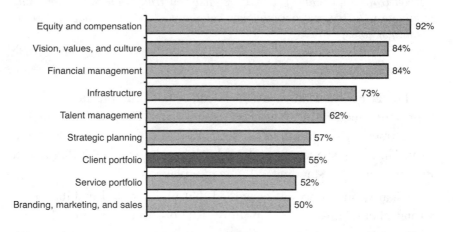

Equity and compensation	92%
Vision, values, and culture	84%
Financial management	84%
Infrastructure	73%
Talent management	62%
Strategic planning	57%
Client portfolio	55%
Service portfolio	52%
Branding, marketing, and sales	50%

Virtually all firms, whether global enterprises or niche players, allow for opportunistic client acquisitions. However, many believe they have erred too much in that direction and are far too ad hoc in their approach to acquiring clients, allowing partners to bring in new business at their discretion or reactively responding to pitch opportunities with little or no strategic planning. Traditionally, professionals have sought and served clients as part of their personal book of business—and this "lone ranger" mentality is alive and well throughout the professional service industry.

By nature, professionals like to own and protect their client relationships. They possess a natural reluctance to sever ties with clients, particularly those with whom they have long-term working relationships. This reluctance often goes hand in hand with an unwillingness to conduct an objective profitability analysis that many consulting firms routinely recommend their clients undertake to prune and upgrade their business portfolios.

A healthy number of respondents observed that they have fallen prey to the Golden Goose syndrome: overreliance on a handful of clients who provide a major contribution to the firm's revenues but who also result in dangerous vulnerability. We heard a number of sobering war stories about near disasters from firms that unexpectedly lost a key revenue-generating client. Everyone who runs a professional service firm understands the danger of keeping too many eggs in too few client baskets, but it is difficult not to be lulled into complacency when deep-pocket, long-term client assignments come your way. Small firms in particular tend to throw all hands on deck to manage these engagements, while long-term planning and business development to keep the new-client pipeline active are put on hold.

"If you compared us to a corporate structure, we would fail abysmally in terms of the amount of time and thought we put into portfolio planning."

"There was a very strong belief amongst partners that the more clients you have, the better. And we had to convince them that the opposite was true."

Five Essentials of Client Portfolio Management

"We're continuously assessing what sectors and what clients are likely to perform best and have the greatest need that we should be able to tap into."

The best approach to developing an effective client strategy is a combination of analysis, focus, measurement, cultural change, process, and technology—all fueled by a healthy dose of continuous market feedback. A comprehensive client portfolio and relationship management program starts with a current-state analysis and follows a continuous cycle of action, review, and reward. A successful program is based on five essential precepts:

1. *Proactively plan and manage the portfolio.* Expecting your business to grow opportunistically with no cohesive strategy underpinning individual efforts is rarely a recipe for success. Firms that adopt this approach run the risk of never gaining critical mass or reputation in any particular market. The best-run firms engage in formal organization-wide client planning and management programs to critically evaluate the current client base on a regular basis. They profile the highest-opportunity target clients; nurture and grow high-value clients; and track and measure the profitability, strengths, and weaknesses of individual clients and the overall portfolio.

2. *Frame the client experience.* Savvy firms spend time discussing and documenting their philosophy and processes to create a client experience that exemplifies the firm's work style, values, and culture. This is an inclusive process that involves partners across the firm in an evaluation of the factors that contribute to a successful client engagement, ranging from client early-stage needs through the quality of interactions throughout a project, to follow-up to identify service strengths and weaknesses from the client perspective. Benchmarks and ROI metrics for determining client satisfaction and client service levels are captured and assessed frequently.

3. *Clearly define roles and responsibilities.* Firms strongly committed to developing a comprehensive client strategy recognize that someone must be responsible for developing and monitoring every aspect of an integrated client program. Although top management owns the overall strategy, responsibility cascades to business unit leaders and individual partners and professionals to manage and monitor client relationships, solicit feedback and review, and measure progress. Everyone in the firm has a role to play.

4. *Establish rewards and accountability.* If building and sustaining vibrant client relationships is viewed as an integral facet of professional development, it follows that individual performance in this area must be monitored. Equally important, rewards and consequences must be clearly defined and communicated—and compensation tied to results. If a positive, relationship-enhancing client experience is to be the barometer of

professional success, a firm must reward those who excel in this area of performance.

5. *Involve clients.* In the best-run firms, client opinions and recommendations are an integral part of service testing and innovation, structure and process improvements, and relationship management. Clients are contacted to solicit their viewpoints formally in periodic surveys or informally during regular engagement interactions. Some firms pilot new offerings and service delivery concepts with key clients to test-run ideas and deepen their commitment to and involvement with the firm.

Mastering the Client Management Life Cycle

Many of the firms we studied have amazingly long-lived relationships with clients—some spanning more than a century. The original founders of what is now the London-based law firm Freshfields, for example, began working with the Bank of England 270 years ago. Interestingly, the ability to maintain client continuity is not just confined to firms with traditional annuity-type businesses, such as accounting or advertising and public relations; it also exists in project-driven segments such as architecture, consulting, law, and executive recruiting. So how do these firms do it?

Based on our discussions and experience in the industry, we have identified five steps to successfully manage the client cycle from concept through acquisition, retention, and renewal. As shown in Exhibit 4.3, the cycle begins with strategically planning and regularly reviewing the client mix. As clients come onboard, they are carefully introduced into the firm and are nurtured and managed throughout the relationship via a well-defined process to sustain, grow, solicit feedback, and improve the client relationship. The cycle is completed with regular reviews of client profitability, partner management, and relationship status. Each step in the cycle is integral to building a profitable client base that sustains and nourishes the firm and its professionals.

EXHIBIT 4.3   The five steps of successful client life cycle management

5. Review
and measure
results.

4. Solicit client
feedback.

1. Strategically
plan and review
client portfolio.

2. Onboard new
clients.

3. Sustain and
grow accounts.

Step One: Strategically Plan and Review the Client Portfolio

Leaders agree that the most effective way to maintain and build a strong client portfolio is to proactively plan and manage it. However, as shown in Exhibit 4.4, just over one-third (36 percent) of our interviewees indicated they formally engage in strategic planning and portfolio management on an enterprise-wide basis. While over half (53 percent) engage in planning and targeting as part of their annual planning process, they indicated that responsibility for this step resides at the practice level; choosing new clients is left to the discretion of key partners, with little or no firm oversight beyond conflict checks. And 12 percent of our interviewees said they do not plan or review their client portfolio.

EXHIBIT 4.4   Client portfolio planning ranges from opportunistic to strategically planned

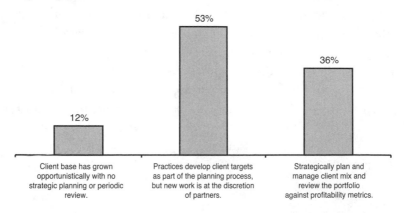

53%

36%

12%

Client base has grown
opportunistically with no
strategic planning or periodic
review.

Practices develop client targets
as part of the planning process,
but new work is at the discretion
of partners.

Strategically plan and
manage client mix and
review the portfolio
against profitability metrics.

Start by Assessing What You Have

We had several discussions about the benefits of conducting a periodic review of the entire client base, which can be relatively easy for a small firm and extremely daunting for a global multipractice organization. However they rank themselves in this area, leaders agree that it is crucial to take their firm through this type of client evaluation exercise on a regular basis. Several of our interviewees said they find the old-fashioned SWOT analysis (Strengths, Weaknesses, Opportunities, Threats) to be a reliable tool for portfolio assessment, and praised its utility in identifying strengths and opportunities to leverage, along with weaknesses and threats to mitigate.

Firms typically begin by assessing their portfolio strengths. They look at their portfolio to determine which clients are the most profitable, which provide the most promising opportunities for cross-selling or integrating additional firm services and what type of client work offers the best platform to develop new services and skills. Finally, they look at which clients and engagements have the greatest sex appeal—brand and cache—in terms of their power to enhance the firm's reputation and strengthen its marketplace image.

After reviewing strengths, the next step in the SWOT analysis is to pinpoint portfolio weaknesses. Most firms have some clients that don't make sense from a variety of standpoints. Perhaps the most obvious is low profitability, but this can sometimes be justified if current work has the potential to lead to future, more lucrative engagements. Less obvious weaknesses are strategic and cultural mismatches. Too many pieces of business that are off target and out of sync with the firm's traditional skill base can confuse the market, dilute positioning, and fragment services. Some clients are simply a poor fit: they just don't mesh with the firm's team, always complain, or require a great deal of senior time—often unbillable—to manage and keep satisfied. The opportunity cost of continuing to serve such clients is high and should be evaluated, with the obvious caveat that it is often a tough political job to "fire" a long-term client.

In the next phase of a SWOT analysis, new business opportunities are identified. Almost every professional service firm that we have consulted with has multiple opportunities to expand business with current clients. Time and again when we talk to clients of the firms we are working with, we uncover potential new business. And in fact, a significant number of our interviewees admitted that they do not do a good job of identifying the potential for growing current client relationships. Happy clients are pleased to buy additional services from professional service providers who have done good work for them. But all too often, professionals are reluctant to ask for more work. Equally damaging, the firm's professionals can be so protective of their relationships that they hesitate to tell their clients about the full complement of service offerings that their firm can provide.

Finally, a classic SWOT analysis can pinpoint inherent weaknesses in a client portfolio. Relying on too few clients creates dangerous vulnerabilities, but other threats also can seriously affect a firm's profitability and positioning. Volatile markets and tough economic times are particularly challenging for some professional service segments, such as consulting and executive search, which are often viewed as discretionary purchases. The best-run firms say they strive for a mix of offerings and a diversity of clients that will enable them to remain viable in both vibrant and slow market conditions. It is always difficult to predict an economic meltdown, an unexpected merger or acquisition of a key client, or the departure of a partner with a large book of business, but top firms are fully aware of their vulnerabilities to these threats and make every effort to ensure that they are not caught off guard.

Decide Where to Focus

"We are not disciplined in profiling our clients. Are we going after the multibillion-dollar clients or the midmarket? Which industries make the most sense? Are we targeting the CIO or the CFO or both?"

"We had a client we resigned from because they were very disrespectful of our values and our people. We are just not going to work for people like that."

Once the current client mix has been thoroughly reviewed and assessed, the next step is to create a vision of the ideal mix of clients that will drive the firm's strategic direction while meshing with its values and culture. Responses to this topic ranged from "We don't do that" to descriptions of in-depth strategic profiling and planning processes. Most leaders agree that too much structure can have a negative impact on the entrepreneurial nature of professionals who want to grow their own practices and work on the things they love to do. Others, particularly leaders of multipractice, multibusiness unit firms, disagree with this strategy—or rather, the lack of one. They say that the larger and more diverse the firm, the greater the potential to spin your wheels and dilute your focus if decisions about a firm's client base are left in the hands of practice leaders.

Finding the right balance is difficult, but we recommend erring on the side of planning and focus. The most successful firms—both large and small—focus services around well-defined functional and industry areas of expertise. Their strong service focus dictates the profile of the clients that make the most strategic sense for the firm to pursue. Equally important, the marketplace overwhelmingly supports the vote for focus. Broderick & Company conducts a periodic study of hundreds of top executives who buy professional services. Repeatedly, these senior buyers rate industry and functional focus and expertise as their top reason for selecting specific professional service providers. (See Exhibit 6.8 in Chapter 6, "Finance.") Sophisticated buyers are looking for depth of commitment and knowledge, background and bench strength of teams, relevant work experience and credentials from professional service firms.

Savvy firms take a rigorous approach to determining their optimal target mix of clients. These organizations review and rate opportunities based on a predetermined set of criteria that reflects both internal and external market considerations. Industry is often the first screen applied to the profiling process, followed by size, geographic dispersion, functional buyers, the competitive landscape, and an assortment of characteristics such as marquee value, emerging growth potential, level of innovation, and degree of distress. We suggest that firms profile the highest-potential buyers for each service area and then create a firm-wide map of buyers by services to focus marketing and sales to identify cross-selling opportunities, as shown in Exhibit 4.5.

EXHIBIT 4.5 Target Client Profile for a Midsized Regional Law Firm by Practice Area

Target Audience	Corporate	Finance	IP	Energy	Sample Companies	Buyer
Midmarket technology companies "about to go public" or growing internationally ($50 million to $1 billion)	✓	✓	✓		Autodesk Novellus SGI	CEO COO CFO General Counsel
Large global technology companies headquartered or doing significant business in the region ($1 billion +)	✓	✓	✓	✓	HP Intel Cisco	General Counsel or direct reports
Private equity companies	✓	✓			Weston Presidio TPG Genstar Capital	Managing Director
Venture capital firms	✓	✓			Citigroup Venture Capital	Managing Director
Large banks and financial institutions	✓	✓			Wells Fargo Bank of America Charles Schwab	Managing Director/SVP
Large companies with significant energy assets; energy companies or companies with cogeneration facilities	✓	✓		✓	Mirant Chevron Duke Reliant	General Counsel
Large global nontechnology companies headquartered or doing significant business in the region	✓	✓			Bechtel McKesson	General Counsel or direct report

Firm leaders say that it is important for clients to be cultural fits for the organization as well as profitable revenue generators. As Steve Gunby, former Chairman of North and South America for The Boston Consulting Group, summed it up, "The question we always ask is, where can we find the type of work where we can make a difference, build our brand, and energize our people?"

Step Two: Onboard New Clients

"I always call clients and thank them for the business. And four out of five will say to me, 'I can't believe you're calling me and thanking me for the business. Nobody in Wall Street has ever done that before.' They are just blown away."

Given the importance of clients in the life of a professional service firm, we are continually surprised and dismayed by the fact that so few firms have formal "welcome aboard" programs for new clients. Accounting firms have rigorous risk-assessment procedures to evaluate the potential risk of taking on a new client. Law firms have conflict committees that review each new potential piece of business to make certain that the firm does not currently represent an opposing party. But these are screening processes, not welcome programs.

Most firms rely on partners to introduce new clients to the firm. This casual approach works reasonably well for many of the firms studied because professionals typically don't become partners if they can't retain and expand client relationships. Many firms spend considerable time and resources teaching client care to professionals throughout the course of their progression in the organization. And in many firms, partner compensation is positively or negatively affected by the longevity and growth of key accounts.

Yet even the most seasoned partners readily admit that engagement start-ups can be rocky, both for the professional service team and its new client. They also acknowledge the importance of ensuring that the transition to a client/provider relationship is a smooth and satisfying one.

An effective onboarding program creates positive expectations, builds familiarity and trust, and demonstrates value to a client early on with the goal of transforming an initial engagement into a long-term relationship. The best-led PSFs use a carefully selected mix of onboarding approaches that go well beyond standard "let's get acquainted" letters and meetings. They view the initial honeymoon phase as the launchpad for a carefully orchestrated relationship-building strategy. Grant Thornton International Ltd.'s U.S. member firm, for example, introduces its client experience programs at the start of a relationship, setting client expectations, documenting progress, and reporting results to both the client and firm management. Based on our survey findings, there are several hallmarks of a strong onboarding program:

- A *formal project-launch plan* designed to set service expectations, establish mutually agreed-upon criteria for success, introduce key players to each other, and identify hot-button issues
- *Frequent face-to-face meetings* with the goal of building trust, encouraging collaboration, identifying key client contacts, and confirming a desired plan of action
- *Regular progress reports* providing accurate, timely information on project milestones and initial results to foster strong communications and allay predictable start-up concerns
- A *touch-point strategy* designed to create a profile of key project players and maintain consistent contact with them as valued information sources and stakeholders
- *Client feedback outreach* aimed at assessing client perception of service quality and identifying potential problems or barriers to strong performance
- *Client exposure to firm expertise*, with the goal of introducing client stakeholders to firm professionals outside the firm's immediate service team
- *Deploying advanced technology* by building client portals, conducting online training, developing shared systems for project tracking, and utilizing other digitally driven activities to support outstanding communication

Step Three: Sustain and Grow Accounts

Interviewees gave their firms higher ratings on client relationship management than on portfolio planning. As shown in Exhibit 4.6, 41 percent said they have a formal firm-wide process in place that is "taken very seriously" by firm leaders.

Grant Thornton Client Experience Program

Audit, tax, and advisory firm Grant Thornton, the U.S. member firm of Grant Thornton International Ltd., is committed to delivering high-quality personalized services to its clients. To formalize this commitment, the firm has developed a client-centric program to deliver a consistent experience for clients that the firm calls the Grant Thornton Client Service Cycle. The program is a multiphase series of activities that walks engagement teams through the process of working with the client from pre-engagement through post-engagement. Highlights of the cycle include the following:

- A meeting with the client in advance of each engagement to discuss expectations

- A customized service plan for each client based on the client's expectations on everything from timing to definition of value

- Regular check-ins to ensure that the team is delivering as expected and to share any relevant technical, regulatory, industry, or general market intelligence that the client may find valuable

- Annual review programs to measure service quality, led by an independent third-party vendor

- A customized portal containing Grant Thornton ideas and business and industry knowledge on an assortment of topics tailored for an individual client's needs and shared through a secure extranet website

Success metrics are clearly defined, and responsibilities for executing the program are documented and emphasized for the firm's professionals. Each partner receives a dashboard report on service reviews and performance ratings from his or her clients. A monthly client service metrics report is provided to all office managing partners, and all employees receive an annual report that documents the program's results across practice areas and that outlines improvement priorities for the coming year.

"The program is definitely working," said Ed Nusbaum, former CEO of Grant Thornton in the U.S., now CEO of Grant Thornton International Ltd. Since launching the initiative in 2006, the firm has seen steady improvement in client satisfaction and loyalty. And the firm's analysis has confirmed that a definite correlation exists between increased client loyalty and higher fee growth and realization. "The program has been a key component of the firm's strategy to create a competitive distinction," says Nusbaum. "We have significantly strengthened our client relationships, our brand, and our market share. It's well worth the effort."

EXHIBIT 4.6   Client relationship management is most often driven by the partners

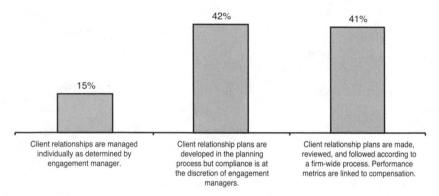

| Client relationships are managed individually as determined by engagement manager. | Client relationship plans are developed in the planning process but compliance is at the discretion of engagement managers. | Client relationship plans are made, reviewed, and followed according to a firm-wide process. Performance metrics are linked to compensation. |

Within the top-ranked group of firms interviewed, we found several excellent programs for managing and nurturing key clients. Although the processes varied from firm to firm, we identified three common elements that are integral to each program and form the basis for the success of their client relationship activities: portfolio segmentation, assigning lead account managers, and developing and implementing formal client plans.

Portfolio Segmentation

Portfolio segmentation involves dividing a firm's client roster into established categories or tiers based on their level of value and potential. Top-ranked firms view segmentation as a key management tool for prioritizing investments in people, services, training, marketing, and business development. Segmenting enables a firm to visually map the enterprise-wide landscape of its client base. As one firm leader told us, "I can glance at a map of our entire portfolio with accompanying metrics for each tier and get an instant pulse on the lay of the land."

Portfolio segmentation is enormously valuable for several reasons. It offers a 360-degree view of a firm's client activities across industries, geographies, and service utilization. It enables a firm to evaluate each client in terms of profitability and growth potential. And it lets a firm create profiles of its different types of clients, from loyal core accounts to event-driven "walk-ins." Finally, portfolio segmentation can reveal potentially damaging service gaps and/or lucrative service opportunities. Despite all these compelling benefits, we consistently find that many firms resist the idea of categorizing their clients in any way, shape, or form. Behind this resistance is a deep reluctance to acknowledge a sometimes painful, but necessary, truth: All clients are not equal. Although firm and practice leaders know this intuitively, they are often unwilling to bite the bullet and adjust their resource deployment and levels of investment for low-profitability clients.

Client portfolio categories typically cascade from the largest and strategically most valuable clients to transactional clients. Top-tier clients receive high levels of investment in both time and dollars. Most are given white-glove treatment, with designated formal programs of special activities such as in-house customized seminar programs, quarterly knowledge-sharing meetings, visits from the firm leader, and invitations to special social gatherings and sporting events. Account leaders of these clients are expected to—and do—spend a great deal of nonbillable time tending these relationships.

The approaches that the best-run firms use to segment their client bases vary somewhat, but in general they divide their clients into four categories:

- *Strategic clients* are major contributors to a firm's revenue streams—so much so that their loss could materially affect the firm's profitability. For larger, multinational firms, these strategic contributors are often global enterprises that the firm may serve across multiple geographies and practice areas. These are the clients that most firms leverage to grow their business by expanding their relationships and work assignments across product lines, service offerings, and geographies.
- *Core clients* are solid bread-and-butter accounts—loyal, ongoing service users who contribute to a firm's bottom line year in and year out. These clients consistently request work and, as they mature, usually require relatively low levels of investment and maintenance. This type of client often represents high comfort

level work for the professionals who know and serve them over time. In this category, relationships tend to plateau at some point in time; as a result, core clients may or may not also be "strategic clients" with significant growth potential.

- *Emerging-growth clients* are companies that the firm has decided to monitor with an eye toward new business development in the near or distant future. They may be fast-growing firms, companies in dynamic growth markets, or innovators pursuing game-changing strategies or technology breakthroughs.

- *Transactional clients.* With most firms, a portion of their client base consists of one-off assignments that "fall from the sky" which they take on as the opportunity presents itself (see "Black & Veatch Client Portfolio Mix").

The Critical Role of Lead Account Managers

The account manager has primary responsibility for orchestrating the firm's services to a single key client. The role is challenging in a multipractice global organization that serves multijurisdiction, multifaceted clients. The points of entry to these global organizations are vast and varied, and many large-scale professional service firms are siloed into regions and practices, making it difficult to effectively manage and monitor a global client relationship. According to interviewees, the key to addressing this challenge is finding the right balance between a centralized command-and-control structure and a decentralized eat-what-you-kill approach to client management. Too much centralized control and bureaucracy can create bottlenecks and lost opportunities. On the other hand, a decentralized structure can lead to chaos and confusion. One law firm leader told us that he had only recently discovered that 1,000 lawyers across his firm were working on various matters for one major client!

There is no single best approach to the client ownership issue. How firms manage top clients depends on their culture and organization style. Many interviewees said they take a hard line within their organizations on the issue of client management. In these firms, no one partner owns a client: Instead of being viewed as entries in individual partners' books of business, clients are considered to be institutional assets. To make certain that clients don't walk out the door with a departing professional, some firms assign a team of at least two partners to comanage

Black & Veatch Client Portfolio Mix

Strategically planning and managing a balanced portfolio of clients is a critical task, according to Mike Elzey, Senior Vice President of Management Consulting at engineering, consulting, and construction firm Black & Veatch. "It's a huge effort to get multiple operating units and lines of business all on the same page to plan and coordinate the acquisition, maintenance, and growth of the client base," says Elzey. To focus and facilitate the management process, the firm segments its client base into four major categories:

1. **Strategic clients**—Thirty percent of the firm's client mix represents high revenue generating clients, which, if lost, would damage the business. The firm's goal is to continue to grow strategic clients into very large ongoing revenue streams so that, as Elzey explains, "the firm becomes a trusted business advisor serving multiple parts of their operations with multiple parts of our business."

2. **Core clients**—Fifty percent of the portfolio are core clients that Black & Veatch has worked with for many years and established a steady business stream and strong relationships. In 2009, the consulting division selected 12 to 15 of the firm's core clients to transition to strategic clients. Elzey and his team met with each client to express their interest in deepening the relationship and discuss potential areas where Black & Veatch could add value. Based on these discussions, the firm developed relationship plans for each client and are measuring and tracking progress.

3. **Target clients**—Target clients, who represent about 10 percent of the base, are potential clients that the firm is planning to pursue and penetrate. "These are new companies on our radar screen that we're going to approach, get to know, and introduce our services to," says Elzey. "Our ultimate goal is to figure out how to appropriately serve them, win a few initial assignments, and begin the relationship development process."

4. **Opportunistic clients**—The remaining 10 percent are companies not on a proactive target list that have approached Black & Veatch with interesting projects that the firm decides to bid on and pursue.

The firm deploys a sales team to focus exclusively on expanding services to the strategic client base and invests in a CRM system to better manage the firm's contacts and services around major accounts. Elzey refers to the firm's client management process as the "zippering strategy." "We try to zipper our side of the organization to the side of our client's organization," says Elzcy. "It's, of course, harder to do than it sounds, but very effective if you can do it successfully."

a top-tier client. This practice, they say, benefits both the firm and the client, who appreciates the additional touch points and service continuity. In almost every interview conducted on behalf of our clients, senior executives at leading companies have repeatedly told us that they appreciate having one or two point people whom they can contact for service needs, advice, and direction. Our advice is to err on the side of central coordination; clients definitely prefer it, and it gives firm management greater control over its client base.

Several firms prefer the third-party approach to account leadership. In this model, top management intentionally selects a partner from a practice area that does not work frequently with the client to manage the account. The goal is to bring a more objective and cross-functional eye to relationship building. Again, this approach has the advantage of preventing one partner or one practice group from dominating the client.

For most firms, account managers or lead partners are assigned to the top-tier client group. The lead role in managing a valued client is a highly coveted position and generally is entrusted to the most senior professional on a service team. Almost all the firm leaders we interviewed managed one or more of their firm's top clients during the course of their careers. Most said it is an important training and grooming ground for future leaders. Client relationship manager responsibilities run the gamut from serving as a third-party resource or point person for clients to contact during engagements to acting as an orchestra leader who coordinates a fully integrated complement of services and teams.

Several of the advertising and public relations firms that we studied have adopted the orchestra-leader approach (see "Account Management at Burson-Marsteller"). These firms have established key global

Account Management at Burson-Marsteller

Global public relations and communications firm Burson-Marsteller serves its largest global clients through a 15-year-old program it calls KCR, Key Client Relationships. The program was designed to deliver the highest levels of service to the firm's most important global clients. Approximately 20 KCRs represent about one-third of Burson's revenue and include the firm's top global accounts based on size, growth, length, and depth of the relationship.

KCR client leads include members of the firm's senior leadership team and other highly experienced professionals who are pulled out of the bureaucracy. "Their only accountability is to make the client happy," says Burson-Marsteller Worldwide COO Richard Powell. They operate outside the geographic and service line P&Ls, and have the authority to command firm resources around the globe to serve their clients.

The firm carefully tracks the profitability and other financial metrics of KCRs with a dedicated financial manager for each client. Powell conducts formal reviews with KCR client leads at least twice a year and often quarterly. Using a structured process, client leads report on progress, relationship status, financial metrics, and areas of potential vulnerability. As a further management oversight mechanism, each KCR leader has a management committee sponsor who stays in touch weekly with the client's performance and is available to provide additional resources or intervention as needed.

In addition to creating the structure to deliver the highest levels of service to its most strategic clients, the firm sees the KCR program as a laboratory to advance their business and incubate new ideas and programs. Part of the KCR leads' role is to team with large clients to generate new services and programs. In weekly conference calls and regular face-to-face meetings, account leaders share their client successes and challenges, further extending the reach of innovations developed at client sites across the globe.

"The key client relationship program has been very successful for the firm," says Powell. "The special attention clients receive sustains and deepens the relationships, and the new service ideas that have resulted from the program have fueled the firm's growth and supported its positioning as a provider of high-stakes communications campaigns."

accounts as a separate dimension of their matrix governance model. In these firms, top-revenue clients are managed by global account lead professionals who operate independently of the service team system and are not held accountable to any practice or P&L. Account leaders have the clout to pick and choose talent and resources from throughout the organization to ensure that the quality and level of service remain high.

Client Plans

"We tend to be strategic at the high end, pretty targeted in the middle, and opportunistic and entrepreneurial around the edges. You never want to completely take away that entrepreneurial edge."

"We are trying to layer an account management strategy on top of our regional and practice structure like a 3-D matrix. The account strategy draws on the expertise from the regions and practices to better serve the clients."

We often consult with clients to develop client relationship segmentation and planning programs. In this role, we are constantly surprised at the fragmented information and lack of a coordinated client management approach that we find throughout the industry. In what can only be described as a typical scenario, we facilitated a meeting for a client in which every partner who had provided substantial work for one of the firm's top revenue-producing clients came together to discuss the account. The 20 partners who participated were "shocked and astounded" to discover the depth of work and the scope of relationships with this company that resided within their firm. The collective knowledge about the client's business was powerful, but until that point, it had not been leveraged to anyone's advantage. As one partner observed, "We probably know more about their business than they do."

Independent financial advisory and investment banking firm Duff & Phelps insists on client plans being shared among managing directors to ensure a coordinated approach to both service provision and analysis of additional business opportunities. Peppercom conducts weekly relationship management reviews as part of its client planning process. As Steve Cody, Managing Partner and Cofounder, notes, with such discipline, there is "no place to hide." Other firms have plans reviewed by nonteam members to ensure an objective, fully leveraged client management strategy. Not surprisingly, firms with decentralized client ownership structures do the least amount of client planning. It is difficult to develop a master plan when you have multiple relationships and touch points with one client.

Forward-thinking firms have a detailed plan for each of their high-performing clients—that 20 percent or so of their client base that typically provides most of their business. The primary goal is to build a framework for a consistent, firm-branded client management plan aimed at cultivating optimal clients. These clients will enhance the firm's reputation, provide rich service and cross-selling opportunities on an ongoing basis, and refer additional work to the firm (see "Client Management at Ernst & Young").

A robust client plan features a clearly delineated profile of client resources and service needs, includes a service progression map built around an enhanced revenue strategy, and has a tracking process and benchmarks for measuring progress against objectives. In a formal client plan, roles and responsibilities are carefully laid out. Client ownership is well defined—not just from a service perspective, but also in terms of accountability for expanding the client relationship and generating additional business, as shown in Exhibit 4.7.

Some firms prefer to take an informal approach to developing client plans. They depend on bottom-up client management and allow primary responsibility for client relationships to remain with partners in their traditional role within the matrix organization. However, as the needs of global clients increase in complexity and PSFs themselves grow across every dimension, more and more firms in every sector of the industry are seeing the value of a formal, coordinated approach to planning and implementing client management programs.

EXHIBIT 4.7   Client Planning Template

Establish goals for client relationship
- Objective with this client
  - —Specific 12-month objective
  - —Specific longer-term objective
- Client's objective
  - —What does the client want to achieve with the firm?
  - —Feedback from client interviews

Inventory the current status
- Current projects under way with this client
- Other projects with the client in the past 5 years
- Key relationships matrix (who knows whom)

Understand the client's business needs
- Client profile
  - —Organization chart, 10-K, other filings
  - —Analyst reports, news feeds, competitive analysis
- Current business needs and challenges for each operating segment
- Market conditions and external factors (regulatory, competitive pressures, technology disruption) affecting the company's need for services now and in the future

Identify and map target opportunities
- Key services to sell to the client
- Decision-makers and influencers to reach for each service

Develop marketing and business development activities
- Key vehicles to deploy to build the relationship
  - —Thought leadership
  - —Events
  - —On-site continuing education presentations
  - —Calls/meetings to introduce other services and firm partners
  - —Other

Manage the process
- Select team and assign overall responsibility
- Assign responsibilities for each activity
- Establish a timeline
- Set regular team meetings to review status
- Monitor and track
- Reward performance

Client Management at Ernst & Young

According to Jim Turley, Chairman of Ernst & Young Global, "At EY, the client is the center of the universe." As a major global PSF, the organization's client base is large and diverse with a wide spectrum of needs. To deliver consistent service across the portfolio, EY adopted a multi-level, account-centric client approach to service delivery:

- **Account segments**—The organization strategically classifies its clients into several categories based on the size and service needs of the client. The objective is to calibrate service levels to client needs or, as Turley explains, "to better serve clients where and how they need to be served." Major multinational clients, for example, require seamless service across the globe from a well coordinated account team, whereas an emerging growth client needs hands-on attention from a team that is familiar with the needs of fast-growing companies. The segmentation helps EY deliver the types of services required for each client. EY reviews the segment distribution on an annual basis and makes adjustments based on changing client needs.

- **Coordinating partner (CP)**—Every client has a CP who is responsible for overseeing the delivery of services and managing the overall client relationship. The CPs are selected based on their specific skill sets and usually reside in close geographic proximity to the client—account teams for multinational companies are typically led by a partner based at the company headquarters. For the largest accounts, the CPs are required to develop an annual client plan to address the client's service needs and deepen the relationship. Account plans are reviewed and approved by senior leadership and are monitored regularly for service quality and staffing consistency.

- **Assessment of service quality (ASQ)**—EY monitors client satisfaction throughout the year through a formal and rigorous process called ASQ, which is executed locally and monitored at the global level. A person independent of the account team meets with several senior executives—including the audit committee, board members, and senior management—to assess the relationship status. The ASQ leader files a written report, and any risk areas are promptly communicated to the CP and quickly addressed. For the firm's largest accounts, the reviews are conducted annually; other accounts are reviewed on a rotating basis.

Turley emphasizes that, to grow the business, EY is looking for profitable work with clients it can serve in a quality way. The client management program supports this goal and creates a win-win situation for both the organization and its clients.

Step Four: Solicit Client Feedback

"Clearly, getting feedback from your clients is like gold dust. It's of immense value."

"We found the only thing that really matters at the end of the day when everything's said and done, you're past the honeymoon, you've gone through the hell part of the project, you've turned it all around, they're happy, and then you go back to them and say, 'Would you hire us again?' That is the litmus test of the satisfaction."

Listening to clients is key. Virtually all firms solicit feedback as a way of monitoring client work and needs; here again, both the scope and formality of programs vary. Nearly all firm leaders say that a significant part of their job is spending time with clients, whether billable or not. As David Childs, Global Managing Partner at law firm Clifford Chance, notes, "I think the challenge for all professional service organizations is keeping in touch with clients in a meaningful way, particularly because your entry point is going to be all over the place."

The most common feedback tool is some form of survey, whether face to face or online. Many years of conducting interviews both in person and via telephone have given us a bias toward having conversations rather than relying entirely on an online survey. However, some firms use online surveys as a first step, with in-person or phone conversations as a second-level vehicle if the initial online survey uncovers less-than-satisfactory results.

A number of firms across the industry have well-defined and well-executed programs to regularly obtain feedback and mine it for relationship-building data. Some rely on their leadership team and staff to spearhead the feedback process, and others use third-party interviewers. Most who survey their clients do so annually, although some, like ghSMART, survey every client every six months, asking them to rate their satisfaction on a five-point scale. Others survey clients quarterly.

Euro RSCG Life utilizes a tool called the rapid response system, which triggers automated e-mail surveys to all clients once a quarter. The survey has five simple questions, which may vary by client. A client's responses are aggregated, and if any response rates a satisfied or less, the Euro RSCG co-presidents automatically get a real-time-generated e-mail. When this happens, according to Worldwide Managing Partner Donna Murphy, "We pick up the phone and say, 'Hello, Mr. Client. We'd love to come and see you. Do you have time to discuss this?' The client is thrilled that we do it. They know that we're paying attention to their business." The firm also does formal annual reviews for each client.

When it comes to monitoring client satisfaction, again, some forward-thinking PSFs go the extra mile. The accounting firm Wipfli, for example, has a formal program that uses a number of feedback vehicles, including client advisory boards and win-loss studies. Its client advisor boards meet every four to six months and provide objective input on potential new service offerings and service delivery structures. Wipfli has also introduced a Client Satisfaction Index, described by Chief Growth Officer Ulrike Harrison as an extensive client analytic program. The firm randomly chooses 10 to 15 percent of its clients for the survey. Scores are analyzed on a firm and industry basis, and the feedback is used to create action plans. On an individual basis, the scores are included in performance evaluations. Edelman also takes a thorough approach to client feedback, as discussed in "Edelman's Client Feedback Program."

Many firms use third parties to inject objectivity and discipline and a consistent approach to all client interviews. More firms are embracing automated tools, such as sophisticated customer relationship management (CRM) software, to develop client profiles, track relationships on a firm-wide basis, and gather data to fine-tune their client management programs.

Edelman's Client Feedback Program

Client service has historically been a top priority at global public relations agency Edelman. In 2001, the firm revitalized its commitment to making quality its number one business goal and appointed Janice Rotchstein as its Chief Quality Officer to lead the effort. Under her guidance, the agency's quality initiative has evolved into an award-winning program called Edelman Excellence (E2), which is aimed at creating a global client service strategy that transcends geographies and cultures.

Integral to the E2 client quality program is a carefully structured firm-wide system for soliciting and analyzing client feedback gathered at different stages of each client engagement. The cornerstone of this system is its "Right from the Start" meeting—a quality-driven approach for launching a new client relationship or reintroducing Edelman's service team when the client contact changes on an existing account.

When a client is introduced to the firm, it automatically enters the client quality program. New clients are asked to complete an online survey twice during the first year, and retainer clients are surveyed annually on the anniversary of their signing with the firm. The survey includes 40 closed and open-ended questions, including a Net Promoter Score® question. Edelman analyzes its Net Promoter Scores® globally, by region and by office. Questions cover quality of service, quality of thinking, quality of performance, quality of people, and quality of the relationship. Before launching the survey, the firm piloted the questionnaire in Chicago and Beijing to ensure that it was understandable and user-friendly on a global scale.

A client's anniversary date triggers the system to e-mail the client relationship manager, who selects a language and approves the release of the questionnaire. If the client manager does not approve the release, Rotchstein is alerted. "Some people get a little nervous about sending out the questionnaire," she says. "I tell them this is not only about results; it's about the relationship." Absent a compelling reason, the questionnaire is sent to the client.

Clients typically respond within two weeks, according to Rotchstein. She sends an e-mail summarizing the review to the client relationship manager, that person's managing director, the global practice leader, the regional president, the HR director, and others who "would benefit from knowing the client's response." Once a month, Rotchstein analyzes the cumulative results and presents a report to the executive committee. Regional reports go to all general managers and client leaders.

The quality program has become an integral part of Edelman's client service methodology, according to Rotchstein. "It's all about recognition and accountability." By intentionally identifying exceptional client service as its overriding objective and creating a portfolio of tools for generating client feedback from day one of an engagement, Edelman has gained an outstanding reputation as a client-focused firm.

Step Five: Review and Measure Results

"We don't trust our data on client profitability. We're working toward it. I'd say we do it well enough to be directional. We're continually pushing to make our systems better."

"I can go into any client and find out where we are, what the projects are, how profitable they are, what the history is. I don't know how you would run your business if you didn't have that."

By far the most politically challenging stage in client life cycle management is assessing and fine-tuning performance. This involves reviewing client service results, taking definitive action based on feedback and financials, and rewarding good performance and mitigating average or poor performance. In general, firms review and measure performance across three dimensions: Are the clients happy? Are the partners doing a good job? Is the firm making any money?

- **Relationship status**—Most firms with a formal client feedback program are well aware of the importance of using the input they receive to aggressively address problems and make needed service improvements. As a result, they typically share client-specific feedback with the client service partner and team, and then aggregate the results and share them with a broader group of partners.

- **Partner management**—One of the most sensitive, yet critical, aspects of assessing client service results is evaluating how adeptly or poorly lead partners manage key client engagements and relationships. Partner performance is always a loaded issue, but in today's intensely competitive environment, few firms have the luxury of tolerating behavior and results that jeopardize valued client relationships. That said, many firms continue to find it a major challenge to tie client feedback and other service data to compensation.

  Some firms, however, have taken significant strides in this direction. On a broad level, they may factor relationship results into personnel evaluations and flag areas for improvement. Those with formal client relationship plans review plans against performance. Advertising agency, McCann, for example, reviews client plans during partner performance reviews on an annual basis and links performance to compensation. Wipfli generates client feedback reports for each of its industry groups, which are then required to develop action plans to address significant service gaps. The results are monitored on a quarterly basis and factored into performance evaluations.

- **Profitability**—To complete the client service cycle, it is important for firms to review clients from a profitability perspective as well as in terms of relationship quality. A few firms indicated that they actually conduct a formal profitability review of each client, but they are definitely the exceptions. By and large, PSFs continue to tread lightly when it comes to evaluating their client relationships from a purely financial standpoint. If serving a client is clearly a losing proposition financially, firms are more likely to gently adjust their resource deployment rather than sever their connection.

We did find one firm that has attempted to weed out the weak members of its portfolio through a program called "The Bottom 500." Every year, the firm reviews its economically challenged engagements. The responsible partners must evaluate the relationship across several parameters—economics, cultural fit, degree of risk, and others—and either justify or terminate the work. According to the firm leader, empowering the partners to think strategically about their business has enhanced leadership development and netted tangible economic returns. The first year that the firm launched the program, it found that servicing these low-return engagements was the financial equivalent of having 45 staff members working for free. As the firm leader explained, "We resigned from 100 accounts, and all of a sudden we had enough staff and a nice jump in growth."

Technology is markedly improving data gathering in this area. Dashboards that offer real-time reporting highlight the impact of increased profitability on effective portfolio management and spotlight the negative effects of low-return clients on the firm's bottom line.

CHAPTER SUMMARY

Portfolio

- A PSF's client base, in effect, defines the business it's in. As a result, acquiring and retaining clients is in many ways more crucial and complex in professional services than it is in a product-based business.

- Effective client portfolio management consists of five essentials:
    1. Proactively plan and manage the portfolio
    2. Frame a desired client experience
    3. Clearly define roles and responsibilities
    4. Establish rewards and accountability
    5. Involve clients

- The process of successfully managing the client cycle from concept through retention and renewal has five steps. The cycle begins with strategically planning and regularly reviewing the optimal client mix and continues with introducing new clients, managing client relationships, and reviewing and measuring results (see Exhibit 4.3).

- Hallmarks of a strong onboarding program include a formal project-launch plan, frequent meetings, regular progress reports, a touch-point strategy, regular client feedback outreach, broadening client exposure to firm expertise, and deploying advanced technology.

- Top firms use three common elements to manage and nurture clients: portfolio segmentation, account leadership, and client planning.

- Soliciting client feedback is critical to relationship management.

- Many firms find it difficult to review and measure client profitability.

5

Services

Strategy, innovation, and knowledge sharing

"There's no question that an important part of the equation for leading a professional service firm is the ability to ignite and then sustain innovation. It's a key fundamental business process—easy to talk about and really hard to do."
—Jim Quigley, CEO, Deloitte Touche Tohmatsu Limited

"Without productization, intellectual capital just builds brand; it doesn't create a new service portfolio."
—Stephen Rhinesmith, Senior Advisor, Oliver Wyman

"The best services are developed in the field, and then the back office puts sophistication and scale to it."
—Paul Reilly, CEO, Raymond James

If talent is a firm's lifeblood, an effective service portfolio strategy represents the arteries through which that talent is channeled—and innovation keeps the whole system healthy and energized. Keeping services fresh and relevant to clients is an important differentiator in highly competitive fields. Service innovation can enhance brand, add value to clients, and create valuable new revenue streams. Plus, new services are growth catalysts, enabling firms to expand their offerings and tap new markets. A robust service portfolio strategy is fueled by three interdependent sources: service relevance, innovation, and knowledge transfer.

Service relevance involves maintaining a holistic view of all offerings to ensure that they are market-responsive, that there are no gaps or missed opportunities for competitors to exploit, and that no weak sisters are in the mix—low-demand, low-profitability services that siphon valuable professional time and energy. A strong innovation process ensures that promising new ideas are systematically identified, vetted, and, if appropriate, commercialized with the ultimate goal of energizing a firm's service base. Finally, a strong knowledge-transfer program ensures that best practices, winning client solutions, and leverageable tools are shared.

The leaders we spoke with are well aware of the critical importance of service strategy and management. Close to 80 percent of our interviewees rated service management and innovation as an important activity on their leadership agenda, as shown in Exhibit 5.1. Although 52 percent gave themselves relatively high marks, as shown in Exhibit 5.2, only 5 percent placed themselves at the highest point in the chart.

EXHIBIT 5.1   Over three-quarters place service strategy and management high on management agendas

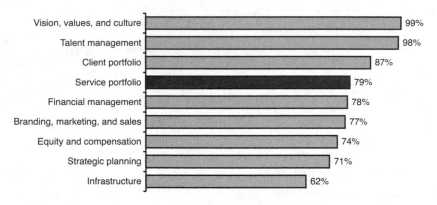

EXHIBIT 5.2   Performance reviews on service strategy and management are mixed

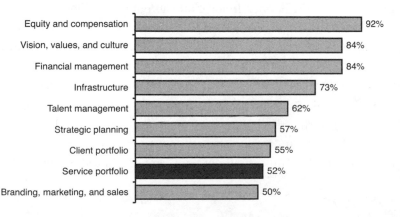

Four Essentials of Successful Service Portfolio Management

"The challenge is capturing the ideas, selecting those that have applicability to broad populations of clients, and then driving the investment and development process."

"There are probably 20 client meetings and valuable discussions happening right this minute in this building alone which could positively impact our current service offerings."

"The magic is to flip a switch and move from innovation to capitalizing on what you've developed. The mantra is to build something once and use it 100 times rather than building 100 things once as a stand-alone solution."

Over the years, we have found that developing and managing a service portfolio is challenging for many professional service firms. Even in the most sophisticated PSFs, service portfolio management is often at best reactive rather than a proactive strategic priority. Few firms review their current service portfolios regularly, and even fewer have processes in place to capture, select, and commercialize innovative new offerings.

And, of course, change is difficult. Professionals, like all human beings, are often reluctant to change how they do things. Services and methodologies become entrenched, and even with compelling market reasons to upgrade or exit current approaches and offerings, it can be a painful process to convince people to do things differently. Retiring services is particularly difficult for many firms. Legacy work for long-term clients, even if it is no longer profitable, is hard to give up. And moving professionals from a low-margin to a higher-margin practice requires not just a new mind-set but retraining. Rocking the service boat can be dangerous; a firm runs the risk of losing highly skilled performers who have an "I'll do it my way" mentality.

So, how do you do it? Based on our interviews with leaders across all industry segments, we've identified four essentials for effective service portfolio strategy management:

1. *Strategically plan and manage the service portfolio.* The best firms incorporate service strategy into both their long-term and annual planning cycles. The portfolio is regularly reviewed and

analyzed to assess the service's continued market relevance, identify gaps, and purge nonproductive services. Criteria are clearly established that provide the rationale for making tough decisions to jettison offerings that are not profitable or that are of marginal value to the marketplace.

2. *Establish and follow a protocol for innovation.* The firms that excel in this area have a well articulated and communicated process for stimulating, capturing, selecting, and transforming the best ideas into market offerings.

3. *Validate offerings with the market.* Astute firms talk to clients and prospective clients to test and validate current services, identify gaps, and uncover ideas for new services. Some firms integrate clients into the service innovation process to provide advice and direction on development and to test, debug, and validate a new offering.

4. *Assign ownership and accountability.* Like any other important activity with bottom-line impact, successful service management requires ownership and accountability. Responsibility for keeping current offerings fresh and generating potential new service offerings must be clearly defined.

Follow the Service Strategy Cycle

Firm leaders agree that successfully managing service development and renewal is a continuous cycle of activities, as shown in Exhibit 5.3. The process begins with a portfolio review to identify gaps and retire services that are no longer relevant. It continues with ideation, the often-complex task of stimulating and capturing new ideas. Then comes selecting the best candidates for development. And finally, ideas are transformed into viable service offerings, the troops are trained on delivery, and the services are launched. Gathering and sharing knowledge and client experiences is integral to the ongoing success of a service strategy. Each step of the cycle is important in creating a consistent engine of innovation.

EXHIBIT 5.3   The most successful firms in service strategy follow a five-step service development and renewal cycle

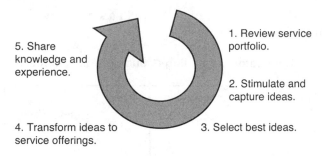

5. Share knowledge and experience.

1. Review service portfolio.

2. Stimulate and capture ideas.

4. Transform ideas to service offerings.

3. Select best ideas.

Step One: Review the Service Portfolio

"Today's good service offerings will be commodities in five years. I don't want to stay on a train that's slowing down."

It is critical that services are fully aligned with the firm's vision, strategic, and financial goals. As discussed in Chapter 7, "Positioning," a firm's services can either support or undermine market positioning and brand development. A firm seeking to become a premium high-value provider, for example, probably should not offer highly leveraged, more commoditized services. Understanding the strategic impact of the service portfolio on structure and governance, recruiting and training, pricing and profitability, and values and culture, and managing them accordingly, are important leadership priorities.

The first step is an inventory and review of the current mix of service offerings. Each service should be assessed on an assortment of criteria: revenues generated, revenue and profitability trends, market use, the buyer's degree of influence, and the competitive landscape.

The Boston Consulting Group developed a useful portfolio analysis tool for mapping services along two dimensions: market attractiveness, or the rate of growth of the market in which the service is sold, and market share, reflecting the firm's ability to compete in the market. Based on those two dimensions, firms assign services into one of four categories, as shown in Exhibit 5.4:

- **Star**—The firm has a high share in a fast-growing market
- **Cash cow**—The firm has a high share in a low-growth market

- **Question mark**—The firm has a small share in a fast-growing market
- **Dog**—The firm has a small share in a slow-growth or declining market

EXHIBIT 5.4   The Boston Consulting Group portfolio approach

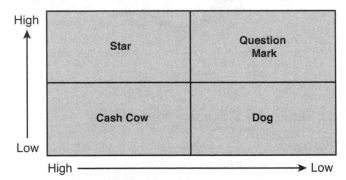

Source: The BCG Portfolio Matrix from the Product Portfolio Matrix, © 1970, The Boston Consulting Group

Firms then allocate resources to services in each category. Stars, which present the greatest potential, typically are considered areas of investment for staff, research, marketing, and sales to leverage the opportunity. Cash cows should be carefully nurtured, because they provide the revenue to maintain cash flow and fuel new investments. Services in the question mark category need to be seriously explored and debated. If they aren't terminated, they need to be monitored for performance and reevaluated periodically. Absent any compelling reason to keep them alive, the dogs should be retired.

Although this exercise yields an actionable profile of existing services, it doesn't identify gaps—services the firm should consider offering to the market. Philip Kotler, in his book *Marketing Professional Services*, provides a framework to identify opportunities for new services as well as opportunities to modify the services that survived the initial assessment (see Exhibit 5.5).

EXHIBIT 5.5 Service/Market Opportunity Matrix

	Existing	Modified	New
Existing	1. Market penetration	4. Service modification	7. Service innovation
Geographic	2. Geographic expansion	5. Modification for dispersed markets	8. Geographic innovation
New	3. New markets	6. Modification for new markets	9. Total innovation

Source: *Marketing Professional Services*, Second Edition, by Philip Kotler, PhD and Thomas Hayes, PhD, Paul N. Bloom, PhD. Copyright © 2002 by Learning Network Direct, Inc. Used by permission of Berkley Publishing Group, a division of Penguin Group (USA) Inc.

Using this tool, a firm would first evaluate existing services (cell 1) for the potential to increase revenues through market penetration, or deepening the use of the service in existing markets. An accounting firm, for example, may focus on introducing its consulting services to tax clients. Taking a more ambitious approach, the firm then considers any existing services that could generate more revenue by being introduced to new geographic markets (cell 2) or to a new industry segment or type of buyer (cell 3). While market penetration, or cross-selling, is well within the comfort zone of most PSFs, geographic and new-market expansion are riskier approaches, requiring more investment of time and money.

The next level of analysis is reviewing existing services to determine if modifying the service would increase market potential. This can happen through expanding or making changes in the service offering itself or repackaging the service to be more attractive to either existing clients (cell 4), new geographic markets (cell 5), or new industry or buyer segments (cell 6).

Finally, the firm examines ideas for new services to offer to existing and potential new clients (cells 7, 8, and 9). These can be either services offered by others in the marketplace but not yet offered by the firm or entirely new service offerings generated by a vibrant innovation program. The next phase of the service portfolio cycle—stimulating and capturing new ideas—sows the seeds of innovative services.

Step Two: Stimulate and Capture New Ideas

"The way we have gone from one business unit to five has been because some-one inside the company raises their hand and says, 'I want to start a new business.'"

"We begin with an idea or an insight and chase it at a high conceptual level without much regard to whether there is a market for it."

Regardless of industry segment, PSFs have two basic approaches to service innovation. They can build it themselves by incubating and developing new ideas internally. Or they can acquire it by buying or merging with businesses or practice groups that bring new or comple-mentary experience and knowledge.

Acquisitions can be time-consuming and fraught with complexi-ties. Therefore, the buy-it option is used predominantly by larger firms that have the resources to devote to integrating new services in conjunction with internal development efforts or by midsized firms hoping to enter new markets quickly. In addition to creating brand-new services, innovation encompasses redesigning or updating cur-rent services to better address market needs, repackaging or bundling of services across practices to create an integrated new offering, and upgrading service delivery to more efficiently and effectively serve clients. Many of the firms we studied include all of these innovation options in their service management process.

Stimulating smart, ambitious professionals to think creatively about what they do and how they do it would seem like an easy task for firm management. Yet the leaders we interviewed agree that there is definitely an art and science to innovation and that it is, in fact, not easy. For some firms, the innovation process may be informal— encouraging professionals to submit ideas for service creation via online community-based tools, for example, or encouraging small groups of key client relationship managers to brainstorm ideas on a weekly basis. Other firms are committed to a formal, systematic inno-vation process.

Most firms choose to develop services through a variety of formal and informal internal vehicles. The firms that do this best deploy a combination of cultural reinforcement and an appropriate amount of structure and process. It is extremely important to create a culture that supports exploration and rewards and recognizes good ideas. But without a well-defined process to capture and nurture ideas and manage the development process, a tremendous amount of value can be left on the table. As Lem Lasher, Chief Innovation Officer at consulting firm CSC, says, "The best approach is to assume that professionals are creative by nature. They want to innovate and do new things, and it's our job to create the ecosystem—the governance, the leadership, the structure, and the process to support and nurture a culture of innovation."

Deloitte has proactively focused on embedding innovation into its organizational DNA. In our discussions with Deloitte's leaders across the globe, we discovered a host of formal and informal programs to support and stimulate innovation and create an innovation mentality throughout the enterprise (see "Deloitte Australia's Innovation Program"). Edelman, known in the public relations sector as a prolific service innovator, has a section in its policy and procedures manual devoted to the process of developing new products and capabilities, and participation is encouraged and recognized within the company. Steve Cody, Managing Partner and Cofounder of Peppercom, says that although his firm does not have a formal process for managing innovation, he very effectively drives a constant stream of new ideas through awards, such as plane tickets and gift cards, which he gives out at every staff meeting for good creative concepts. Whatever the process for stimulating ideas, the trick is to create the ecosystem that works within your own unique organization.

Several firm leaders say they utilize a combination of approaches to foster innovation. Some ideas bubble up from clients, and others are top-down, driven by professionals and firm-wide programs. The majority of the firms studied, 60 percent in all, said that service innovation is primarily reactive and is driven by professional and client work (see Exhibit 5.6). Over a third of interviewees indicated that they are proactively driving service innovation on an institutional basis with formal processes and programs.

Deloitte Australia's Innovation Program

"We define innovation as fresh ideas that create value," says Giam Swiegers, CEO of Deloitte Australia. Swiegers was elected CEO in 2002 to take the helm during a particularly difficult time for the business. "The firm was in the unenviable position of having a really weak market position, a very damaged brand, and a very damaged practice," explains Swiegers. After stopping the bleeding and making sure the firm would survive, Swiegers decided to focus on innovation as a catalyst for the rebirth of the firm. In 2004, he took his 11-man executive committee to Harvard for a course on organizational change and renewal, focusing on managing innovation in a conventional organization. "What they did for us was make the concept of innovation tangible," Swiegers says. Following the course, the executive committee started working with small groups of influential partners and account directors looking for breakthrough ideas.

As people gained confidence that innovation was an effective competitive differentiator, the ideas began to flow and the concept gained momentum. Since its initial commitment to innovation, the firm has launched a series of new initiatives, such as innovation brainstorming sessions for key clients which, according to Swiegers, "unleash the brain power of 4,500 Deloitte people to solve problems and offer creative ideas to positively impact our client's business." The Deloitte Innovation Academy is an online resource where companies can collaborate, share knowledge, and learn how to launch and run an internal innovation program. And the Deloitte Innovation Challenge, launched at two important recruiting campuses, provides students with coaching from Deloitte professionals and challenges them to come up with innovative ideas.

Swiegers offers the following advice for firms looking to stimulate innovation:

- *Drive change through a combination of culture, structure, and processes.* Deloitte Australia started by stimulating creativity and motivating participation on a grass roots level, and then added the technology and processes to help people connect and share ideas. For example, Swiegers described a program suggested by a young professional to send graduates to interview partners with flip cameras and capture their ideas on new services for a YouTube video collection. "The partners were highly motivated to come up with something to say," says

Swiegers, "and this simple idea turned out to be very effective for stimulating creativity."

- *Create a no-fear atmosphere.* Encourage and embrace every idea. After the innovation concept took hold, Swiegers received suggestions on everything from how to recruit to how to manage the culture; some were tried and failed, and some stuck. "It's ok to fail," says Swiegers. "Our goal is to fail fast and fail cheap."

- *Go viral.* Deloitte has effectively leveraged the power of social media to spread the word, and capture and share ideas. The firm's head of Deloitte Digital in Australia, for example, has 26,000 people following his views on innovation, and the firm has more than 1,000 internal Yammer users in the country.

- *Start small.* "Start with baby steps," says Swiegers. "Spread some ideas and get people excited in a smaller format before taking it on a global stage; once you fail globally, it's very hard to get a second chance."

The Australia firm's innovation strategy has been extremely effective. Eighteen months after launching the program in 2004, the market voted Deloitte the most innovative professional firm in the country, and in 2006, the firm was rated the most preferred employer in Australia by commerce students. "The ultimate goal is to take good ideas generated in one area of the organization, rapidly propagate and share them, and get them to market across the enterprise," says Swiegers. In 2006, the firm established an Innovation Council to explore all ideas for potential and move the most marketable along to the next level. "Innovation," Swiegers is convinced, "is now a part of Deloitte's DNA."

EXHIBIT 5.6 The service innovation process varies from random events to formal programs

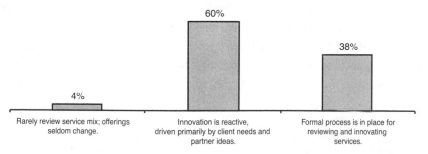

4%	60%	38%
Rarely review service mix; offerings seldom change.	Innovation is reactive, driven primarily by client needs and partner ideas.	Formal process is in place for reviewing and innovating services.

In most firms the senior leadership team is responsible for looking at the lines of business to determine which to exit, which to upgrade, and what to add. Some firms embed new-service discovery into employees' job descriptions and tie performance to evaluations. Subject matter experts, typically practice and service line leaders, are expected to present new ideas to the leadership team annually.

For the majority of firms whose approach to innovation is entirely reactive, individual cheerleaders are critical. The onus is on entrepreneurially inclined professionals to step forward and pitch a business case for a new idea to management and to be prepared to invest significant personal time and energy in leading the initiative. In some firms, particularly in the highly creative advertising and public relations segments, ideas are generated on a much more informal basis, and employees have the freedom to take an idea and run with it.

Some firms solicit potential service options through a range of channels—from websites where professionals at all levels can make suggestions, to innovation forums and global specialty teams charged with scanning the horizon for promising concepts, to client surveys that elicit feedback on service gaps and market opportunities. In other cases, a practice or global specialty group may take a futuristic approach to service design, interviewing thought leaders in a specific field for their insights into the most promising ideas for new service options. For example, SmithGroup, an architectural and engineering firm, launched a project called "Lab 2030" that involved interviewing the top 50 U.S. research institutions. Based on its findings, the firm identified and analyzed the components of the ideal lab facility of the future and began sharing results externally with clients.

There were a few impressive formal programs for incubating and driving new services. These programs typically are developed and managed by a dedicated team, their methodology is established and well articulated, and participation is encouraged and rewarded. The best programs weave clients directly into the service ideation and development process, incorporate significant proprietary market research, and include a formal process for selecting the best ideas and turning them into service offerings (see "CSC's Office of Innovation").

CSC's Office of Innovation

CSC, a global business solutions, technology, and outsourcing firm, is committed to continuously improving products and services to keep pace with changing client needs. CSC's Office of Innovation was created in 2005 as a way to bring existing innovation ideas and programs under one umbrella. According to Lem Lasher, President of the Global Business Solutions Group and founder of the program, the office develops and administers a number of organization-wide innovation programs and works with business units and individual professionals on their innovation agendas.

The program mix includes the Leading Edge Forum, a multiclient subscription-based research network that issues research reports on client-generated ideas and conducts forums and strategic study tours for clients; Custom Research, which conducts market-based analysis on any subject that anyone in the firm wants to examine, whether for a client project or an internal initiative; and Global Solutions, which takes ideas generated by the Leading Edge Forum that have been validated by the research network and turns those ideas into investment opportunities for CSC. The Global Solutions Group, along with other business groups, manages six global innovation centers—physical spaces where clients and CSC professionals work together on innovative solutions.

The Office of Innovation reports to the Chairman and CEO and is run by a full-time cadre of professionals—60 worldwide—working across all the business groups. One of its main functions is to foster a culture of innovation; the Office administers the Chairman's Innovation Award program, which rewards professionals for creative ideas and accomplishments and inspires others to make creative leaps and experiment. Nominations for the award are collected from across the organization and then are filtered by the chief technologists for each of CSC's 28 business units before finalists and winners are chosen by the office in consultation with several hundred internal and external adjudicators. The office also conducts annual call-for-papers and grants events, in which employees and clients submit papers on technological or management issues for recognition.

The office maintains a balanced scorecard of innovation metrics. Results are reported to senior management on a quarterly basis, and the measures are subject to periodic review by leadership. A yearly anonymous survey that asks all employees for their opinions on current innovation programs is factored into the scorecard metrics.

Steps Three and Four: Select the Best Ideas, and Take Them to Market

The approaches that firms pursue to select the best new ideas vary widely by culture, size, and organizational style and range from a "gut decision" to a formal committee review and analysis. Arguably the most difficult step in the innovation process—and the one that leaders struggle with the most—is translating ideas into action.

Several years ago my team was conducting an assignment for one of our global consulting firm clients. Our task was to speak with 50 CFOs of Fortune 1000 companies in the high-tech field, spot trends, and develop a thought leadership series to position the client as an innovative thinker in the industry. It was clear to us fairly early on in the engagement that a significant, unfulfilled service need in major high-tech companies had potential to generate substantial revenues.

We presented the opportunity to our client, mapped out the service, and even suggested a game plan for rolling it out into the market. Our client was pleased and eventually developed the offering, deployed a team, and sold quite a few engagements. But the path from concept to execution was arduous. Our client did not have a formal process in place to proactively identify and create new service opportunities, and once the need had been identified, there was no official path to launching the service. We had to go door to door to find a partner advocate to take it on and drive it through the organization.

Based on our interviews, we've identified a ten-step strategy for moving from concept to commercialization:

1. *Develop criteria for service viability.* The first hurdle a possible new service offering must jump over is satisfying a predetermined set of criteria for applicability, marketability, and profitability. In the applicability arena, key questions typically

include the following: How big an idea is this? Does it have cross-practice potential? Can it go global? Does it meet a compelling and substantial client need? Does it have enduring value from a service perspective?

In terms of marketability, key questions are likely to include the following: Does this idea have potential for enhancing our brand and reputation as a thought leader? Is it easy to sell both internally and to clients? Will it be a major competitive differentiator? Can we get it into the marketplace quickly and efficiently enough to make it worth the investment of time and energy required? Does it have breakthrough, best-practice, performance-boosting potential?

From a profitability standpoint, a baseline ROI analysis generally is conducted that objectively reviews direct development expenses, top-line revenue projections, gross margin, and other financial performance metrics. If an idea is given the green light for development, results are carefully tracked and measured against projections.

2. *Build a business case for potential service.* After an idea is vetted for service viability, most firms construct a business case to sell it to a review committee or top management group. The business case may be an extremely detailed multiple page proposal or a concise summary. Whatever form it takes, generally the business case covers the service viability considerations just outlined and includes a development timeline and ramp-up requirements.

To drive innovation within the firm, Booz Allen Hamilton created a formal service campaign program. When senior leaders in the market surface new service areas that they think will be big opportunities, such as fiber or systems engineering and integration, they can garner investment dollars from the leadership team if they put together a good business case to justify the investment. To do so, they must spend time thinking about methodologies, people requirements, and projections for growth. Campaigns have a two- or three-year lifetime. The campaign either grows up and becomes an embedded service offering—such as cyber security—or it becomes what Booz Allen calls a sunset: It makes a splash, but the result doesn't rise to the level of refreshing the firm's core service offerings. Partners are highly motivated to build a successful business, which can mean promotion within the partner ranks.

3. *Select the best ideas.* The management team responsible for the selection chooses the ideas that best meet the firm's criteria for viability, timing, budget, and resources.

4. *Test-market for receptivity.* At this stage, firms with well-developed innovation programs move from internal to external review. This may involve a range of activities: brainstorming with clients, submitting service concepts to a client advisory board, consulting with independent experts, researching the competitive landscape, and evaluating potential market use.

5. *Establish benchmarks for the launch plan.* After the business case has been presented and the development process approved, the next step involves determining a time frame and project milestones. The time frame from planning to launch can extend anywhere from a matter of months to three years, with clearly defined benchmarks to measure progress along the way.

6. *Pilot service offering.* As with any standard product or service, the next step generally involves testing with a limited number of client implementations and then rigorously evaluating the road test results. In most cases the original service viability criteria are revisited.

7. *Refine and blueprint offering.* When the testing process is complete, the next step is to fine-tune the offering and map it fully, with an eye toward market introduction. At this stage, a marketing plan for communicating the new offering and its client benefits is developed. If the offering has brand enhancement and/or thought leadership potential, promoting these assets will be integral to the marketing communications mix.

8. *Train teams.* As part of their go-to-market strategy, the best programs make sure that internal support and expertise are fully mobilized to give the new service offering the best possible chance for a successful market introduction. Practice leaders and their teams are fully briefed on the offering, instructed in effective service delivery, and given the communication tools they need to promote it to their client base.

9. *Launch.* If all the other pieces are in place, the launch stage should unfold smoothly. In some cases the launch may involve introducing the service on a limited basis and then rolling it out nationally or globally. A strong marketing communications strategy and its aggressive implementation are critical for maximizing market impact.

10. *Monitor and refresh.* The service is tracked and reviewed on a regular basis to continuously test its market acceptance and

financial performance against plan. Clients are interviewed on the offering pros and cons, and adjustments are made as appropriate.

Step Five: Share Knowledge

For many, the toughest part of the innovation cycle is knowledge management. Forty percent of firm leaders claim they have made investments, sometimes significant, in systems and resources to capture and track knowledge and service expertise. However, the degree of satisfaction with those processes is fairly low. And surprisingly, even some of the most sophisticated service innovators give themselves very low marks on the process of gathering and sharing client experiences and knowledge, as shown in Exhibit 5.7.

EXHIBIT 5.7 Firm leaders acknowledge that the knowledge management process is important, and many struggle to get it right

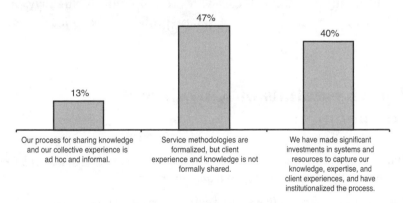

Of course, this seems crazy in a professional service firm, where the assets walk out the door every night. A great deal of a firm's intellectual capital and service know-how resides in the heads of professionals, which unfortunately for many firms represents a vast untapped treasure trove of knowledge and ideas.

Why Is Knowledge Management So Challenging?

As is the case with service innovation, there are several obstacles to capturing and sharing knowledge. Some professionals are reluctant to share their client experiences, preferring to closely manage their own book of business. They view their client relationships and service acumen as a portable asset that they can leverage to secure a better position in a new firm should they decide to make a move. Professionals often don't trust the skills that others have developed and tend to rely on their own base of experience. Pitches to prospective clients, for example, often focus only on local teams' experiences and do not capitalize on the collective experiences of professionals throughout a firm.

Even if the motives are not self-serving, busy professionals are challenged to add "yet another bureaucratic nonbillable task" to their very full plates. Many leaders agree that time is the single biggest deterrent to knowledge management. As one senior partner told us, the easy part is building the system; the hard part is getting the team to "feed the beast." Finally, quite a few interviewees cited familiarity with technology as yet another challenge to sharing knowledge. Some professionals aren't as computer-savvy or comfortable with the concept of inputting data as those who grew up with technology. It is difficult to motivate self-reliant senior professionals to learn a new system.

Four Essentials of Knowledge Management

"Whoever is able to capture the implicit knowledge that exists among the professionals will have an incredible advantage over competitors."

"Our younger colleagues live on the keyboard, so while they are on the phone talking to people, they are capturing insights and ideas. It goes into the system, and it's coded and accessible, which is wonderful."

"You can access every subject area that we work in. It lists people who are the experts in each area. It includes references, books, bibliographies—everything. And most of us never look at it. These damned internal websites get so complex nowadays you can't figure out where anything is."

So how do you develop a successful knowledge management program? Given the challenges of knowledge sharing, we were pleased to discover some good knowledge-management processes. All these programs shared several common characteristics that are critical to their success:

- *Create a culture of sharing.* Perhaps the most important characteristic, and undoubtedly the most difficult, is building and reinforcing a culture of participation and sharing. No amount of technology or process will create an effective program if people aren't encouraged to cooperate and participate. If busy professionals don't believe it's important, they simply won't do it. As Ralph Baxter, Chairman and CEO of law firm Orrick, explains, "Evangelism is the only answer. You have to get people to understand that this is expected, required, and important. It's like with any change process—you have to make it part of every conversation."

  Several firms use rewards and recognition to remind everyone that knowledge sharing is important. As part of its award series, Landor issues the One Landor Award, which recognizes the team that best leverages the firm's skills and knowledge. Deloitte's leaders recently introduced an award for "Best Steal of the Year" for the professional or team who adapts a great idea and delivers it to the marketplace to create value. The idea is to get people motivated and excited about sharing and leveraging knowledge.

- *It's about people, bricks, and clicks.* The best knowledge management programs incorporate a combination of people, process, and technology. As Rajat Gupta, former managing partner of McKinsey, told us, "Effective knowledge management is about people and networks, bricks and clicks." Several firm leaders claim that their collaborative and supportive environments are so effective that they don't need systems and processes to share knowledge. An e-mail or phone call asking for help or advice from colleagues will always net a quick response. Others say that their organizational knowledge gets passed from generation to generation through on-the-job training on client teams and through face-to-face meetings and formal training programs in almost a tribal fashion.

  But there are inherent problems in relying solely on the network, even in small firms. Professionals leave, partners retire, and everyone gets intensely busy, and valuable intellectual capital and service knowledge walk out the door or never get shared. As one CEO told us, "The days of standing out in the hall and yelling, 'Does anybody know anything about this subject?' are long gone." A cultural willingness to exchange information and ideas can be leveraged dramatically using technology that is user-friendly and content-rich. Cohn & Wolfe promotes global brainstorming via its Creative Catalyst Network, an intranet where people describe a new business or client situation and solicit ideas and concepts from around the firm. The agency's creative director filters the responses and funnels the best ideas back to the consultant or account team. According to Donna Imperato, Cohn & Wolfe President and CEO, the agency has won new business as a result. Edelman's intranet, called Fusion, features not only access to new business data and winning presentations, but also best practices on a monthly basis. Supplemented by a weekly electronic newsletter and e-mail videos, it offers professionals a dynamic, interactive view of the firm's business. It also underscores the importance of knowledge sharing in energizing the firm's performance.

Some firms are using social networking media with great success to promote self-organized knowledge sharing around best practices and service delivery. Using highly sophisticated software, they are sharing intellectual capital among multidisciplinary teams and creating an "ecosystem" of sharing communities that arise spontaneously and then solidify over time. Since these groups are forming of their own volition and technology is being used to support rather than drive them, they often put down strong roots and thrive.

Many firms with a global geographic footprint have also realized that innovation can get buried or localized without a dynamic approach to knowledge sharing that is global in its reach. As a result, they are finding creative ways to enable client teams to easily find the right people with the right expertise anywhere in the world via digital tools. Online profiles of consultants, examples of their work, staffing and pricing strategies, and research data are all available 24/7. In many cases, knowledge sharing begets more knowledge sharing as people begin to tap into these systems and realize their value in winning and implementing client engagements.

Just as finding the right mix of formal and informal knowledge management approaches depends on your firm's culture and organizational style, so should finding the right software technology to facilitate firm-wide knowledge sharing be an organic process. Many costly, sophisticated software options are available—and the temptation to grab one and get it up and running quickly is huge. However, the firms with the most fully integrated and successful knowledge management systems take ample time to investigate capabilities and navigability to find the right fit for their firm before they sign on the dotted line. These firms know that even the most advanced technology will remain undervalued and underutilized if it's a poor match with their firm's culture, service values, and operating style. They also recognize that technology is best leveraged and most widely applied when it supports knowledge management rather than attempting to drive it (see "Knowledge Management at Grant Thornton").

• *Keep it simple.* Another key component of the most effective knowledge management programs is simplicity. The knowledge input and outtake process must be very user-friendly to succeed. Complex, onerous technology and burdensome processes simply fail and are a waste of time and money. Tapping into the wealth of knowledge residing in your firm doesn't have to be a complex process, according to many of the leaders we spoke with. It can be as simple as bringing together groups of people to form quality improvement teams and encouraging them to talk about lessons learned and ideas for improving client services. Or it can involve creating team sites on a firm's intranet, where people share information and post engagement profiles and results.

Firms that have learned from experience recommend avoiding buying a sophisticated knowledge-management software package and suddenly introducing it to the troops with a flashy internal marketing campaign. Instead, they say, start small and be selective. Design a low-key, high-impact knowledge management initiative that really makes sense for your organization and offers an early win. Some firms slip into a knowledge management frame of mind simply by having all their professionals submit, to a centralized site, profiles of their backgrounds, areas of expertise, most valued assignments, and innovative strategies. Everyone across the firm can instantly access background on their colleagues' expertise worldwide and begin to appreciate the vast intellectual capital they can tap into right in their own backyard. Other firms ease into knowledge management by inviting professionals to submit "best practice" candidates on a weekly or monthly basis on the firm's intranet. Creating a special annual award to recognize a team or service approach that leverages knowledge management effectively on behalf of a major client/high-profile engagement is another powerful but low-cost vehicle that some firms have used very successfully to highlight the benefits of sharing information.

- *Make certain someone owns it—and is accountable.* Finally, as with other initiatives, assigning responsibility and accountability is the make-or-break factor. Several firms have dedicated knowledge management staffs who manage the program tools to ensure that information is up to date, accessible, and being used. Others designate professionals within practice groups to champion the sharing process. Ownership of knowledge management programs can reside with a knowledge committee, with knowledge managers who report to each market sector, with professional support staff, or with full-time knowledge management officers. The best approach is a combination: staff support to keep the machine running smoothly, and professional champions to stimulate participation.

Knowledge Management at Grant Thornton

According to Ed Nusbaum, former CEO of Grant Thornton in the U.S. and current CEO of Grant Thornton International Ltd., "You can't be in the professional service business without sharing knowledge." In 2007, the audit, tax, and advisory firm decided that it was time to formalize its knowledge-management activities to "get everybody on the same page with the same technology, a common language, and a defined way to share," says Nusbaum.

The firm hired Tamara Smith to become the firm's Chief Knowledge Management Officer and spearhead the development effort to build an effective program. Smith led the firm through a multi-step process of assessment, planning, and implementation:

1. *Conduct a current-state assessment.* Smith and her team conducted 180 interviews with both the subject matter experts who develop the knowledge and the day-to-day users who apply the knowledge in their work. They also reviewed the firm's current technology platform. Finally, they performed a deep-dive assessment of 75 of the firm's over 200 knowledge bases to "get under the hood" and see what was being shared and why, what information was the most useful, how it was organized, and who used it.

2. *Define the desired state.* Smith worked with the firm's leadership and a cross-functional working group of 24 people to agree

on the vision and goal for knowledge management at Grant Thornton. They decided that the program should focus on three major information components: knowledge from the practices; profiles of all employees and their backgrounds and capabilities; and up-to-the-minute news on clients, industries, markets, and a wide range of business topics. "We named the program KSource and created an overarching mantra—'Seek, Share, Succeed,'" says Nusbaum. "The goal was to position the program as the source of our organizational knowledge."

3. *Establish the knowledge management foundation.* The team developed a content classification scheme to categorize each piece of information by service line, industry, geography, internal function, business issue, business topic, and content type to organize all the knowledge in the context of how a user works and thinks. This provided flexibility so the knowledge content can be connected into existing business processes. The firm selected SharePoint as the technology platform and worked with Accenture to customize it for the Grant Thornton program.

4. *Identify communities of practice.* With multiple service lines, industries, and local offices, and an array of internal support functions, the job of organizing the knowledge and content was enormous. To facilitate the process, the team identified 85 communities of practice that represented groups of people with ongoing specific business needs.

5. *Launch in phases and begin by rounding up the knowledge.* The plan was to bring ten communities of practice onboard every 4 months over a 3-year period with all 85 communities up and running in January 2012. A key step in the community building process is what Smith calls the "knowledge roundup"—gathering valuable and reusable content from across the firm. "There were 20,000 documents on the firm's intranet, 200 separate knowledge bases that didn't talk to each other, 5,500 individual hard drives and e-mail boxes, and thousands of shared drives on local area networks," says Smith. To make it more manageable, the team is tackling the task on a community-by-community basis. The final phase of the program will be the launch of personalized homepages where each person can customize their knowledge needs based on the communities they belong to, delivering key updates and knowledge to each person daily.

Based on her experience in knowledge management and business and technology strategy, Smith offers several suggestions for firms considering a knowledge management program:

- *Make knowledge sharing everyone's responsibility.* Contributions to and usage of the knowledge management system are monitored and considered in performance evaluations.

- *Decentralize the knowledge management team and processes.* Only five of Smith's 40-person dedicated team operate on a central basis; the rest sit next to the practice leaders in the line.

- *Make certain it gels with the firm's culture.* "'Build it and they will come' never works," says Smith. "It's 80 percent people and process, and 20 percent technology; the seeking and sharing of knowledge and expertise must be 'baked in' to existing processes."

- *Track and measure ROI.* The firm tracks usage for each community and incorporates feedback and recommendations directly within KSource and the firm's regular employee survey process.

- *Don't underestimate change management.* Smith highly recommends a phased approach to roll out the program, always starting with the "low-hanging fruit where you've got enthusiastic sponsors who will make it happen."

CHAPTER SUMMARY

Services

- PSFs widely recognize the importance of developing an effective service portfolio strategy, yet reviews on performance are mixed.

- Effective service portfolio management and innovation consists of four elements:
    1. Strategically plan and manage the service portfolio
    2. Establish and follow a protocol for innovation
    3. Validate offerings with the market
    4. Assign ownership and accountability

- A five-step service management cycle begins with a portfolio review and progresses through knowledge sharing (see Exhibit 5.3). Each step of the cycle is important in creating a consistent engine of innovation:
    1. Review the service portfolio
    2. Stimulate and capture new ideas
    3. Select the best ideas
    4. Transform them into service offerings
    5. Share knowledge and experience

- Transforming ideas into revenue-generating services and solutions is a ten-step process:
    1. Develop criteria for service viability
    2. Build business cases
    3. Select the best ideas
    4. Test-market
    5. Set benchmarks
    6. Test pilot service offerings
    7. Refine and blueprint
    8. Train teams
    9. Launch
    10. Monitor and refresh

- An effective knowledge management program has four essential components:
    1. Create a culture of sharing
    2. Incorporate a combination of process, people, and technology
    3. Keep it simple
    4. Make certain that someone owns it—and is accountable

6

Finance

Planning, metrics, and reporting

"Financial management is the bedrock. You can't be successful if you don't end up with competitive earnings, whatever metrics you use."
—Steve Harty, North American Chairman, BBH

"The most important metric we look at in analyzing financial performance is profits per partner, because that's ultimately what it's all about."
—Rodge Cohen, Chairman, Sullivan & Cromwell

"We've got to make sure that it's not just about the metrics—it's about exceeding our client's expectations and doing innovative design. If we do great design, the money follows."
—Andy Cohen, Co-CEO, Gensler

Although it is true that most professionals in PSFs enjoy what they do and are driven by their work more than the money, let's not kid ourselves: Money does matter. In an environment where people are the product, talented professionals can shop around for a good "home" to practice their skills. The culture and values of the firm they choose must of course be a mutual fit, but the compensation package, the equity ownership potential, and the firm's financial stability and growth trajectory are clearly part of the decision criteria.

A strong, steady bottom line is critical to attracting and retaining the best people, fueling growth and innovation, and creating a compelling return on investment for the firm's shareholders. As Ray Kotcher, Senior Partner and CEO of Ketchum, said, "Strong financial performance and management gives you the ability to do everything else."

121

Financial management ranks high on the senior management priority list. Seventy-eight percent of interviewees gave it a top rating in terms of importance, as shown in Exhibit 6.1.

EXHIBIT 6.1   Financial management ranks high on the leadership agenda

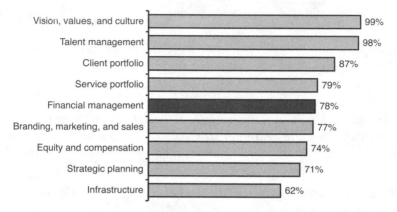

Not surprisingly, given their level of sophistication, the leadership of the best-of-breed firms that we studied believe they are doing quite well in financial management, with 84 percent giving their firms a top mark (see Exhibit 6.2).

EXHIBIT 6.2   Most firms give themselves high marks for financial management

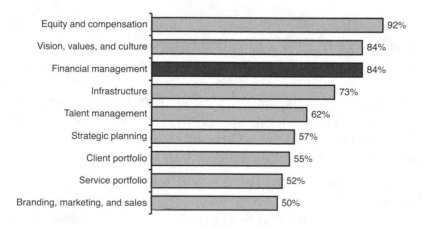

How Do the Top Firms Manage Finance?

"If you make money, then you can make decisions independently of financial considerations. Poor financial performance boxes you in and forces you to make decisions you'd rather not make."

"Professionals enjoy doing the work, but they don't like collecting the money."

On the surface, professional service firms seem like simple businesses to manage financially. As one leader told us, "It's mostly a time and materials business driven by rates, revenue, utilization, realization, and expenses." But there are nuances that make it challenging. In the short-term project-based PSF environment it is almost impossible for many firm leaders to see beyond the window of a few months, which makes revenue forecasting a distinct challenge. The fluid and uncertain nature of the market makes it difficult to determine where and when to place investments in practices, geographies, and people. Decisions must be made quickly to capitalize on opportunities, which is not easy in a PSF governance environment where partners and equity owners must all weigh in on key financial decisions. And finally, most professionals don't like what they perceive to be tedious, bureaucratic processes—such as timekeeping, billings, and collections—that keep them from focusing on their clients. One CFO admitted that getting partners to send out their bills—or, even worse, call clients to collect if they don't pay—is one of his biggest problems.

So what do the best firms do? In the course of our research, a number of common best practices for disciplined financial management emerged:

- **Strong planning and budgeting**—The top firms have a clearly articulated financial strategy that establishes revenue and earnings goals that reinforce their strategic business plan. Financial planning and budgeting is done in conjunction with annual operating plans and is a collaborative process between the management team and business unit leaders.

- **Rigorous tracking and reporting**—Leaders of the best firms receive very thorough, timely reports of the relevant metrics needed to run their businesses efficiently and effectively. Many have 24/7 access to executive dashboards providing an up-to-the-minute picture of the firm's financial health.

- **Careful management of cash flow**—The most successful firms have effective and timely billing functions and closely manage cash flow from collections and working capital. As one CEO told us, "If a firm has cash, it is a well-run place. If they don't, it isn't." Strong firms are adequately capitalized and maintain close banking relationships.

- **Forward-looking versus purely historical**—Savvy firm leaders use a combination of both lagging and leading indicators to manage the business. Traditional metrics such as revenue, profitability, utilization, and realization are paired with trend-spotting data such as talent retention, declining billings, client satisfaction ratings, and sales pipelines to spot early warning signs that the firm may be heading toward financial trouble.

- **Transparency to partners**—Firm-wide financial goals and results are shared with partners in most of the PSFs we studied. Firm leaders believe that a transparent, open reporting environment is important to building the ownership mentality and encourages participation and accountability from the partnership team.

- **Accountability**—The best PSFs hold business unit leaders accountable for the financial performance of their practice areas. Financial goals have clearly established metrics, and performance against plan is closely monitored and tied to compensation.

- **Investment in people and tools**—Even the smallest firms in our study have made investments in experienced financial professionals—either full- or part-time or outsourced—to work collaboratively with partners to manage planning, budgeting, tracking, and measurement. The best PSFs use sophisticated analytical tools that provide timely, action-oriented management information.

Financial Planning and Budgeting

"Our budget is a top-down/bottom-up process and, hopefully, the bottom up equals the top down. If not, we start negotiating."

"Good financial planning and management is the ability to influence a good outcome."

With few exceptions, the PSFs we studied had strong business planning and budgeting processes. Most firms prepare the annual budget in conjunction with the preparation of the annual operating or business plan and conduct monthly reviews and quarterly reforecasting. Financial planning typically is a top-down/bottom-up process, with management and business unit leaders working together to achieve an agreed-upon goal. Although it often takes many months to complete, the planning process involves three basic stages, as shown in Exhibit 6.3:

- *Stage One: Management establishes financial parameters.* The management team analyzes historical financial performance data, assesses the market to determine which services and geographies may grow or decline, and estimates the levels of investment across the firm. Based on this analysis, they establish parameters for growth and revenue for the firm overall and for each business unit.

- *Stage Two: Business unit leaders develop plans and the budgets based on parameters.* The business unit leaders take the financial targets from the management team and develop the detailed financial plans for their groups, setting goals for top-line revenue, gross margin, headcount, utilization, operating expenses, and bottom-line profitability. They then submit these plans to the leadership team.

- *Stage Three: The leadership team reviews, adjusts, and finalizes the financial plan.* The management team reviews the individual unit plans and works back and forth with the unit leaders to reach a final agreement. As one CEO told us, "If the budget doesn't come out to the right number, we go back to our people and tell them what they need to do, whether it's to increase revenue or margin targets or reduce operating expenses. We know what the levers are and where to point people in the right direction."

This three-stage process works best when the following are true:

- Management team goals are realistic and based on sound analysis.
- Business unit leaders have the data and resources they need to develop their budgets without being micromanaged by the management team.
- The communication between business leaders and the management team is open and productive, resulting in effective collaboration.

EXHIBIT 6.3　Stages of financial planning

Management team establishes financial parameters	Business units develop plans	Management team reviews, adjusts, and finalizes financial plan
Management reviews historical data, assesses market opportunities, and determines investment levels	Based on management parameters, unit leaders develop financial plans to submit to the leadership	Management works back and forth with unit leaders to finalize goals
Based on above, management establishes financial expectations		

Forecasting

"In a volatile economic climate, I think that a Ouija board might be the best way to forecast revenue!"

"Other than people, heat, light, rent, promotion, and some other stuff, I don't want to say budgeting costs is pretty straightforward, but it's pretty straightforward."

Participants in our research agreed that expenses are relatively simple to estimate in PSFs. Roughly 50 to 70 percent are people costs, and the rest are a combination of real estate and back-office support. Sixty-eight percent of respondents gave their firms a top mark in estimating the costs associated with the business, as shown in Exhibit 6.4. Forecasting revenue, however, is a different matter; only 12 percent of interviewees placed their firms at the top of the chart, as shown in Exhibit 6.5.

Exhibit 6.4　Most are confident in their ability to forecast costs

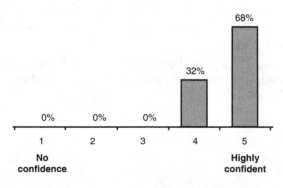

EXHIBIT 6.5   Forecasting revenues is a challenge for many firms

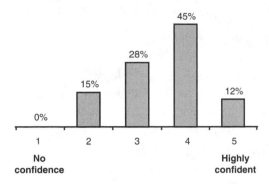

The challenges of financial management in the short-term, project-driven world of PSFs makes predicting the future difficult. As one CEO said, "It's almost pure guesswork. So much of our business is driven by responding to events, and we can't predict when those things are going to happen." Many firms indicated they could accurately forecast 60 to 90 days out—some three to six months—but few had confidence beyond that. Revenue forecasts and budgets are estimates derived from analyzing historical data; assessing current and expected workload, staffing commitments, proposal pipeline, and an assortment of other leading indicator metrics; and gathering as much information as is available on the probable future client demands affecting business units and geographic markets (see "Black & Veatch Forecasting Process"). Most firms reforecast the budget each quarter, which firm leaders say is a critical factor in predicting and managing the firm's financial stability.

Metrics to Monitor the Business

Most leaders look at a host of financial metrics to track, measure, and manage the financial health of the business. As one CEO told us, "You name it, we measure it." Most firms studied use a fairly standard set of metrics. As shown in Exhibit 6.6, 93 percent of respondents place revenue at the top of the list of key metrics, followed by profitability, utilization, realization, costs, margins, pricing, leverage, and performance efficiency.

Black & Veatch Forecasting Process

Global engineering, consulting, and construction giant Black & Veatch manages very large, multiyear, multimillion-dollar projects that generate a fairly stable predictable revenue stream and performance schedule. When the company launched its consulting division in 2003, it was not used to the short duration, high transactional volume services of a management consultancy. "The company struggled a bit initially with the stop-and-start aspect of project-based consulting work," said Mike Elzey, Senior Vice President, Black & Veatch Management Consulting. "They wanted us to have the same level of predictability in the way we forecasted our revenue as the rest of the business, and that was a challenge for us."

The company deploys a rigorous financial planning process to track and manage revenue and costs across the organization. "The white lines on the road are determined by the CEO and the executive committee based on the market parameters they see," says Elzey, "and then we try to make that real in terms of the way we are actually going to perform the work and drive the growth." All divisions are required to develop an annual budget, which is managed monthly and reforecast every quarter if needed. According to Elzey, his division had to build a host of different mechanisms to strengthen their forecasting ability. His budget predictions are based on a number of components: current workload, expected workload, staffing commitments for the work, project end dates, proposal pipeline and a weighted probability of winning the work, and staffing needs for potential new work.

These components are analyzed by individual consultants and by practice area. They are merged into an overall forecasting model of annual and "reasonable" month-by-month revenue expectations for the division. Everyone from the lowest-level consultant up to senior management participates in the forecasting process. Accurate and detailed weekly timesheets that track both current and future workload are required to provide the raw data to plug into the report. Every Monday, Elzey reviews the past week's productivity and forward-looking forecast. Each division head meets individually with both the CEO and CFO at a set time every month to review the division operations, financial results, and the sales pipeline.

The process takes a great deal of focus and effort for the company's leadership and financial team, but Elzey acknowledges that it creates a sense of stability and helps manage the business better. "I am able to more accurately predict hiring needs, anticipate downturns, and more efficiently plan everyone's work, vacation, and training time," says Elzey. "It's tough, but it's worth it."

EXHIBIT 6.6   Top economic metrics that leaders watch

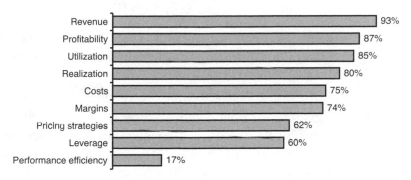

Firm managers sort and analyze each of these metrics by a variety of categories, including for the firm overall, by partner and professional, by business and geographic units, and by client and engagement. The weight that leaders place on each metric varies by type of business. For example, in highly leveraged models with many people working for one partner, utilization is critical. For less-leveraged, higher-value types of services, revenue per professional is important to watch.

Revenue

The ability to generate revenue is fundamental to growth and survival. New clients and new work from existing clients are powerful indicators of the firm's long-term viability, its brand power in the market, and the abilities and skills of its professionals to find and execute new business and nurture enduring client relationships. As Peter Stringham, CEO of Young & Rubicam Brands, said, "For the advertising business, if you're not growing, you're shrinking." Firm managers closely watch the revenue numbers—some with daily reports. However, savvy firm leaders realize that top-line revenue is only the first step in financial health and management. One hundred million in revenue is pointless if nothing ends up in the net bottom line to distribute to shareholders.

Profitability

"If you get the work and you don't produce it profitably, then you're dead."

"The real number that you want to know is profitability."

"Profit and profitability trump everything else."

The most important measure for professional services is profit per partner or per equity shareholder, depending on the ownership structure. For PSFs, the profit generated per partner or shareholder is the equivalent of earnings per share or return on equity in a traditional corporation. The partners' time and effort represent the firm's equity investment.

Financially successful firms convert a high percentage of revenue into bottom-line profits per shareholder. This bottom-line number—pretax earnings before partner bonus distribution—varies across and within the segments studied. Architectural and engineering firms reported the lowest margins, ranging from 3 to 15 percent; advertising and public relations, 15 to 20 percent; consulting, 10 to 35 percent; and law and accounting, 20 to 40 percent.

Mark Scott, in his book *The Professional Service Firm*, describes the conversion of revenue to profits per shareholder as a multistep management process (see Exhibit 6.7):

- **Fee capacity**—The process begins with a determination of the firm's total fee capacity. This is based on the number and level of professionals, the average rate or fee at which they can be billed, and their utilization or billability on client work.
- **Realization**—The percentage of fee capacity that is turned into revenue. Realization, according to Scott, is a measure of whether the professionals are efficiently utilized, whether the price of the service is attuned to the market's willingness to pay, and whether the firm's billing and collection process is managed effectively.
- **Contribution**—The efficiency with which the firm converts revenue per professional into contribution per professional. Contribution is calculated as revenues less direct costs of the engagement, which in PSFs is primarily the cost of the people doing the work.

- **Operating profit**—The bottom-line profit per partner is determined by subtracting an allocated cost per professional for non-staff overhead costs such as property, expenses, and support functions and the cost of any interest expense on debt.

Successful firms create shareholder wealth by generating enough top-line revenue to consistently operate at close to maximum fee capacity, efficiently deploying professionals on engagements and carefully managing costs. The conversion rate from top line to bottom line is consistently high in the best-run firms.

EXHIBIT 6.7 Simplified stages of conversion of fee capacity into profit in a PSF

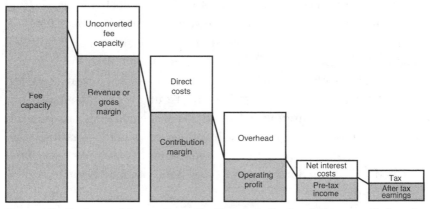

Source: *The Professional Service Firm: The Manager's Guide to Maximizing Profit and Value*, Mark C. Scott, 2001. Used by permission of John Wiley & Sons, Ltd.

Utilization

Utilization—the amount of time that professionals are actively billing work for a client—is a closely watched number for the PSF leaders interviewed. Utilization times the rate or fee at which the professional is billed equals productivity, one of the primary drivers of profitability in a PSF.

Keeping the staff billable makes eminent sense in a people business, but according to Michael Broshar, Chair and CEO of architectural firm Invision, "Utilization doesn't tell the whole picture." Headcount is an important part of the equation. Determining the right number of people to manage the workload is difficult in a short-term project-based business.

Too many people drive costs up and profits down. Too few can impact quality and the ability to take on new assignments.

Target utilization varies across the professional hierarchy. For the most junior ranks, utilization targets are high, typically close to 100 percent if possible. This number decreases as you move up the ranks to partners, where utilization can be as low as 30 to 40 percent, depending on the sector. Leaders warn that an obsession with high utilization levels across the ranks usually means that there is not enough time for partners to focus on marketing and selling to replenish the pipeline. It's seductive to have everyone billing at maximum capacity, but in the long run it can create a roller-coaster effect on work and revenue.

Reported utilization numbers often don't reflect the actual time spent on a client. Partners may decide to overinvest in a client—particularly in new clients—to ensure that the relationship gets off to a good start. Plus, indirect staff costs—a range of nonbillable people who are associated with executing an engagement—often are unaccounted for on a per-engagement basis. This results in a lower-than-actual utilization or billability number, which in turn can lead to poor pricing and staffing decisions on future work. Most leaders watch utilization numbers often, typically on a weekly and monthly basis. As one CEO summed up, "If you don't get your supply-and-demand balance right, it causes huge problems."

Pricing

"We are struggling with pricing strategies. All our clients are coming to us for fee relief, and many of our competitors are willing to do the work."

"I'll tell you what we're not looking at which is important—pricing strategies and margins."

"We are very strategic about pricing, but it's not at the global level, it's situation by situation."

A firm's pricing strategy is much more than a financial lever to manage the business. It is, in fact, a key decision for the PSF leadership team. Pricing is a powerful branding tool that supports—or undermines—the firm's positioning in the market. Pricing must accurately reflect the value of the service. A PSF that chooses to position itself as an efficiency-based business offering high-leveraged, routine services, cannot charge the same high fees as an expertise-based practice that provides "unique solutions to unique problems."

Determining a value and a price for a service is not an easy feat. Buyers of professional services are sophisticated and knowledgeable about the services to be purchased—many began their careers in PSFs—and they know how to shop for what they need. Interestingly, Broderick & Company has found that in a normal economic market, price is not the primary purchasing criterion. In fact, it is often at the bottom of the list. In a 2008 study, we conducted of consulting firm buyers, 240 senior executives of Fortune 1000 companies in the U.S. and Europe named demonstrated expertise in their industry (43 percent) as their top selection criterion for hiring a consulting firm, as shown in Exhibit 6.8. This was followed by specific functional and technical expertise (23 percent), understanding of the business (13 percent), and a collaborative style (13 percent). The cost of services was tied for last at 1 percent.

EXHIBIT 6.8　Most important criteria for hiring a consulting firm

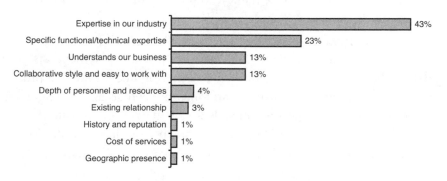

Source: 2008 Broderick & Company study of buyers of consulting services

Not surprisingly, the cost of services moves up the purchasing criteria priority list in a down market. The 2008–2010 economic crisis was an enormous speed bump for just about every segment of the professional service industry. Many study participants were forced to reexamine their pricing, staffing, delivery methodology, and mix of services. Firms were forced to lay off people and eliminate service lines with marginal rates of return. The traditional bill-by-the-hour segments, such as law and accounting, were pressured by clients to seriously explore fixed-fee and alternative-fee arrangements. Retainer-based businesses such as advertising and public relations firms were challenged to produce "more for less" or to restructure fees to either pay-for-performance or fixed project fee models. In an effort to stay afloat and keep staff intact, some firms chose the "lowball fee strategy" in an attempt to retain long-term clients, buy a few competitive proposals, and keep professionals busy until the economy recovered. As one CEO told us, "Typically, we price for a 15 to 20 percent net margin on each engagement, but in this market (2009), 5 percent is looking pretty good."

The accounting firms' reaction to the economic downturn of the mid-to-late 1980s is an example of the negative impact of allowing price versus quality and value to drive the purchasing decision. The "Big Eight" firms at the time collectively started a price-war frenzy in the industry, offering to conduct audits at bargain-basement prices in the hope of attracting new clients who would then buy expensive tax and consulting services. The strategy backfired; firms lost their shirts on these low-fee assignments, and audits became commodity services in the minds of the buyers. It took years to reposition the service and adjust pricing levels.

The best-run firms—whether bill-by-the-hour, fixed fee, or retainer businesses—maintain a tight link between pricing and the costs to deliver the service. They carefully price each assignment to reflect profitability targets and track, manage, and measure actuals against plan for each engagement. Partners responsible for client work are measured and rewarded based on both top-line revenue and bottom-line contributions.

My firm learned this lesson the hard way through a few painful, unprofitable engagements that were not priced to reflect our delivery costs or managed efficiently. We have subsequently developed two simple planning and budgeting tools to price and manage assignments that have been quite effective for our business. The project planning template, shown in Exhibit 6.9, is an effective tool for both pricing and engagement management. It is used to map the activities and timeline of each assignment and the responsibility of each team member for each phase of the engagement. The second tool, shown in Exhibit 6.10, is a budget worksheet used to price and budget each project. The numbers from the project plan are plugged into this template to appropriately price each assignment. Even though we traditionally charge a fixed-project fee instead of an hourly fee for our assignments, we price each project based on the number of anticipated hours times the direct cost—base plus payroll and insurance—of each professional. Like many of the firms studied, we price based on a three to four times cost multiplier to cover payroll, overhead, and profit margin.

EXHIBIT 6.9　Broderick Project Planning Tool

ASSESSMENT PLANNING	Responsible	Participants	Hours	Wk of 5/7	Wk of 5/14	Wk of 5/21	Wk of 5/28
Project Kick-off							
Internal kick-off							
Develop work plan							
Develop research brief							
Kick-off meeting with client							
Finalize research framework							
Internal Interviews							
Develop internal interview guide							
Schedule internal interviews							
Conduct internal interviews							
Develop Target Database							
Profile target market							
Gather target database from client							
Analyze database for missing data							
Consolidate databases and upload							
Supplement database if necessary							
Develop External Interview Guide							
Draft outline for client							
Develop questionnaire							
Gain initial approval from client on discussion topics							
Gain approval from client on key questions							
MARKET ASSESSMENT							
Continue for each phase...							

EXHIBIT 6.10   Broderick Budget Planning Worksheet

Instructions: Fill in the boxes when proposing on/or planning a project. The formulas will do the rest. Once the project is underway, use the planned-to-actual dashboard to monitor results.			
	Planned	**%**	
Proposed Fee	$		
People Costs	$		
Net Fee			
Target Profit			
Hours Summary			
Phase One – Internal Assessment	**Hours**	**Cost**	**Time to Complete**
Project Director			
Senior Manager			
Associate			
Administrator			
Total			
Phase Two – External Market Research	**Hours**	**Cost**	**Time to Complete**
Project Director			
Senior Manager			
Associate			
Outsourced Research Associate			
Database Coordinator			
Analyst			
Administrator			
Total			
Continue for each phase...			
Planned-To-Actual Dashboard			
	% Hours Planned	**% Hours Used**	**Hours Remaining**
Remaining Project Hours			
Remaining Hours by Person			
Project Director			
Senior Manager			
Associate			
Administration			
Total			

Leverage

Leverage, the number of professionals per partner on an individual engagement, varies depending on the type of work. A consulting firm with multiple practice areas, for example, can have a significant variation in leverage. For its IT-related work, the ratio of the project team to partners can be as high as 30 to one, while the firm's strategy practice may operate at close to one to one.

The key to managing leverage is to make certain that the skill levels of the project team are appropriate for the type of work delivered.

Board-level strategic consulting assignments cannot be performed by junior staff. Clients who buy these types of services are retaining the organization's most experienced brainpower. On the other hand, large-scale, long-term projects such as systems integration or outsourcing engagements, in which the delivery methodologies are more routinized, can and should utilize lower-cost, less-experienced professionals. Both types of work can be equally profitable if managed appropriately. Bill Hermann, former managing partner of Plante & Moran, said his firm lets each practice determine the appropriate leverage and pricing model based on its type of work. According to Hermann, "There are two ways to get to the contribution margin. It can be high charge hours at a lower rate or fewer charge hours at a higher rate, but everyone has to get to the same number."

Several respondents discussed the importance of not allowing partners to hoard work. Most firms reward partners for both billable hours and the length and duration of client relationships as part of their compensation criteria. Partners are often fearful that junior professionals or even fellow partners might jeopardize their billable numbers or their relationships with clients and are reluctant to delegate the work to others in the firm.

The failure to properly leverage the partners has several negative implications for the firm. When high-value partners are spending precious hours doing lower-value work, junior professionals are underutilized, marketing and business development to keep the pipeline full are probably neglected, and the mentoring and training of the next level of firm leaders probably aren't taking place. All these factors can significantly impact short-term profits per partner and the business's longer-term viability.

Performance Efficiency

"Most professional service firms are process-avoidant."

"We are starting to look at what it cost us to do that, what did we collect, and could we be more efficient in the delivery."

We were disappointed to find that only 17 percent of respondents listed performance efficiency as one of the top metrics that leaders watch to measure financial health. It is, as discussed in Chapter 1, "Professional

Services," a weakness of the industry. Unlike their counterparts in the industrial and service sectors, PSFs typically have little interest in improving the process efficiency of delivering services to clients.

Firms that bill by the hour have little incentive to improve efficiency as long as the clients continue to pay the bills without complaint. It would seem logical that PSFs charging a fixed project fee or annual retainer fee would be extremely interested in controlling the costs of delivering services. Even a slight improvement in the efficiency of the behind-the-scenes support work typical in each engagement can have a direct impact on the bottom line. However, few firms truly understand or bother to assess the cost of the activities to deliver the work. The excuse for some, particularly premium-brand low-leveraged firms, is that because no two engagements are the same, it is impossible to standardize and improve processes. We do not agree. We would be willing to wager that 80 percent of the work—even for a "one-of-a-kind strategy" consulting assignment or a "bet-the-company" litigation engagement—follows a well-developed path of development, execution, and deliverables.

Early Warning Signs

"Having the right analytics is critical. You can look at the same old data the same old way and not spot the issues coming down the track."

"If you're not selling work and building a backlog of work to be done, that's your 'going out of business' notice."

"It's less about being a historian. It's a lot about being able to predict what's going to happen around the turn."

In assessing the organization's financial health, astute firm leaders at the top PSFs look at both leading and lagging indicators. Lagging indicators are metrics that measure the results of financial performance that has already occurred, such as revenue, utilization, realization, and costs. These are important metrics in running a business, but they are only part of the equation. Leading indicators, such as declining revenue growth per client and professional turnover, facilitate the ability to forecast future outcomes to make adjustments or change direction before a serious problem occurs, or take advantage of an opportunity emerging on the horizon. As one managing partner said, "It doesn't do me much good to get a report in mid-July that tells me we had capacity the second week of June."

Firm leaders described a variety of red flags or early warning signs that they monitor to stay on top of their firm's financial health. Most of these indicators coalesce around four components of the business: clients, the partnership, talent, and financial management (see Exhibit 6.11). Dennis Nally, Global Chairman of PwC, said that it is important to remember that financial results are only one aspect of firm management. "Our dashboard at PwC is focused on a balanced scorecard approach. It starts with our people strategy—how are we doing in terms of recruitment, turnover, and employee satisfaction? Second, we talk about the quality and value of our client work and relationships. And finally, we look at classic financial performance metrics—revenues, cost structure, profitability, margins, and so on."

As you can see from the list of warning signs in Exhibit 6.11, respondents watch a host of important indicators to ensure that clients are happy, paying their bills, and buying more work; talented people are joining and staying; partners are united and contributing; and the firm is financially stable.

Reporting

Many firm leaders expressed the need for more streamlined and better synthesized reporting. Persistent problems cited by respondents in the reporting area ran the gamut from poor data quality to gaps in data flow from system to system to the sheer volume of data, which can often result in "phone book-sized" reports. Even among those who feel they have a fairly effective data-gathering process, many agree that reports are often irrelevant and not useful for business decision making. Firm leaders believe that aggregating the data is only the first hurdle. The more difficult step is reviewing, analyzing, and synthesizing the reports to understand the correlations and interrelationships across the organization. As one COO admitted, "We have a tremendous amount of financial information. The question is from a management standpoint, what do we do with it?"

EXHIBIT 6.11   Warning signs of failing financial health

Clients	Partnership	Talent	Management
Declining billings	Partner departures	Declining satisfaction and enthusiasm per employee surveys	Low cash position
Declining revenue growth per client	Lack of consensus among leaders on key strategies leading to inaction	Unplanned employee attrition	Declining revenues and margins
Declining realization or clients not paying on time	Insufficient collaboration in business development and client service across geographical lines	Difficulty attracting top talent; losing to competitors	Declining utilization
Instability in client relationships; declining satisfaction	Principal glue is financial results		Lack of timely action on negative metrics
Low backlog of work	Partner compensation is greater than their contribution		Potential legal exposures and contract liabilities increasing
Fewer proposals in the pipeline	Inability to improve or exit undercontributing partners		Poor/unstable relationship with banks
Fewer wins/higher losses to competitors	Eclectic collection of practices		Unwillingness to cut back when demand flattens
Little cross-selling	Decline in intellectual capital development		Deferring expenses; artificially accelerating collections
High client turnover	Partners have no understanding of financial requirements		

Most leaders reported receiving monthly reports on firm financial activity, but several say they review data more frequently. David Childs, Global Managing Partner at Clifford Chance, receives daily, detailed information on performance for the firm's London headquarters, weekly or monthly reports from other offices, and a weekly flash report on the whole firm. Latham & Watkins uses a financial and practice management software product called Elite Enterprise, a web-based user platform that can track a host of data on a multi-office global scale. According to LeeAnn Black, the firm's COO, "Full, real-time access to financial information is central to our culture of transparency and our 'one firm' ethos. Giving our partners the ability to view a wide range of financial data on a daily basis, at their desktops, is important to us from a cultural, operational, and business performance perspective." ghSMART's CFO, Ron Zoibi, prepares a one-slide state-of-the-firm dashboard report that is distributed to everyone in the firm (see "Metric Management at Gensler").

Metric Management at Gensler

As the world's largest architectural firm, outstanding design and innovation are the hallmarks of Gensler's global leadership. While metrics are certainly important to running the firm's 35 offices around the world, it's the understanding of what's behind the metrics that really counts. "Numbers are just indicators. They're not the meat—the day-to-day reason why a project is working or not or why a client is happy or not," observes Co-CEO Andy Cohen. With this caveat in mind, Gensler uses the data it captures via its financial dashboard not just for at-a-glance reporting or a snapshot of short-term performance, but for strategic planning and forecasting. The goal is twofold: to use its constant stream of data to fine-tune its operations in the short term, and to steer its enterprise successfully from a global economic perspective.

Key aspects of Gensler's holistic approach to leveraging its financial dashboard data and managing its metrics include:

- **Flexibility and focus**—Gensler constantly gathers lots of data—and slices and dices it across many dimensions to gain an understanding of current performance, global trends, and market indicators. Groups of 25 to 30 people, which the design sector refers to as studios, are the firm's building blocks. Each self-sustaining studio has a set of metrics that roll up to the firm's offices and regions. Revenue, growth, and other metrics are also tracked by project, within and across the firm's 16 practices, and by client relationship. As a global enterprise, eight or more Gensler offices may be working for a particular client at any given time, so having a full picture of the firm's ongoing projects, costs, and revenue for each major client is critical.

- **Transparency**—The firm is exceptionally open about sharing metrics. Important financial indicators are presented at monthly all-staff office meetings, along with new assignments and potential projects. "At year's end, management talks candidly about profit and loss and the general health of the firm so that everyone understands the numbers and what's happening from a global perspective," said Cohen.

- **User-friendly systems**—The data that management has to work with is only as accurate and complete as the information that people input into a firm's financial dashboard. For this reason, Gensler is constantly fine-tuning its data-gathering tools and technology to make them as easy and painless to use as possible. The goal is always to minimize the input time involved and maximize the value of the output that results.

- **Forecasting**—Tracking dashboard metrics by project, studio, office, region, practice, and client is valuable in monitoring performance on an ongoing basis. But, as Cohen notes, most of this data gathering is "looking in the rearview mirror." Looking behind and beyond the data to project future demand and how the firm should move forward strategically is a far more critical aspect of metrics management in Cohen's view. In addition to looking at booked and projected revenue, the firm closely analyzes its win and loss rates for lessons learned. Beyond this, it factors global metrics into its planning process, such as unemployment, GDP, and country-by-country growth rates—all with an eye toward projecting areas for the firm to focus on in meeting Gensler's vision to "Redefine What is Possible Through the Power of Design."

Ultimately, Gensler's goal in managing the metrics it gathers is not just to gauge short-term performance, but to guide long-term growth and the firm's vision. "We're constantly measuring to ensure we are a leading innovative design firm," notes Cohen. "We're trying to see where global trends are in relation to our practice area growth strategy, what's working, and what areas of the firm we need to improve on."

Transparency and Accountability

"We're very transparent on the financial information distributed to our partners. They get everything."

Transparency is not only a financial management decision, but also a cultural one. As organizations grow and become more geographically dispersed, there is a tendency to move away from total transparency. While transparency can support the sense of partnership and teamwork, it can also create the distractions of internal competition and divisiveness.

Most of the firms in our research share overall firm performance results with the partners, but in some of the largest PSFs, partners see only data for their own projects, clients, and office or business unit. Some firm leaders say that sharing financial data is all well and good, but often pointless if partners don't understand the reports or know how to respond when the metrics are bad. Making certain that professionals are educated on the numbers, their implications, and the actions appropriate to deploy to address problems is a task for the CFO and the training programs. Employee-owned Black & Veatch runs a day-long training program called Value-Based Management that every person in the company attends. The program's goal is to raise the level of understanding of the financial data and drive consistency around the use of terminology and metrics to manage the business. The company created a board game to simplify the learning process and engage the professionals. "It's actually a lot of fun," said Senior Vice President Mike Elzey. "It's a great tool to help professionals understand how to interpret and get value out of the financial reports."

For the top PSFs studied, accountability around financial goals is carefully tracked, and performance against goal is one of the key criteria in compensation decisions. Seventy-one percent of respondents rated their process for managing to revenue and cost targets as rigorous, as shown in Exhibit 6.12.

EXHIBIT 6.12   The firms studied place a great deal of accountability around financial goals

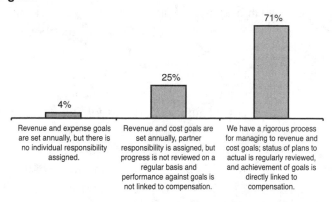

ghSMART's Budget, Dashboard, and Review Process

Geoff Smart, Chairman and CEO of ghSMART, said that he hired a CFO "way before I needed one. I knew it was critical to have a sophisticated finance executive on board early on to help me grow the business." When the firm's CFO, Ron Zoibi, joined in 2003, there were three full-time employees—Smart, Zoibi, an administrative assistant—and a handful of part-time independent consultants. In 2010, the firm has grown to 27 full-time consultants and support staff and more than $10 million in revenue. Over the past 5 years, ghSMART has grown revenue and profits an average of 25 percent per year.

According to Zoibi, financial planning and budgeting is a bottom-up process at the firm. The culture is very much a "choose your own path" philosophy, said Zoibi. On an annual basis he reaches out to all the consultants to ask them "what they want to do this year." There is a minimum revenue threshold of about $600,000 for principals and $1.5 to $2 million for partners, but beyond that consultants can choose their growth trajectories in the firm. Smart is a tough recruiter and targets "very driven people." (See "Recruiting at ghSMART" in Chapter 3, "People.") Plus, 100 percent of the partner's compensation is based on personal and firm performance, so no one typically signs up for the minimum. The strategic leadership team aggregates the individual consultants' revenue goals and adjusts the numbers to reflect market and client predictions and the firm's growth expectations and ambitions.

Zoibi tracks results against plan "365 days a year" and prepares a weekly report for the chairman and CEO, a monthly dashboard report that is distributed to everyone in the firm and quarterly individual reports for each consultant. "We are passionate about communicating the five metrics that we believe are the key drivers of our business," said Zoibi. The five metrics the firm tracks are client and team satisfaction, EBITDA growth, growth in number of consultants, and average revenue per consultant. Client and team satisfaction is measured every six months. Zoibi personally contacts each client by phone or e-mail to discuss services and asks them to rate the firm on a scale from 1 to 5. Each person at ghSMART receives an anonymous satisfaction survey to determine the good and bad things the firm is doing from the team's perspective. Quarterly individual dashboards include stats on personal client satisfaction scores, revenue contributions, clients and targets, and professional development—"the things they need to do to get promoted," said Zoibi. Individual stats are rolled into a quarterly state-of-the-firm summary slide that everyone reviews (see Exhibit 6.13).

On at least a quarterly basis, Zoibi meets with each consultant to review that person's plans and results. "It's developmental," said Zoibi. "It's not about being punitive or forcing anyone to go harder or slower. The theme is all about helping them stay close to their goals and helping them amp up or down accordingly."

Both Zoibi and Smart agree that having happy clients, satisfied and energized people, and steady team growth are the ticket to a successful EBITDA and revenue outcome.

In most PSFs the leadership team meets regularly with the business unit heads and partners to discuss progress and make adjustments and recommendations as needed. The quarterly meetings in many firms are used to reforecast the budget, while monthly meetings cover immediate performance results (see "ghSMART's Budget, Dashboard, and Review Process").

EXHIBIT 6.13 ghSMART State of the Firm Report

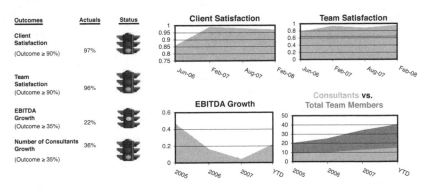

CHAPTER SUMMARY

Finance

- Eighty percent of leaders interviewed ranked financial management as a high priority.
- The best-run firms share seven noteworthy characteristics:
  1. Strong planning and budgeting
  2. Rigorous tracking and reporting
  3. Careful management of cash flow
  4. Forward-looking versus purely historical
  5. Transparency to partners
  6. Accountability
  7. Investment in people and tools
- There are three typical stages of annual financial planning and budgeting (see Exhibit 6.3).
- Successful leaders watch a host of financial indicators to monitor firm financial health (see Exhibit 6.6).
- Firm leaders monitor a variety of indicators to ensure that clients are happy, talented people are joining and staying, partners are united and contributing, and the firm is financially stable (see Exhibit 6.11).

7

Positioning

Brand, marketing, and sales

"Your brand is the place you occupy in the consciousness of your constituents."
—Frank Burch, Chairman, DLA Piper Global Board

"How you use marketing to convey the value you're capable of delivering to your client is the real challenge."
—Dennis Nally, Global Chairman, PwC

"In a professional service firm, every one of your people out doing the work is a reflection of the brand."
—Marie Lerch, Vice President, Marketing and Communications, Booz Allen Hamilton

In professional services, positioning is what you stand for. It's based on the organization's vision, values, and culture and represents the firm's promise to the marketplace. Positioning defines what the firm does, how it does it, and why it is different from other organizations. Brand is the image the clients have of the firm. It is essentially the grade you receive from clients and the marketplace on your ability to fulfill the need you promised to address. Building a strong brand is a cycle of setting expectations and delivering on or exceeding those expectations repeatedly over time.

Marketing is the process of identifying, targeting, and approaching clients and prospects to build awareness of services to attract and retain business. It involves a set of integrated activities that include market research, segmentation, market strategy and planning, brand management, market communications, sales support, and program tracking and management. Sales is the process of identifying potential clients, establishing credibility, closing engagements, and retaining and expanding client relationships. It is a continuous cycle of finding ways to grow the business.

Throughout the industry, there is a good deal of controversy surrounding the processes to position the firm, establish a brand, market the business, and ultimately sell services. In the course of our interviews, we heard a variety of definitions for each of these concepts, and an even wider variety of descriptions of how these activities are tackled and managed inside the organization. The firm leaders we spoke with do agree that positioning, branding, marketing, and sales are important ingredients of firm success. Seventy-seven percent of interviewees placed them at the top of their management agendas, as shown in Exhibit 7.1. Ratings on performance in this category, however, were mixed. Although 50 percent of the leaders we spoke with gave their firms fairly high marks in this area (as shown in Exhibit 7.2), most said they were best at brand management and spotty on marketing and sales. Or, as one CEO confessed, "I would say we are substantially underinvested in these areas."

Exhibit 7.1   Branding, marketing, and sales ranks sixth in order of importance for firm leaders

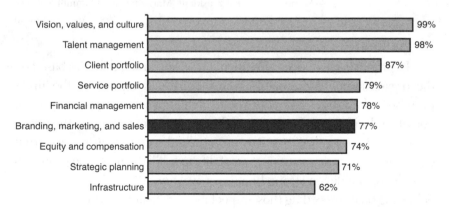

Exhibit 7.2   Reviews on performance for branding, marketing, and sales management were mixed

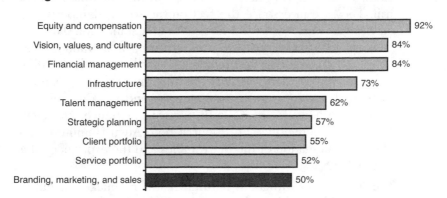

Five Elements of a Successful Market Strategy

"The brand is all about the importance of the value and the integrity with which we do work. And that's every person from top on down."

"We deliberately formed a view that our brand is all about how our clients and others perceive us—and we have to make sure all the time we're doing what we can to improve that perception."

"Most firms are not very specific, and they're bland in general. So, we have to say here's what we do and here's what we don't do. Here's how we do it, and here's what the value proposition is for you. And here's why we think it's not just hot air."

We have found several fundamental elements of a successful brand-marketing and business-development program. Specifically, the most savvy firms do the following:

- *Know who they are and what they do.* Positioning is the foundation of a successful brand. The firm's position in the market must flow, like all other elements of firm management, from the axis point of the PSF leadership model: shared vision, values, and culture. The internally galvanized view of the firm—its character, talent, enthusiasm, and direction as an organization—should permeate all interactions with clients, colleagues, and the communities and markets it serves. A focused positioning attracts both top talent and top clients and steadily builds a distinct brand.

- *Mobilize their people as the key brand managers.* In PSFs, professionals are the product, the voice, and the champions of the firm. They are in essence the feet on the street, demonstrating daily to the world what the firm does and stands for. The best firms spend a great deal of time nurturing and training their teams in both technical and relationship skills, carefully instilling and enforcing the firm's values. The way the professionals interact with clients—the partnerships, trust, and working relationships they establish—creates a distinctive experience. As Reggie Van Lee, Executive Vice President at Booz Allen Hamilton, said, "It's the combination of the deliverables and the experience that differentiates a service firm."

- *Plan.* Some firms with a few naturally gifted rainmakers might be able to build a steady, stable crop of clients. But for most PSFs, this formula doesn't work in the long run. The best firms step back, assess, and test the market for opportunities. They focus on the most effective target clients and service offerings and map out an approach to get in front of these targets to tell their story, build credibility, and sell business. The plan is collaboratively developed and agreed on, and progress is tracked and managed.

- *Talk to the market.* "Build it and they will come" is not a good idea for selling professional services. It always amazes us when our clients are reticent to approach their clients and contacts to find out what they need and what they might be buying. The most effective firms are constantly out in the market talking to clients, testing new service concepts, assessing and reporting on trends, and asking for advice and direction. This pulse on the client's business fuels thought leadership and new services and establishes the firm's professionals as innovative thinkers and experts in their sector.

- *Hold people accountable.* Accountability across all areas of firm management is a recurring theme throughout this book. It is definitely a best practice and an important lesson from the top firms that we studied. The market strategy and plan must come with assigned roles and responsibilities, specific goals and timelines, and a formal review and monitoring process that ultimately links performance to compensation.

The Power of Brand

Frank Burch, Chairman, DLA Piper Global Board, aptly described brand as "the place you occupy in the consciousness of your constituents." Virtually all the firm leaders interviewed understand and value the power and impact of brand in the professional service business. Unlike product companies, which have something tangible to sell— something you can see or touch or taste—PSFs are challenged with the difficult task of selling an intangible. The product we sell is talent, skills, insights, and ideas. Brand for professional services, therefore, is essentially a promise to deliver a value. Selling intangibles is not easy in a highly competitive field of players who look much the same to the buyers of these services.

Determine the Market and Brand Positioning

The key to building a successful brand is positioning. Positioning, as discussed at the beginning of this chapter, defines what the firm does, how it does it, and why it is different from other organizations. Why would prospective clients pay money for the firm's services? What benefits are they hoping to receive? And why would they select one firm over another that offers similar services? To succeed, a PSF must identify a credible position to occupy in the market. Determining positioning involves decisions on a number of fronts.

Spectrum of Practice

Firms must decide where to play on what industry consultant David Maister calls the Professional Service Spectrum of Practice. In his book, *Managing the Professional Service Firm*, Maister has identified three points on a continuum that represent different positioning and service options—efficiency-based, experience-based, and expertise-based practice models. Efficiency-based practices such as systems integration provide efficient solutions to common problems. Typically, they are low-margin, highly leveraged assignments that utilize a team of relatively low-cost junior professionals performing well-developed routinized methodologies. Profitability is achieved through a high volume of low-fee engagements.

Experience-based practices offer customized processes and solutions to certain types of problems that, according to Maister, don't require an expensive "start with a blank piece of paper" approach. These models usually are lower leverage—one partner to five to ten professionals versus one partner to 30 or 40 in an efficiency practice. Fees and margins are higher, and the work requires an experienced "been there, done that" team of professionals.

Expertise-based practices provide unique solutions to unique problems such as a turnaround or a mergers and acquisitions strategy for a *Fortune* 100 company. These assignments require a top-notch team and are very low-leverage—often one partner to one professional. Because clients are willing to pay for the "best minds in the business," fees and margins are high.

The decision of where to practice on the spectrum has critical implications for all the management areas of focus illustrated in our PSF Leadership Model and discussed throughout the book. The choice to position and price as an expertise-based premium provider of top-of-the-line services, for example, must be reinforced with what the market perceives as high-value services delivered by senior top-notch professionals, who provide a high degree of one-on-one service. The target profile, revenue, and status of the buyers of these high-price/high-value services will look different from those for the buyers of lower-cost PSF services. The premium brand model creates a distinct culture and values within the firm that, together with a high skill requirement, impact recruiting and retention of professionals. To attract experienced and top-schooled professionals, compensation is at the high end of the market. Brand building and marketing in this model focus on establishing credibility and value through thought leadership development and knowledge sharing. Business development will most likely be conducted exclusively by the partners or equity owners.

However, the bottom line of a premium brand model does not differ from a lower-cost, high-leverage, efficiency-based service model if both businesses are managed well. Profits per shareholder can be lucrative for both, but each calls for a very different strategy and team. Some of the major firms studied have a mix of all types of practice areas within the firm, and the leaders of these PSFs acknowledge that it can be challenging to manage them all effectively under the same roof.

Services

The firm must determine the focus, depth, and breadth of the practice areas or service sectors in which it hopes to compete. Deciding what to sell may seem basic to those outside the industry. Lawyers practice law, architects design, executive search professionals recruit and place. But it is not that simple. PSFs do, of course, begin with a professional skill acquired after years of study and training, so the basic service focus is a given—lawyers do practice law, not engineering. But the mix of potential service areas of focus under the legal umbrella is broad. We counted 15 different practice areas for one 10-attorney law firm and 60 areas of expertise for a 2,000-attorney global law firm in our study.

Deciding on the mix of services usually begins with the founders' specific skills and areas of interest. One person might gravitate toward working in mergers and acquisitions, another toward tax planning, and still another toward litigation services. As the firm grows, new services are added, sometimes solely based on who comes onboard and what they want to do. The best firms have evolved services based on a strategic analysis and perspective on market trends, client needs for services, and the competitive environment. As showcased in Chapter 5, "Services," savvy firms continuously talk to their market to test and validate current service areas, spot gaps or weaknesses in offerings, and identify potential new services. Choosing what to sell and identifying whom to sell it to is pretty much a chicken-and-egg predicament—it's difficult to say which comes first. In fact, both typically evolve together.

Segment Focus

Some firms choose to establish themselves as specialists in a specific industry or type of work. A consulting firm may specialize in the retail industry, for example, or an architectural firm might include a focus on airport design. An executive search firm may recruit only CEOs and boards of directors. Specialization is a good way to differentiate from competitors and simplifies the process of defining and approaching the market.

Geographic Reach

Will your firm offer its services globally or locally to your immediate community? Each of these choices dictates a different strategic approach to positioning as well as to just about every area of focus listed on our PSF Leadership Model. Many firms, of course, have morphed over time from local to global. This is terrific as long as the firm makes the appropriate adjustments to remain aligned with its vision, values, and culture.

Markets

Accurately profiling potential buyers of the firm's services is a critical task that many firms do not do well. Some believe that anyone who can afford the fee is a viable client. We once asked a law firm team who specialized in labor law who the market was for their services. We knew we had a lot of work to do when the reply was, "Anyone with five or more employees." It is impossible to launch an effective marketing and sales initiative if you cannot pinpoint the highest-opportunity buyers for the firm's services. Particularly when the budget and resources are limited, every dollar and partner business development moment must be appropriately focused on the top clients, prospects, and markets. Profiling the buyers most likely to buy your services—by segments, geographies, revenues, companies, and specific buyers within those companies that make the purchasing decisions—is a critical component of the positioning process. The steps to assess the current client portfolio, and segment and profile the prospective market, are detailed in Chapter 4, "Portfolio."

Service Delivery and Buyer Experience

When your product is a service, clients view your brand as both what they receive and how they receive it. It's both "What do I get?" and "How do you deliver?" Within the professional service arena, the experience—the how—matters as much to clients as the results delivered. For example, how the firm interacts with a client, the partnership it creates—the "roll up our sleeves" attitude, or, as discussed in "Brand Management at Skadden, Arps," a "walk through walls" mentality creates a distinctive experience for clients and prospects. Deciding on the service experience the firm will create for the client—whether it's efficiency, speed, availability, practicality, or something else—is a critical component of positioning.

Unfortunately, you can't just aspirationally develop your service philosophy in a conference room. Saying it is so doesn't necessarily translate into reality. The attributes selected must realistically demonstrate the firm's ability to deliver. Failure to do so can backfire if you set false expectations with clients and prospects. The task of establishing the service promise begins with an honest internal assessment of the firm's culture and environment to identify the values and characteristics that will resonate with the market. Some firms, such as advertising agency Euro RSCG Life, conduct regular "anonymous and candid" surveys of employees to gather the internal perspective on what the firm does best and worst. This feedback is used to both improve life at the firm and define the client experience (see "Euro RSCG Life Culture Scan").

Embed and Build the Brand

"When you look at the decision criteria that clients use for selecting service providers, a lot of it has to do with your reputation, your track record, the experience they've had with you, and what their peers are saying about you."

"We want to be viewed as the consultant of choice to our clients. We want to be viewed as the employer of choice to our people and our potential recruits. And we want to be viewed as a good corporate citizen."

The top firms that we studied focus their brand-building efforts on several key constituencies: the internal team and potential recruits, clients, and the markets and communities they serve. As Ted Burke, CEO of Freshfields, explained it, "We have to build our brand by impressing everyone that comes into contact with us, and we have to tell them here's what we do, here's how we do it, and here's what the value proposition is for you."

People are the firm's brand ambassadors. The value that PSFs deliver comes directly from the knowledge, skills, and behavior of the professionals. As emphasized in Chapter 3, "People," the best firms invest significant resources on recruitment to select the people who best embody the firm's values and culture and on training to embed these values. Being considered an "employer of choice" that attracts top professionals in the field is an important component of brand building.

Professional services is largely a word-of-mouth business. Happy clients tell their colleagues about their experience and are pleased to serve as references when asked. The key to building a strong client brand

Brand Management at Skadden, Arps

"Brand for us is our reputation," says Eric Friedman, executive partner at Skadden, Arps. The roots of the firm's brand were established in 1948 when four lawyers—Marshall Skadden, Leslie Arps, John Slate, and Joe Flom—launched their law firm in a tiny suite of offices on Wall Street. They established a reputation as a scrappy and entrepreneurial practice that would tackle the tough assignments—such as hostile corporate takeovers—that the old-line Wall Street firms did not do at the time. Since then, the firm has grown to 2,000 attorneys based in 24 offices around the world and is one of a handful of global law firms posting revenues of more than $2 billion.

The firm continues to embrace the values of its founding fathers and very rigorously manages its brand and reputation in the market. In connection with messaging, Skadden considers four constituencies: current and prospective clients; the internal audience; potential recruits; and the broader legal, business, and social communities. Accordingly, the firm focuses its brand strategy and management on the following:

- **Highest-quality legal advice and innovative solutions**—Although Skadden is best known for representing clients on their most challenging, "bet-the-company" issues, the founders' vision was to provide best-of-breed lawyering for every engagement. This is an integral part of the firm's brand, crosscutting all practices and geographies.

- **Client service**—Skadden's founders were steadfast in their commitment to providing unparalleled client service, and that dedication is unwavering today. "Other firms make similar claims," says Friedman, "but the buzz on Skadden always has been—and hopefully always will be—that we walk through walls for our clients." Friedman believes this philosophy is a critical component of the firm's brand differentiation. As an example, he describes the firm's "Return each call every day—no exceptions" policy. No one—from partner to staff person—goes to sleep until they've returned all calls received that day.

- **Recruitment**—Friedman says that perpetuating and managing the brand start with recruiting. Skadden paved the way for major firms to look beyond the top five or ten law schools to recruit the most talented associates. According to Friedman, "Our goal is to hire lawyers whose qualities reflect our philosophy and brand. We look for really smart lawyers with a problem-solving orientation. And we seek a true diversity of skills, experience, background, and perspectives."

- **Training**—At Skadden, training is considered a very important vehicle to instill the firm's brand at all levels of seniority. The program combines a formal curriculum with on-the-job training in team environments and one-on-one mentoring. To ensure that brand messaging is incorporated, Skadden's marketing team works collaboratively with the attorney development, recruiting, and human resources groups.

- **Public service**—Social responsibility is one of the firm's core values, for which Skadden is widely recognized. In addition to an unusually broad base of pro bono activities, Skadden invests a significant amount of both attorney time and money into two major public service programs. Since 1988, the Skadden Fellowship Foundation has annually provided two-year paid fellowships to 25 young lawyers to help them pursue the practice of public-interest law on a full-time basis. The Skadden Honors Program in Legal Studies at the City College of New York is a $10 million, 10-year commitment to fund and support talented students from diverse racial and socioeconomic backgrounds with the education and groundwork they need to gain admission to and succeed in competitive law schools.

In connection with brand messaging, Sally Feldman, Director of Global Marketing and Communications at Skadden for 20 years, says that how the firm communicates, both internally and externally, is as important as the message itself. "We strive to capture Skadden's commitment to excellence and convey it to our clients, lawyers, staff, and recruits. Our brand is not just a message; it's at the heart of the firm."

Given the increasingly competitive marketplace and commoditization of many types of services, brand and brand management are more important than ever before. "The challenge for professional service firms is to constantly differentiate themselves and deliver the best value proposition. To survive and thrive, we must remain relevant and our brands must embody that relevance," says Feldman.

Euro RSCG Life Culture Scan

Euro RSCG Life is a diverse global healthcare communications network of 60 agencies and 2,000 employees worldwide. In 2003, the firm launched an initiative to bring together its network of agencies under one P&L to unify the organization and to harness and leverage the best ideas and services for its clients around the world. According to Donna Murphy, Worldwide Managing Partner, "Even though the agencies were all part of the same healthcare network, working under the same parent company, they all operated independently. We needed to pull everyone together under one management structure."

Once the global financial objectives were established, the firm began the process of creating a consistent overarching culture throughout the organization. To strategize and help implement the initiative, the firm turned to an outside consultant who suggested they launch a culture scan as an initial step to take the organization's pulse. The scan provided an overview of the firm's culture through focus groups, interviews, and an online survey. The goal was to identify and leverage the firm's strengths and create a more coherent culture by soliciting candid feedback from employees at all levels about what the firm did well, what it needed to work on, and how effective it was at achieving its strategic priorities.

Each culture scan is carefully planned to encourage maximum input from employees; it takes about 2 months from launch to presentation of the results. As a first step, the leadership team sends out a brief e-mail describing the rationale and scope of the scan. They invite employees to participate by logging onto a special site and completing a 15-minute anonymous online survey that is monitored by the outside consultant. The firm supports its initial announcement with an internal ad campaign of frequent e-mails and signage in local offices to heighten interest and increase participation.

In conjunction with the survey, the firm conducts regional focus groups that bring together people at all levels, as well as one-to-one interviews with about 50 employees from a cross-section of practices and geographies.

The data from all three activities is analyzed and presented to management at a series of regional meetings. The report highlights results, identifies problem areas, and lays out a strategic framework for the future. Senior management then selects the top three cultural issues to address and maps out a game plan for implementation. The firm rolls out all the results locally by agency. In most cases, agency presidents present the findings and plan in a town-hall format so that employees can ask questions and make suggestions.

"The results have been very gratifying," says Murphy. Euro RSCG Life has made significant strides in creating a collaborative, unified enterprise from a diverse network of agencies, and employees feel much more connected to the company as a whole. The firm's efforts have won recognition outside the agency as well. *Medical Marketing & Media* named Euro RSCG Life the 2010 Network of the Year, and *Adweek* named the firm the 2009 Healthcare Agency of the Year.

brigade is, of course, client service. Bringing the firm's service philosophy to life every day in every interaction is vital. Most of the firms studied carefully nurture their client relationships, and clients are contacted often to solicit feedback on service satisfaction and future needs. The loss of a client is carefully studied to understand the reasons and to make certain that any flaws in the service or deliverables are improved.

As mentioned in "Brand Management at Skadden, Arps," social responsibility is a critical component of many firms' ethos and philosophy. It is also a powerful tool to position the firm in the market and demonstrate its skills, values, and culture. PwC, for example, has leveraged its deep commitment to training, education, and open innovation into a broad-based knowledge-sharing initiative called PwC Open University. The program provides business executives, faculty, students, and regulators around the world with open and free access to the firm's expansive and growing library of training courses.

This first-of-its-kind corporate learning and education resource builds upon steps taken by leading universities such as MIT and Yale to make their courseware freely available. PwC Open University launched with an initial portfolio of 150 courses across multiple industries; delivered via webcast, podcast, or eLearn. According to Mitra Best, PwC Innovation Leader, the firm plans to expand the library based on market needs and requirements, establishing PwC as a trendsetter in open and free corporate education.

Keep the Message Clear and Consistent

Rodge Cohen, Chairman of Sullivan & Cromwell, expressed a warning to all PSFs, "The brand that a firm has built up over many years can be dissipated in a blink of an eye. All it takes is one or two mistakes of any magnitude, and you can destroy the brand."

As previously discussed, it is critical that everyone in the firm, from back-office support to chairman, understand the firm's positioning: Here is what we stand for; here is how we interact every day with each other and with clients and our communities; here are the words we use if anyone asks; and here is how we package ourselves in all our written materials and communications. Ensuring consistency across the firm requires two important steps:

- Clear articulation and communication of the positioning message so that everybody knows what it is, and what their role is in delivering the message
- A strong enforcement of the rules to ensure compliance

As discussed in Chapter 2, "Shared Vision, Values, and Culture," the best firms invest time and energy in articulating and instilling their values and enforce the rules through performance evaluations, compensation, and promotions or dismissal. For many, the values indoctrination process includes instruction on the dos and don'ts of brand management. Some firms put brand rules in writing. Latham & Watkins, for example, issues a simple four-page brochure to "every single person" in the firm that outlines the brand guidelines. These guidelines are reviewed with new hires and all employees on a regular basis. SmithGroup has been working for the past seven years to make certain that "anytime a client interacts with us, they will feel the same way and get the same quality," said firm President and CEO Carl Roehling. The firm developed an annual in-house seminar program to discuss brand strategy and the firm's service policy and to establish the rules for all graphics and public relations.

Regularly Test Brand Strength

"Gathering very regular, detailed feedback and making sure that we are responding as best we can to what the clients want and what the clients need is very important."

Firms of all sizes should conduct regular checkups of their brand awareness, perceptions of services and capabilities, and standing vis-à-vis competitors. Some firms studied have formal brand testing programs conducted by a third party on a regular basis, typically every 18 months to 2 years. Some firms test brand informally. One firm leader asks all partners to regularly poll their seatmates on airplanes to see if they have heard of the firm and, if so, what their opinion is; partners are asked to report the results. Some PSFs conduct semiformal testing: Partners talk to a selection of clients, everyone asks the same questions, results are collected in writing, and the information is shared and discussed.

Some believe the best way to get an unbiased view of where you stand is to conduct a third-party blind study in which interviewees do not know the name of the firm conducting the survey. Be aware, though, that it takes some serious "donations to a charity of your choice" and a tenacious recruiting program to persuade busy senior executives to take time to answer questions from some unknown entity. Answers given are usually guarded and not very revealing. There are numerous benefits to picking up the phone and asking clients to candidly rate the firm's brand and services. They love being asked, and it's a terrific relationship touch. From years of experience conducting these studies for PSFs, we can attest to the fact that the senior executives who buy professional services are not timid about sharing their viewpoints.

We suggest incorporating a brand-testing section into the annual client satisfaction survey process if the firm has one. Most brand tests incorporate similar types of awareness, usage, and perception questions. The key is to ask the same set of questions year after year to establish a benchmark and track progress over time.

Marketing

"Marketing is something we have done an absolutely dreadful job at. I think we are doing a much better job at it now, but we're not there yet."

"It's so terrible; it's awful, but I'm doing a marketing plan this year, and I'm going to stick to it. We really need to do that."

"The challenge is marketing and branding are not in our DNA."

PSFs have a wide range of perceptions about the concept of marketing. To some, marketing means sales: What do I need to close a sale? To others, marketing is business development: What do I need to do to target the right people and start a conversation with them? And to still others, marketing means brand and awareness: How do I build name recognition with the target audience? Some think marketing is PR, some advertising, some pitch packages. In reality, marketing is all these things and more if done correctly. As defined at the beginning of this chapter, marketing is the process of identifying, targeting, and approaching clients and prospects to build awareness of services, with the ultimate goal of attracting and retaining business. Tom Stewart, Chief Marketing and Knowledge Officer at Booz & Company, believes that the role of marketing in a professional service firm is "pretty classic. It's to create and sustain the brand and build the umbrella under which the partners can do their work." He described a marketing funnel that starts with awareness, which drives leads, which eventually turn into proposals and sales, and for PSFs, the process continues with ongoing client relationship management.

A firm's idea of marketing often depends on where the business is in its life cycle and the current state of the environment. In a booming market, little may be needed in terms of sales support, because the focus is on building brand recognition. In a tight economy, the focus is on sales—on getting and closing a transaction. If the firm is mature, the marketing approach focuses on client relationship management, maintaining and deepening brand strength, and supporting business-development activities.

Sales

"None of it's rocket science, but it's all about seeking out opportunities to get in front of clients."

"We all sell. We don't have any folks whose only job is to identify and cold call. Every single person in this organization sells."

"The nature of what we deliver to our clients is very sensitive and very close to the heart. They want to talk to people who are actually going to do the job, and understand the issues, and can give them sound advice."

Sales—or the softer term, business development—is a thorny topic in professional services. Many are of the opinion that only the professionals can sell the firm's services. As one managing director told us, "To sell what we do, you have to understand the work. The client must have the trust and the assurance that the person they are buying from will be there through the experience." We fundamentally agree with this concept, but the process is complicated by the fact that many professionals can't find or close a deal.

All too often firms rely on a few powerful "rainmakers"—professionals who have a natural ability to sell business—to provide work and revenue for the firm. In a professional services environment, all the senior professionals are expected to play a role in bringing in business. However, even though their compensation is linked to revenue generation, many professionals are uncomfortable with the process and are not very skilled at selling.

The pressure on a firm's senior professionals is immense. They are expected to find new business, do the work, manage client relationships, profitably manage their practices, recruit, train and mentor staff, innovate service offerings, and, in many cases, participate in firm governance. Although professional service firms invest significantly in skills training, very few spend much time teaching their professionals to sell and, even more importantly, to find new business. Finding new business-development opportunities, particularly with prospective clients who have never used the firm's services, is often the most difficult part of the selling process. And the more senior the prospective client, the more difficult the effort.

Some firms have experimented with nonbillable internal sales teams to formalize, manage, and support the business-development process. These teams often include fairly senior people with sales savvy who are deployed to generate new business leads and work with professionals to nurture potential opportunities through the sales pipeline. Or they are assigned to major account teams to walk the halls at the client sites to build relationships and spot new work opportunities. Although we like the concept of sales support teams, the jury is still out on their effectiveness. As one CEO admitted, "We are getting rid of our nonbillable sales team. The delivery people don't call on the leads the team generates, they don't want to follow up on any meetings, and they don't want to be bothered with it." Nonbillable sales teams work best in the most productized, highly leveraged end of the professional services spectrum. This kind of team does not work well for the experience and expertise-based models discussed earlier in the chapter.

Sales activities typically are conducted in siloed pockets throughout the organization, often with little connection to the firm's business focus and goals, let alone the marketing function and its activities. Sales is much more impactful when integrated into a multichannel marketing plan and program. Marketing builds brand awareness and credibility and stimulates interest in the firm and its services. Sales generates leads and closes deals. Together they support and enhance each other and become powerful tools to build the firm. To realize the highest return on investment, the marketing and business development activities need to be consolidated under one roof, with one leader managing the process.

Building a Marketing and Business Development Plan

The marketing and business development plan is an important component of the firm's strategic planning process and should be incorporated into the annual planning and budgeting cycle. Although many of the firms studied require detailed marketing and sales plans from their business unit leaders, we are willing to wager that the majority of firms in the industry do not proactively plan these activities.

Exhibit 7.3 illustrates a marketing planning pyramid. It begins with the market strategy decisions on services, markets, and the service promise, which have already been discussed. The marketing and business development plan, which represents the lower half of the pyramid, is designed to march the firm's professionals out into the marketplace in an organized way to promote the services and the service promise to the target market, with the ultimate goal of selling business.

Firm-wide Brand Initiatives

The marketing and business development planning process begins with a selection of firm-wide initiatives to raise awareness and build brand and reputation with key constituents—previously described as

EXHIBIT 7.3 Stages to develop the market strategy and the marketing business development plan

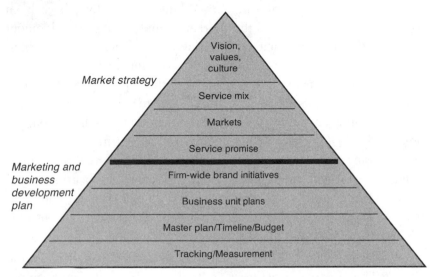

Market strategy

Vision, values, culture
Service mix
Markets
Service promise

Marketing and business development plan

Firm-wide brand initiatives
Business unit plans
Master plan/Timeline/Budget
Tracking/Measurement

professionals, clients, target markets, and communities. We recommend that firms annually target one or two specific new activities to improve their standing with one or more of these important groups. While activities can range from low-cost, easy-to-execute ideas to global programs, the point is to proactively think through and plan what to do. Here are some examples:

- *For professionals*, an award or recognition program for the internal team; a partnering program with a university to improve recruitment statistics (you read about on-campus recruiting in Chapter 3); a leadership role with an industry trade association to raise the firm's stature in its professional community.

- *For clients*, periodic onsite briefings for the client's internal teams on important topics; a special client-only Web cast or event; a holiday charitable donation on behalf of clients.

- *For target markets*, a thought leadership piece or program that contributes knowledge to the firm's market and raises awareness of capabilities (this book is a good example); an expanded media outreach program to a relevant trade press; a speech at an annual industry conference.

- *For communities*, a pro bono activity; a local fund drive; participation on a civic board.

Business Unit Plans

As soon as a few firm-wide brand-building initiatives have been agreed to, the firm develops the marketing and business development plans for the operating units. The many constituencies—geographies, practices, industries, and account teams—of the typical PSF matrix structure and the natural tensions among them pose particular challenges for planning. Some firms develop separate plans for each practice area, geography, and industry, which are executed in silos throughout the organization. The result is often a series of redundant and potentially embarrassing activities where one hand does not know what the other is doing. Anyone in the professional services business has heard stories of separate teams from the same firm scheduling a meeting with a prospective CFO to pitch services on the same day and finding this out only when they run into each other in the lobby of the client's office.

To work effectively, planning must be driven by the market, not the organization's internal structure. Clients don't care where you sit in the organization; they just want to know what you can do for them. Conducting one well-planned meeting with a prospective CFO to discuss the array of services the firm can provide and carrying out a coordinated follow-up plan is the correct way to build awareness and sell services. But achieving alignment and perfect coordination around business development is tricky in a multipractice, multigeography PSF. The most effective way to go to market is to develop marketing plans by industry focus. Study after study that we have conducted confirms that industry expertise followed by functional skill are the top selection criteria for hiring PSFs. But in most PSFs the geographies and practice areas dominate the matrix and control the P&Ls and are, in fact, the best way to internally govern the firm. Industries are often the third wheel in the power chain (see Chapter 10, "Structure").

We are not suggesting that firms restructure the matrix hierarchy to focus on industry. We do suggest that practices and geographies develop their annual operating plans and budgets as usual, but focus the marketing and business development piece of their plans by target industry segments. The assigned leaders of each industry take the focused plans from the units and weave them into a firm-wide industry plan of attack with specific target buyers. Clients and prospects are identified, and the appropriate array of service offerings from across practices is established.

A team of industry experts from each practice and geography is selected and committed. The top industry issues and topics are determined, and a steady stream of marketing and business development tactics are mapped to approach the market (see "Growing an Industry Program at Ernst & Young"). Industry leaders must have the clout to deploy and manage the industry teams, so we recommend a dotted-line reporting relationship to the industry head to make this work.

Master Plan, Timeline and Budget, Tracking and Measurement

"Our management group put together a statement of our go-to-market value proposition which is mind-bendingly complicated."

After the industry plans have been developed, a master plan that incorporates the firm-wide brand initiatives and the individual industry plans is created with a master budget and timeline. As with the annual planning process, someone must be accountable for the plan execution, and performance against plan must be tracked and reviewed regularly and results tied to compensation.

The critical and very difficult part of the planning process is measuring the program's results. How many articles have been written and conferences held debating the eternal dilemma of figuring out the ROI of the marketing spend? Trust me—many. The partners periodically peer at the overhead cost of their nonbillable marketing team and ask what they have gotten for their investment. And it is difficult to give a concrete answer. As one CMO admitted, "If someone were to say to me tomorrow, 'We're going to pull the plug on all client services, entertainment, and newsletters unless you can demonstrate the direct ROI that all those functions have,' I would be hard pressed to demonstrate the value from a dollars-and-cents perspective."

Over the years I have tried many derivations of ROI sleuthing. There was a time when I would go door to door to ask partners if they had received any calls or talked to any clients about our latest newsletter mailing. Then there was the "assign every partner a seminar attendee to follow up with" plan. I would stalk the partners weekly to see if they had done their assignment. But I became discouraged when we landed a

Growing an Industry Program at Ernst & Young

Ernst & Young in the United States had its eye on the nascent technology industry when it opened an office in Silicon Valley in the 1960s. "Our partners could see and feel the Valley transforming from a leading agricultural region into the epicenter of the technological world. The excitement was contagious," says Steve Almassy, who led the U.S. firm's technology practice for 15 years and now serves as Global Vice Chair for the organization's industry sectors. Over the past five decades, the technology practice has grown with the industry and, in 2010, the number of Ernst & Young technology professionals has grown to more than 10,000 worldwide.

According to Almassy, industry expertise always ranks among the top three most important factors cited whenever EY conducts a client survey, and he believes it's very important for professional service firms to have strong industry practices in the sectors they want to be known for. Based on his many years of building a successful practice, Almassy cites several critical steps for launching and growing an industry program:

- *Build deep expertise.* "Immerse yourself in the industry," says Almassy. In order to serve clients in the emerging technology field, EY professionals had to learn rapidly everything they could about the sector's companies and their businesses. Clients demand that their professional service providers have a solid knowledge of the economics and dynamics of their universe. "You've got to have people that have a deep industry expertise that can walk the talk," advises Almassy, "otherwise you won't be credible."

- *Channel your people's passions.* The nucleus for a new practice is often a handful of professionals who are passionate about delivering their expertise to a particular sector. Currently at EY, for example, a grass roots group has banded together to grow the organization's capabilities in serving the emerging cleantech field. The group bubbled up organically when partners began to share knowledge and solutions tailored to that industry. "Entering a new field can be very exciting for professionals who are intellectually challenged to learn a new industry, explore its issues, and develop solutions," says Almassy. "It's important to build a focused team that is driven to create something new."

- *Create and nurture strong networks.* Fostering networks of people around the world is critical to knowledge sharing and transfer, which is the key to mobilizing expertise on a global scale. When you have connection points, you're well positioned to drive brand and quality around the globe. "Developing strong industry networks that share a common goal and sing from the same hymn book helps create an industry machine to capitalize on new opportunities," asserts Almassy.

- *Position as a thought leader.* "Investing in research and dialogue is how we keep our finger on the pulse of an industry," says Almassy. EY technology practices established its position as an innovative knowledge leader through a strategically planned series of surveys, white papers, reports, and client events. As an example, the U.S. firm launched a program in 1986 called "Entrepreneur of the Year" to acknowledge successful growing companies in the field, which today is hosted in more than 135 cities in 50 countries and is widely recognized as the key event for entrepreneurs worldwide.

- *Gain a foothold.* Don't get so caught up in infrastructure that you fail to enter a promising market. Build traction as quickly as you can, identify industry "gurus" and leading-edge thinkers, and create relationships with them early on. Place some bets, marshal your existing resources, target a few key clients, and win some initial assignments. Build your brand client by client.

million-dollar engagement from an attendee at a luncheon briefing two weeks after the event, and the partner refused to give marketing any credit for the win!

It's easy to measure a formalized lead-generation program, but it is much more difficult to assess the benefits of public relations, advertising, or direct-mail programs, even if they are well targeted. The best measurement method that we have used is to track the number of touches, proposals, and engagements for each industry or segment target. As an example, Broderick was asked to design a 12-month marketing program to raise awareness among and create opportunities with CFOs, COOs, CAOs, and division heads of financial service institutions in North America. We worked with our client to identify 25 organizations and 350 specific individuals as the targets for the campaign. We selected five channels to approach the audience over the 12-month period:

- An industry survey, report, and webcast as the kick-off event
- A quarterly thought leadership mailing and webcast series on hot topics identified in the survey
- A five-city roundtable briefing program
- A calling program to make certain that our target buyers had received the thought leadership pieces with an offer to discuss our point of view
- A public relations outreach to trade publications and industry associations to place articles and secure speaking opportunities

The goal was to touch all 350 targets two to three times a month through our various channels so that in any given four-week period they might read an article, receive a thought leadership publication, attend a webcast or briefing, or take a call and schedule a meeting. All direct client contact—via a Web cast or attendance at a briefing or meeting—was tracked and reported monthly. The campaign cost $350,000 in out-of-pocket expenses (not including our fee to manage), but the results were deemed worth it. Each prospective buyer was "touched" 36 times during the course of the year at a total cost of $1,000 per prospect. The firm conducted a total of 40 face-to-face meetings that resulted in six proposal opportunities and three closed assignments totaling close to $700,000. And quite a few more potential proposal opportunities were brewing at the close of the campaign. Although the indirect benefits of heightened brand awareness were not measured, incoming calls increased substantially for the group overall, and revenue was 20 percent above target the year following the campaign.

Well-planned and well-executed marketing programs should result in tangible bottom-line returns. The key is setting expectations, creating realistic goals, and then carefully tracking and measuring results market by market.

Thought Leadership: The Most Powerful Way to Grow the Business

"It's a relentless drumbeat of repeated messages by management and others until it becomes a part of what everyone says."

For PSFs, thought leadership is perhaps the single most powerful tool to position the business, build brand, and sell services. The term thought leadership implies a collection of valuable and original insights into key issues that the market cares about. It suggests that the people who developed these insights are worth following—in other words, hiring—to think through their toughest problems. Far from brochure-ware, thought leadership includes articles, white papers, blogs, webcasts, podcasts, surveys, and e-mail postings. Whatever the vehicle, intelligent, market-focused thought leadership is an excellent way to showcase and demonstrate this expertise. As a stand-alone program or integrated with other marketing efforts, developing and distributing thought leadership can benefit the firm in many ways:

- *Build awareness.* Thought leadership programs build visibility and connect the brand to cutting-edge thinking. Positioning your firm as the thought leader in a specific field or area is a powerful way to differentiate your services from competitors.

- *Focus service offerings.* Developing content for a thought leadership program is an excellent reason to talk to your clients and prospects to determine trends and test service needs and buying decisions. The market intelligence gathered serves as the foundation for thought leadership pieces and focuses services to address client needs.

- *Facilitate business development.* One of the most tangible benefits of a thought leadership program is its impact on business development. A well-crafted program provides opportunities to touch clients and prospects in many ways. Gathering information for content is a good excuse to call and/or meet face to face with clients and prospects and solicit their input. The finished product can be leveraged into meetings with clients and prospects to share information or can be used as the basis for small, focused briefings or speaking opportunities. Sharing the firm's thinking with clients often unveils new opportunities to sell additional work. For prospects, it is a "nonsalesy" way to introduce the firm and begin the relationship-development process.

To be an effective marketing and business development tool, thought leadership must be an ongoing program that is sustained over time. A single thought leadership piece may pique the interest of some, but awareness, brand building, and business development benefits will result from consistency and persistence. It is important to develop a program plan with positioning goals, a well-defined target audience, topics and messaging, targeted delivery methods, a clear follow-up process, and a coordinated timeline and budget (see Exhibit 7.4). It will be at least 12 months before you can begin measuring a program's results, so we recommend not launching if you are not prepared to sustain the program over time.

EXHIBIT 7.4   Building a thought leadership program: a three-step process

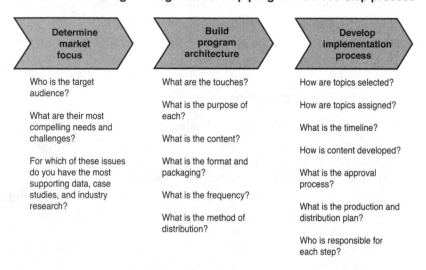

Determine market focus	Build program architecture	Develop implementation process
Who is the target audience?	What are the touches?	How are topics selected?
What are their most compelling needs and challenges?	What is the purpose of each?	How are topics assigned?
	What is the content?	What is the timeline?
For which of these issues do you have the most supporting data, case studies, and industry research?	What is the format and packaging?	How is content developed?
	What is the frequency?	What is the approval process?
	What is the method of distribution?	What is the production and distribution plan?
		Who is responsible for each step?

The firms that are the most skilled at leveraging thought leadership typically incorporate multiple channels of content, each with a different purpose and focus (see Exhibit 7.5). An example would be a short monthly viewpoint series or blog coupled with a less-frequent white-paper series and possibly an annual industry survey and report. The program architecture must be carefully planned with the purpose, content, format packaging, and frequency designed.

For example, under the Korn/Ferry Institute umbrella, the firm generates forward-thinking research and insights that link organizational talent to strategy. This library of intellectual property is the foundation for the firm's informed, consultative conversations with clients. One of the thought leadership initiatives generated from the Korn/Ferry Institute is a quarterly periodical, *Briefings*, delivering

EXHIBIT 7.5   Sample Thought Leadership Program Plan

	Point of view series		Market insights		Industry survey
		+		+	
Purpose	Build awareness Support the sales process		Position firm as industry knowledge leaders Build brand and reputation Support business development		Expand brand Position firm as deep knowledge experts Inform service development Support business development
Content	Topical, practical, "how to"		Insight on topic that addresses industry need Feature interviews with industry leaders		Industry feedback Firm insights
Format	4 pages; 1,200-1,500 words Sidebar case examples 2 charts, introduction, and descriptive headers		8-12 pages; 4,000-5,000 words Quotes from interviewees Sidebar examples; 4-6 charts Introduction and descriptive headers		4 pages; 1,200-1,500 words Sidebar best practice Quotes Introduction and descriptive headers
Packaging	4 color; graphic theme throughout 2-column layout		Ties to point of view 4 color Graphic themes 2 columns		Ties to point of view 4 color Graphic theme 2 columns
Distribution	Every 6 weeks Via e-mail Posted on the Web		Quarterly Via e-mail Posted on the Web		Annually Via e-mail and regular mail Posted on the Web

perspectives on pivotal subjects to more than 35,000 executives globally. Gensler's Web site features an online repository of industry insights—surveys, research, and white papers—that present the firm's thinking on design and its impact on business and society. Booz & Company leverages its intellectual capital through a host of thought leadership programs and channels. Its anchor thought leadership publication, *strategy+business*, a quarterly business magazine launched in 1995, has a circulation of more than 365,000 online and print readers (see "Thought Leadership at Booz & Company").

Thought leadership is an effective tool for both large and small PSFs. Even sole practitioners can create an impressive business and a steady stream of clients by positioning themselves as the industry guru and thought leader in their field.

Thought Leadership at Booz & Company

Tom Stewart, former editor of the *Harvard Business Review*, joined global management consulting firm Booz & Company in 2008 as the Chief Marketing and Knowledge Officer. Stewart's job is to manage the firm's team of marketing and knowledge management professionals and work with partners to build on Booz & Company's foundation of globally recognized thought leadership. Stewart describes his role as overseeing the life cycle of an idea—from ideation through development and publishing, to commercialization and promotion and, finally, to capturing, storage, and reuse.

His team of professionals is divided into four groups:

1. *Intellectual capital directors* who work with partners and practices to identify ideas and then, much like a typical product manager, drive the ideas through development and into the market.

2. *Editorial and publishing professionals* who write, edit, and produce the firm's external publications, including its flagship magazine, *strategy+business*.

3. *Marketing and communications managers* who support regional and local office practitioners.

4. *Knowledge sharing and collaboration managers* who maintain the firm's knowledge management system.

According to Stewart, the intellectual capital at Booz & Company is "prodigious" given its size relative to some of its competitors. Ideas exist at various levels throughout the organization from "little-i" ideas that are focused on solving a specific client problem and delivering good consulting work, to major concepts that try to make sense of the changing world—or even change it themselves. Ideation at the firm is roughly managed in two ways:

1. **Firm-wide**—Booz's "Foresight Agenda" consists of several topics—such as the transition to a low-carbon, sustainable economy—that cross practices in their impact and matter broadly to clients, where it's important for the firm to develop a body of expertise. The marketing and knowledge team puts substantial resources behind developing and marketing Foresight Agenda topics.

2. **Practice priorities**—The firm's industry and functional practices are asked to identify the ideas that they believe are the most

important for their clients. "It's sometimes difficult to get a group of very smart, opinionated professionals to agree on priorities," says Stewart, "but without focus, you will have as many ideas as there are partners." Stewart works with the groups to find convergence and consensus about which ideas can best be leveraged into service offerings, brand building, and sales.

The marketing and knowledge management team harnesses and leverages ideas and concepts through various programs and channels: *strategy+business* magazine; *Viewpoints*, a series of publications that present a point-of-view on a variety of topic areas; practice or industry specific e-newsletters sent regularly to a subscription base; surveys, reports, and white papers; presentations; podcasts and webcasts; events; website content; and press and media placements. The variety of channels utilized depends on the scope of the topic, the audience, and the business development and brand-building potential of the content.

"The bigger, more venerable, and more distinguished your firm gets, the more important it is not to take your brand for granted or to sit on your intellectual laurels," says Stewart. "A strong thought leadership program not only shows you're on the leading edge—it keeps you there."

The Role of the Marketing Professional

"The development of the brand and brand management is a big part of the CMO's job. Business development support is a big part of her job. The strategy comes more from the Office of the Chair. I'm not saying it doesn't come at all from the CMO."

"I don't think marketing has the level of acceptance that it should have, primarily because the keys to professional services are very much focused around delivery and financial operations."

I greatly enjoyed my in-house marketing jobs at the four firms I worked with. I loved that I could wear a multitude of hats, that no day was the same as the day before, and that I was constantly stimulated by very smart and very demanding people. But there is no question that it is a damn hard and often frustrating job, which is why the turnover rate of marketing professionals is extremely high in the industry.

Most of the problem is based on the fact that firm leaders have widely inconsistent expectations as far as what the role is and does. For many firms it's all about tactics: press releases; capability and pitch-book preparation; event organizing; website development; newsletter and publication production; and basically responding to the "squeakiest wheel" on the partnership team. There is typically no rhyme or reason to the instigation or execution of these activities, which is why they so often don't work. Marketing professionals get angry and bored and quit, or the partnership decides that the whole thing is a waste of time and hard-earned money.

To find and keep a good marketing professional, firms must give the top marketing position a seat at the table. This person should report directly to the firm's CEO, participate in annual and long-term strategic business and market planning, and have the ear and support of the leadership team. The responsibilities of the role need to expand beyond the traditional communications function to include a broader brand-management role, client portfolio and key account planning and management, and business development and sales support. This position will attract a very different level of professional who will be engaged, stay longer, and bring more value and tangible results to the organization. A 2007 joint study with Booz Allen Hamilton and the Association of National Advertisers, the leading U.S. trade association for senior marketers, demonstrated that growth in revenues and profitability is strongest among companies that elevate marketing's role to the highest possible level. For all businesses outside of our industry, marketing and sales play an integral and strategic role in the organization. Professional service firms must figure this out.

For firms that have repeatedly tried and failed to hire the right marketing professional and launch a successful program, we suggest that the leadership team first develop or solidify the market strategy and have a fairly clear picture of the plan before the recruitment begins. Knowing where you are going will dictate the skill level and focus of the person to bring on board to manage and drive the execution. Plus, the professional considering the position will know in advance exactly what the job will entail. Too many new hires spend months or years trying to figure out what to do, focusing their time on building an internal team or redesigning the firm's logo and packaging. The key to success is getting the newly hired marketing person externally focused on the clients and the market as soon as possible. The ROI will be much more tangible, and the satisfaction level—both for partners and the marketers—will be significantly higher.

Areas of Focus for the Marketing Department

"A senior partner asked me if any client ever came to the firm because of marketing. If that's the prevailing thought, it's going to take us a long time before we get to the type of role we want to have in the firm."

"We do have corporate marketing resources, but they're support resources for helping prepare collateral material or helping somebody write an article."

There is an enormous amount to do in a typical PSF marketing department. In addition to driving the planned activities and goals in the marketing plan, every day brings a host of unplanned crises of various magnitudes—a major proposal opportunity falls from the sky and must be turned around immediately, a reporter wants to do a story about the firm, a major client threatens to walk, a senior partner needs some tickets to a major sports event for a client. It is difficult to keep the big picture in mind and stay on path.

Over the years, we have managed, observed, and helped construct marketing departments of all shapes and sizes. The number of people and the budgets naturally vary depending on the firm's revenue and complexity, with most firms allocating 2 percent of gross revenue to out-of-pocket costs and the team salary. A sophisticated PSF marketing function should encompass five areas of focus, as shown in Exhibit 7.6:

1. **Market strategy and plan**—The firm's marketing leader should, together with the partners, facilitate and participate in the planning process detailed earlier in the chapter and be responsible for tracking, measuring, and reporting results to the management team.

EXHIBIT 7.6   PSF marketing areas of focus

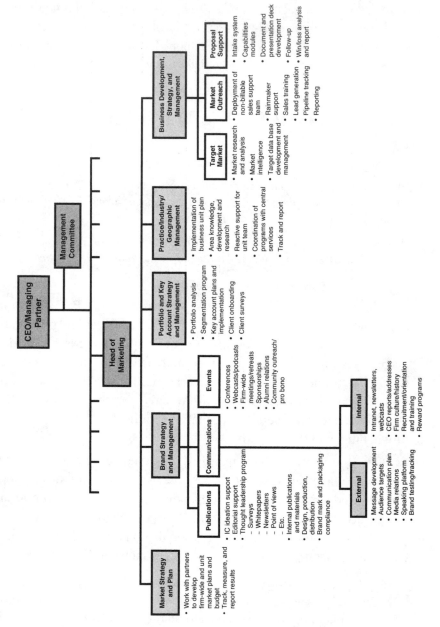

2. **Brand management**—The care and feeding of the brand is an important part of the marketing function. It encompasses a host of responsibilities that begin at a high level with the development of the key positioning and messaging statements that the firm wants to project and continuously reinforce in all of its communications and interactions with the market. How this message is disseminated to all stakeholders—clients and prospects, the firm's professionals and potential recruits, the shareholders and the market at large—requires close monitoring of all internal and external brand touches. The marketing team focuses on several key areas of brand management:

   Publications, which includes ideation support, thought leadership program development and execution, copywriting, editorial, design and production, and distribution of firm materials

   Communications, which encompasses message development for both external and internal audiences, communications planning, media relations and brand testing, and internal communication vehicles and programs—intranet, newsletters, webcasts, and training

   Events coordination of major firm conferences and client activities, firm-wide meetings and retreats, alumni relations, and community outreach

3. **Client portfolio and key account management**—The marketing function should participate in planning and decision making on the firm's client portfolio strategy and management. As discussed in Chapter 4, many of the top firms studied allocate regular time and resources to the analysis of the mix, benefits, and profitability of the client base. The portfolio of clients is segmented by value and potential, and formal investment programs are established for each category. Marketing should support the project management of these programs, working closely with the relationship partners and teams to plan, execute, track, measure, and report the results for individual accounts, each category of investment, and the overall firm-wide client program.

4. **Business development**—Putting the firm's professionals face to face with the highest-opportunity prospective clients and supporting the sales cycle is a high-value activity for the marketing function. Our firm recently conducted a diagnostic of a consulting organization's marketing team, structure, and processes. We launched the assignment with interviews of about 40 of the firm's principals to gather the users' perspectives of the internal market

support efforts. The number one recurring complaint was that marketing did not have a tangible connection to revenue generation. They did understand the importance of brand management, and of course they were delighted when their names hit the trade press. However, at the end of the day, the principals were evaluated and compensated for bringing in and profitably managing client work. They wanted both direction and support from the marketing team.

As discussed, for most PSFs, sales has been the sole purview of the partners and billable professionals. The marketing function, if it is at all involved, is relegated to proposal support—assembling the bios, capabilities overviews, client lists, and so on for the final document. Many years ago at both Price Waterhouse and Brobeck, I ran a bustling proposal support team that sometimes turned around several proposals a day. We often traveled from office to office strategizing the pitch, writing the document and presentation deck, and rehearsing the team. Sometimes we even accompanied the pitch team to the meetings and stood outside the door in case something went wrong with the slide show. We celebrated wins with firm-wide communications and office parties and followed up when the firm wasn't selected to find out why. The firm's partners highly valued these services, which produced tangible results that could be tied to revenue generation.

To effectively support the firm's business development activities, the marketing team must have a clear picture of the target market and the messages and vehicles to approach them appropriately. The business development activities should focus on three primary areas:

Target market tracking. Research and analysis to spot trends and opportunities, market intelligence to monitor competitors, and target database development and management.

Market outreach. Specific activities incorporated into the plan to generate opportunities to meet prospects—from conferences and events, client roundtables and speakers, to formal lead-generation programs and deployment of nonbillable teams. The process includes opportunity tracking and pipeline management.

Proposal support. Development of an efficient proposal intake and production system to process requests and produce the document and/or presentation deck. The process includes win/loss analysis, reporting, and tracking.

5. **Practice/industry/geographic support**—Completely centralized marketing departments do not work well for mid-sized to large PSFs, particularly those with multiple practices and locations. Entrepreneurial and independent professionals won't work with the marketing team if they are too remote or too bureaucratic; they will simply go elsewhere or do it themselves. We often find rogue marketers buried within the business units who have been independently hired by partners to work on their projects. The best scenario is a combination of centralized support services that are leveraged and deployed by a decentralized team of professionals who work close to the practice, industry, or geographic unit leaders they serve. The local professionals often have a dual reporting relationship to both the head of the unit and the head of marketing. These professionals operate in both a proactive and reactive mode. They proactively execute on the marketing plan for their unit while managing the day-to-day needs of their local teams. They tap into centralized services for activities such as public relations, events, proposals, publications, and database management.

CHAPTER SUMMARY

Positioning

- PSFs recognize the importance of branding, marketing, and sales, yet ratings on performance are decidedly mixed.
- A successful market strategy has five elements. The most savvy firms do the following:
    1. Know who they are and what they do
    2. Mobilize their people as brand managers
    3. Plan
    4. Talk to the market
    5. Hold people accountable
- To succeed, a PSF must identify a credible position to occupy in the market. Determining positioning involves several key decisions:
    1. Where should we play on the Spectrum of Practice?
    2. What services should we sell?
    3. Which markets and geographies should we sell to?
    4. How will we define our service delivery and buyer experience?
- Thought leadership is the single most powerful way to grow the business.
- A sophisticated marketing department should have five areas of focus:
    1. Marketing strategy and planning
    2. Brand strategy and management
    3. Portfolio and key account strategy and management
    4. Business development strategy and management
    5. Practice/industry/geographic support

8

Partnership

Equity, selection, and compensation

"There has to be a lot more than money to hold a group of very smart, type-A partners together."

—Evan Chesler, Presiding Partner, Cravath, Swaine & Moore

"The real challenge is how do you create that collegial, collaborative partnership culture within the context of being a performance-based, performance-driven organization?"

—Paul Laudicina, Chairman, Managing Officer, A.T. Kearney

"I think the key to success is to keep the partners excited about their practice and excited about the firm."

—Eric Friedman, Executive Partner, Skadden, Arps

The term partnership has a very special meaning in professional services. Much more than a type of ownership structure, the concept of partnership is both an industry mind-set—a core belief that everyone is in it together, united by a common vision and cause—and a distinctive set of governance characteristics. A partnership-driven governance model is based on many of the professional service firm characteristics already discussed—shared values, collaboration and teamwork, peer relationships, highly participatory decision making, and equity sharing with partner/owners.

A partnership has been the traditional legal form of organization for PSFs since the 1800s and is still the chosen organizational structure for most law and accounting firms. Only in the past several decades have some firms moved from legal partnerships to some form of incorporation. But regardless of the choice of structure, most firms strive to maintain the spirit of partnership. As Steven Tallman, Vice President, Global Operations of Bain, told us, "Legally we are a corporation, but we behave like a partnership." The best-of-breed firms that we studied have managed to retain this partnership spirit even though some are multibillion-dollar publicly traded organizations with thousands of employees.

It is not difficult to see how rapid growth and expansion—particularly global—can negatively impact the partnership governance model. How do you maintain a collegial, peer-based, participatory process when you have 500 partners spread throughout the world as opposed to 50 in a few locations? The firm leaders we spoke with told us that finding the appropriate balance between too corporate versus too consensus-driven is something they work hard to get right.

Creating that special partnership spirit can be just as daunting for small PSFs. In the course of our consulting work, we have encountered many small firms whose partners are quite the opposite of collegial and united. Getting ten independent partners to agree on new carpeting— let alone a vision and strategy—is often impossible.

Six Characteristics of Enduring Partnerships

"That's one of the things that's amazing about this place—we inherit a wonderful firm, and we pass it on to our younger partners over time."

So how do the best-run firms create that partnership ethos? In the course of our research, we identified six common characteristics that are fundamental to building and maintaining an enduring partnership:

1. *Align around shared vision and values.* As discussed in Chapter 2, "Shared Vision, Values, and Culture," 99 percent of the leaders we interviewed rated vision, values, and culture as the most important area of focus for firm management. As our PSF Leadership Model indicates, this area is the anchor and core of a successful professional service firm, and the partnership must be deeply committed to these goals and values. The individual behaviors of the partners—with both clients and other professionals—ultimately define the firm. If the partners have personal priorities and objectives that are not aligned with organizational goals, potential for discord exists. As long as the firm is making money, a divergent partnership

can work. But when times get tough, partners who are not completely onboard with the firm's agenda often won't hesitate to abandon ship for another place to practice.

2. *Foster an environment of integration, teamwork, and collaboration.* Partners must be willing to come together across the boundaries of practices and geographies to serve clients, share work, and collectively manage the organization. The firms that we studied invest heavily to build a culture of teamwork within their partnership—through training, mentoring, performance evaluations, and compensation programs. Particularly for large global firms serving multinational clients, the integration of teams, services, processes, and common standards is a critical success factor.

3. *Treat the senior team as owners.* It is a phenomenon in professional services that regardless of the actual ownership structure, the senior team is regarded as the partners and owners of the business. Becoming a partner—or principal, managing director, or vice president, depending on the designated title—is considered an important honor, awarded after years of challenging work, long hours, and intense training. Partners participate in decision making either actively in small firms or indirectly through a delegated management team in large firms, contribute both sweat equity and capital to maintain and grow the firm, and ultimately share in the business's profits.

   It is a tough job to be a partner. As owners of the business, partners are expected to find work, do the work, manage and grow their practice and teams, constantly update and expand their skills, contribute intellectual capital, and participate in firm management and special initiatives. It is a serious commitment both financially and emotionally.

4. *Create an atmosphere of collegiality and "clubbiness."* A common bond exists in a professional service firm partnership that can be extremely powerful and enduring for organizations that do it right. Becoming a partner should be analogous to being accepted into an exclusive club or organization. A natural collegiality and affinity exists for a fellow partner with whom you share a common cause, skills, and interest. If properly nurtured and harnessed, it creates a strong foundation on which to build the business. McKinsey is a good example of a PSF that has created a loyal team of professionals and devoted alumni who are passionate about and proud of their association with the firm. In small, geographically focused firms, this bond is easier to build and maintain. As firms grow in size and location, the task is more difficult and needs to be actively managed.

5. *Reward contributions appropriately*. Professionals—from junior associates to senior partners—need and value recognition from teammates, clients, and the profession they serve. The best firms understand this and carefully build equity and compensation structures, evaluation and feedback systems, and award programs to acknowledge and appropriately incent their partner team.

6. *Cultivate stewardship*. Partners in the successful long-lived firms we studied are not in it for the short term. They view themselves as stewards and custodians of their organizations, responsible for keeping the firm's vision on track and preserving the values and culture of their organizations. Equity structures and ownership rights are established to effect a fair and orderly transfer of the business from one generation to the next.

Selecting an Ownership Structure

One of the many critical decisions for professional service firms is how to legally structure the organization. The choice of structure has many strategic implications for the firm and should be carefully determined. Structure decisions impact ownership rights and succession; profit distribution and retained earnings; expansion; recruitment and retention; access to capital; and taxation and liability.

There are a wide variety of ways to structure professional service firms, ranging from sole proprietorships to partnerships and corporations—both private and public. The vast majority of professional service firms around the world are privately held organizations. Many start out and remain sole proprietorships or simple partnerships of a few professionals who choose to stay small and locally focused. Growth, if desired, is mostly organic and measured. But, as illustrated in our study, many best-of-breed firms have chosen to pursue aggressive growth paths, expanding their practices nationally and internationally. This growth has been driven by a combination of mergers and acquisitions and rapid internal expansion through intense recruitment and hiring efforts.

Many professional service firms that can do so legally[1] have been making significant changes to their ownership structures. Some have chosen to go public or have merged or been acquired—either completely or

---

[1] Some industry-specific restrictions prohibit public ownership or ownership by anyone outside the firm's discipline. Accounting and law firms in the United States, for example, cannot be publicly held.

partially—by organizations both within and outside of the industry. Many of the firms we studied have changed legal structures over time to reflect stages of growth, the transition from founders, or a reassessment of their ownership philosophy.

Advantages and Disadvantages of Ownership Structures

The majority of the firms we spoke with coalesced around two predominant structure choices, as shown in Exhibits 8.1 and 8.2. More than half (59 percent) are C corporations—both public and private—and 23 percent are limited liability partnerships (LLPs). The remainder are a mix of limited liability corporations (LLCs) (7 percent) and a small number of Swiss vereins, employee stock ownership plans (ESOPs), and subchapter S corporations (S corps).

EXHIBIT 8.1 Breakdown of ownership structures for the firms studied

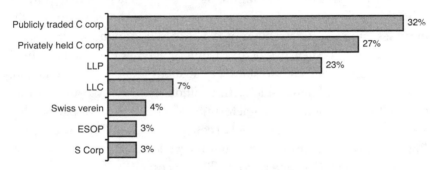

EXHIBIT 8.2 Types of Ownership by Segment for the Firms Studied

Segment	Public C Corporation	Private C Corporation	LLP	LLC	Other
Accounting (U.S. firms)			100%		
Advertising / PR	71%	24%		6%	
Architecture / engineering	15%	62%	8%		15%
Consulting	42%	31%	4%	15%	8%
Executive search	25%			75%	
Finance	67%	17%		17%	
Law			89%		11%

Advantages and disadvantages are inherent in each choice of structure, as shown in Exhibit 8.3. All the U.S. accounting firms and the majority of law firms that participated in the research are LLPs. For many years, U.S. law prohibited professionals such as accountants and lawyers from operating as corporations. As a result, virtually all the largest and oldest accounting and law firms were formed and operated as general partnerships, which dictated that the partners had unlimited personal liability for all the business debts. When the law was finally changed to allow professionals to incorporate, many firms were reluctant to make the change. Converting from a partnership to a corporation was a complex and expensive process that involved retitling all the firm's assets and exposing the organization to potentially significant tax events.

Through a lobbying effort by accounting, law, and other professional service firms, an LLP structure was formed in the early 1990s. It requires a minimum conversion process and grants a form of limited liability similar to that of a corporation. As in the original partnership structure, the profits of an LLP are allocated among the partners for tax purposes, avoiding the problem of double taxation found in the corporate structure. The negative of an LLP in the U.S. is that the liability of partners varies from state to state. Some states grant broad protection, and others only a limited shield. In addition, country-by-country variations in the definition and characteristics of an LLP type of partnership add to the complexity for large global confederations of PSFs, such as the Big Four accounting firms. Often they must adopt a variety of ownership structures to accommodate regional differences.

LLCs and S corps are both good forms of ownership for small to mid-size PSFs. Of the two structures, LLCs offer greater flexibility in ownership and ease of operation. There are no restrictions on the ownership of an LLC, and it is simpler to operate, because it is not subject to the legal formalities of an S corp. An LLC can be member-managed, meaning that the owners run the company, or it can be manager-managed, with responsibility delegated to managers who may or may not be owners in the LLC. The owners of an LLC can distribute profits in the manner they see fit. On the negative side, there is no stock to use for options, so it is not an attractive structure for outside investors. Plus, the income may be subject to a self-employment tax.

The S corp has been in existence for many years and has well-tested case law that supports the rights of officers, directors, and shareholders. It allows income and losses to pass through to the individual shareholders, which, as with LLPs and LLCs, avoids a double taxation event. An S corp has drawbacks, however. It can have no more than 75 shareholders, none of the shareholders can be nonresident aliens or other corporations or LLCs, and it must follow the same formalities and record-keeping procedures as C corps. The directors or officers of an S corp must manage the company, and there is no flexibility in how profits are split up among its owners. Profits must be distributed according to the ration of stock ownership, even if the owners feel it is more equitable to distribute the profits differently.

The C corporation (C corp) is the organizational structure most suitable for firms looking to grow, attract investors, and possibly go public. C corps provide limited liability protection to owners, have no restrictions on the number of shareholders or subsidiaries, and allow for an easy transfer of ownership through the sale of stock. C corps are considered by some to be a more professional and legitimate entity than a sole proprietorship or general partnership. The negative, as already mentioned, is that unlike other forms of organizational structure, the C corp is a taxable entity, which means owners pay taxes at both the corporate and personal level. The corporation's income is taxed, and when earnings are distributed to shareholders via dividends, they are added to personal taxable income and taxed again. Plus, C corps require more administrative complexity—shareholder meetings, records, maintenance of corporate minutes, and so on.

EXHIBIT 8.3   Advantages and Disadvantages of Various Ownership Structures

Entity	Advantages	Disadvantages
Sole Proprietor	No formation formalities Partnership-type tax treatment	Unlimited liability No structure for investors Not suitable if business has other employees All income subject to self-employment tax
General Partnership	Flexible management structure Recognized legal entity with right to contract Partnership tax treatment	Unlimited liability Difficult to add new partners Difficult to raise capital without bringing in new partners Requires two or more partners Any partner can commit the others Death of partner dissolves partnership
Limited Liability Partnership (LLP)	Limits liability of partners Profits not double taxed Each partner can own and/or manage a portion of the partnership	Some personal liability, depending on state in U.S. Some restrictions in some U.S. states on what professionals may choose this form of ownership There are country-by-country variations and restrictions Still liable for partners' actions in furtherance of partnership
Limited Liability Company (LLC)	Flexible structure Can have different classes of stock, different rights and allocations Owners can be persons, corporations, or other LLCs Familiar structure for foreign investors Partnership tax treatment Can convert to C corporation without adverse tax affects	No stock to use for options Not attractive structure for institutional investors Many states require two members Death of member may affect continuity All income may be subject to self-employment tax

EXHIBIT 8.3 Advantages and Disadvantages of Various Ownership Structures (continued)

Entity	Advantages	Disadvantages
S Corporation	Security of corporate structure	Can have only 75 shareholders
	Well-defined law on corporations	Can have only one class of stock
	Death of shareholder does not affect company's continuity	No foreign investors
		Not suitable for institutional investors
	Qualified tax-exempt entities can be shareholders	Limited employee benefits to large shareholders
	Can have corporations and LLCs as subsidiaries	Conversion to LLC requires liquidation and creates adverse tax effects
	Partnership tax treatment	Issues on conversion to C corporation
	Only salary (not profits) subject to self-employment tax	Limited flexibility on allocations of income, leases, credits, and deductions
C Corporation	Limited liability for shareholders	More formalities—board meetings, shareholder meetings, voting issues
	Maximum flexibility on classes of shares, liquidation preferences, voting rights	Double taxation on dividends
	Preferred investment choice for institutional investors	Limits on how much of earnings can be retained in closely held companies
	Suitable for initial public offering	Limits on level of salary to avoid dividends of closely held companies
	Stock options available	No pass-through of net operating losses to personal return
	No limit on the number or type of shareholders	
	Well-defined law on corporations	
	Most favorable structure for employee benefit plans	

Source: Adapted from *The Professional Service Firm Bible*, John Baschab and Jon Piot. Copyright © 2005. Reproduced with permission of John Wiley & Sons, Inc.

Public Versus Private

"We are a public company, but we call equity owners partners, and we have a partnership attitude."

"Just because you're a stock exchange company doesn't mean you have to feel like one. Just because you are a partnership doesn't mean you have to be managed like one."

One of the decisions facing PSFs that have designs on rapid expansion is whether to go public. The financial pressures and complexities of growth—opening new offices, upgrading systems and processes to support the infrastructure, and increasing both professional and administrative headcount—can be overwhelming. Particularly in partnership governance models where most of the annual earnings are distributed to the owners, raising the money to fund a significant build-out is often untenable.

The idea of floating an initial public offering (IPO) to raise capital is seductive to some firm leaders. However, the number of PSFs that choose to go public on their own is, to date, still relatively small. Of the 30 publicly traded firms in our study, 12 chose to launch their own IPO. The remainder were acquired by publicly traded companies and now operate as divisions under their umbrellas. The pluses of a public offering are apparent: increasing capital to expand offices, talent, and services; acquiring new and related businesses; enhancing marketing and branding; buying out retiring founders; and providing a hedge against a future recession. As one managing partner told us, "I can only dream about the top talent we could attract with fifty million or so."

The negatives, however, can be significant. Public investment brings public oversight from shareholders, investors, and analysts who are watching the quarterly earnings clock. There is concern that the firm might be forced to place short-term financial gain over longer-term business decisions or, even more daunting, the best interests of clients. Some fear that the lack of a partnership/ownership opportunity would make it more difficult to attract and retain top professionals. Finally, the potential increased bureaucracy, transparency, and the rigor of financial management and reporting are unsettling to PSFs that are not used to operating in the public spotlight (see "Slater & Gordon Becomes the First Law Firm to Go Public").

Slater & Gordon Becomes the First Law Firm to Go Public

In 2007, Slater & Gordon, a 72-year-old, 650-person Australian law firm with 30 offices throughout the country, became the first law firm in the world to list its practice on a stock exchange. According to Andrew Grech, Managing Director, a number of reasons drove the firm's decision to become a public corporation. Starting in 2000, a series of legislative changes introduced by the government were making it increasingly difficult for the firm to operate at its current scale. To compete effectively, management determined they needed to expand operations from a small ownership structure to a national practice. To do so, the firm needed to increase its capital base.

The firm mapped out a growth strategy that combined an acquisition plan with an organic growth program accelerated by increased marketing and practice development activity. Simultaneously the firm evaluated a variety of financing options to fund the strategy. Slater & Gordon concluded that only an IPO would provide sufficient capital to support the firm's aggressive growth plan. According to Grech, management determined that going public offered many potential advantages. Valuations were likely to be higher. An IPO would provide a stronger basis for succession planning and a mechanism for an orderly shift in ownership from longstanding shareholders. Access to debt and equity post-listing would be easier. Finally, in future mergers, an IPO offered the opportunity to utilize shares as a viable alternative exit mechanism for principals of the merged firms. Plus, the firm would be able to launch an employee ownership plan to support the firm's historically high retention rates and address career advancement aspirations.

In May 2007, Slater & Gordon Ltd. offered an IPO of 35 million shares. They quickly became fully subscribed, attracting strong interest from both institutional and retail investors. As of August 2009, approximately 36 percent of the company was owned by external shareholders, including some of Australia's most respected fund managers. The remaining 64 percent was held by company employees.

"The main disadvantage of incorporating and listing is the increased burden of regulatory compliance," says Grech. The potential for conflicts of interest between duties to shareholders and legal obligations to courts and clients featured prominently in the firm's thinking and planning. To address these challenges, the firm took a number of steps. It engaged regulators of the legal profession early on to work through challenges of potential conflicts. Members of the firm worked closely with members of the stock exchange and shareholders to educate them on the primacy of duties and obligations that attorneys employed by the company have to courts and clients. The firm adopted corporate governance policies to reinforce these primary obligations and has put in place a strong governance framework with the appointment of independent nonexecutive directors to the board.

"In general, the rigor of the due diligence process prior to the float and the increased transparency of being listed have positively impacted the company's approach to compliance," says Grech. "The IPO has improved the level of external accountability, and our internal focus on policies and procedures has moved beyond compliance to best practice."

The capital accessed through the IPO has allowed the company to support its growth strategy. Since May 2007, Slater & Gordon has acquired 20 law firms and has increased spending on marketing and advertising to support strong organic growth. Approximately 80 staff members participate in the employee ownership plan, which has proven to be an effective tool to recruit, retain, and reward talented staff. "By and large, we think it has been a very successful exercise for us and has certainly exceeded our expectations," says Grech. "While most firms have been contracting, we've been growing by about 30 percent year-on-year."

To Sell or Not to Sell

Of the 92 PSFs participating in our study, 16 percent sold their entire business to another entity (see Exhibit 8.4)—typically to other firms in their field or to organizations in related businesses. For example, Thomson Reuters, a publicly traded multimedia news and information company, acquired consulting firms Baker Robbins and Hildebrandt to expand its bundle of products and service offerings to the legal industry (see "The Acquisition Process at Baker Robbins & Company"). Ten percent sold portions of their firms to outside companies, predominantly investment firms. Selling all or a portion of the firm gives the founders and equity owners an opportunity to realize a return on their years of time and financial investment in the business. Like the IPO option, a sale can offer a more stable financial environment and an infusion of capital to jump-start growth. Buying all or a portion of a knowledge-based business, where the product can walk out the door, is somewhat tricky. Most acquiring firms and investors structure the transition to incent the senior team to remain onboard for a minimum time period, typically 3 to 5 years.

EXHIBIT 8.4   PSFs sold fully or partially

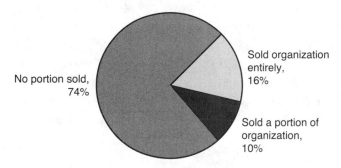

No portion sold, 74%

Sold organization entirely, 16%

Sold a portion of organization, 10%

Life after acquisition or a partial sale depends on the management philosophy of the acquiring firm or investment partner. Some leaders say that their businesses changed drastically and that the imposition of different systems, processes, and culture has been onerous and challenging. For others, the hands-off management style of the acquiring firm or partner has had little impact on their firms. As one CEO told us, "As long as we make our numbers, they leave us alone."

The Acquisition Process at Baker Robbins & Company

Cofounders David Baker and Brad Robbins spent 25 years growing their technology consulting firm, Baker Robbins, into a successful and respected niche provider to the legal industry.

In 2006, the firm was approached by the Canadian-based public company Thomson (now Thomson Reuters), which was interested in acquiring the business. The cofounders decided that the timing was right. Both men were interested in continuing the firm's fast-paced growth and wanted to be able to make bigger investments and provide satisfying career options for employees.

Thomson seemed like a good match. It had already invested in a reputable law firm consulting business and was active in the legal industry. With strong indicators that the move was a win-win situation, both players did their due diligence, and Baker Robbins officially became an independent business unit within Thomson Reuters in January 2007.

As CEO of Baker Robbins, Brad Robbins continued to run the firm until 2010, when Baker Robbins merged with another Thomson Reuters firm, Hildebrandt. He now comanages Hildebrandt Baker Robbins. From a growth perspective, being acquired by a large public company has resulted in powerful benefits. Thomson Reuters gives Robbins wide latitude in overseeing the firm's finances and strategic direction and has provided stability, investment resources, and growing access to its vast client base. Culturally, the smaller firm's collaborative environment remains unchanged, and its reputation as an independent, objective consulting firm has remained strong.

In reflecting on Baker Robbins' evolution from a privately held firm to a division of a large publicly owned company, Robbins offers the following advice for those considering a similar move:

- *Do your due diligence.* Make sure that you understand exactly why a potential buyer wants to acquire you, and reach a thorough mutual understanding of the benefits you each stand to gain. A publicly held firm has responsibilities way beyond those of a small private firm, and it also faces different market pressures. Look very carefully at the company acquiring your business. Does it think the same way you do about key issues? Is it willing to take the same level of risk? Are you willing to change your risk position?

- *Money matters.* Make sure that the acquisition price you negotiate is satisfactory. You never know what the future holds, so it's important that the upfront money is adequate because you may not achieve the negotiated earn-out.

- *Culture is critical.* Can your firm retain its cultural distinctiveness while operating within a larger framework? Thomson Reuters appreciated the firm's culture, Robbins notes, and this has made it easy for the two companies to work together.

Along with benefits such as increased stability and capitalization, Robbins notes that selling a business offers a prime opportunity to rethink how it will operate going forward. "When you have 25 years of history, you can't restructure very easily. But when you sell, it's a good time to restructure for future growth." As Baker Robbins evolves, Robbins believes that its acquisition will continue to have a positive impact in a critical area: recruiting new talent. As he puts it, "I believe people will look at us and say, 'Hey, there's a lot of stability there, but I can still be part of a unique culture.'"

Equity Programs to Attract and Retain the Best

"Our stock has a fixed value. It doesn't pay dividends because we want to distribute the profits based on contribution, not on stock ownership."

"There are some firms that don't exist now because the employees were left with such a burden of debt that they never had a chance, quite frankly."

"When somebody puts their money into the firm, it's completely different than not putting any cash in. They feel much more like partners and owners if they have their money on the line than if they don't."

The opportunity to own a piece of the business is a powerful tool to attract and retain the best and the brightest talent. Many people join a professional service firm with the expectation that they will move through the ranks and someday become a partner entitled to a voice and a vote on firm direction and governance and a share in the organization's equity and earnings.

Deciding on the best equity structure has considerable implications for recruitment and retention, governance, compensation, and ultimately the firm's profitability. Most firm leaders agreed that equity and compensation decisions are an important component of firm management, with 74 percent of respondents giving this category a high ranking on the leadership agenda (see Exhibit 8.5). The majority of our interviewees believed they are doing well in this area, with 92 percent rating themselves toward the top of the chart on performance, as shown in Exhibit 8.6.

EXHIBIT 8.5   Close to three-quarters of respondents place equity and compensation at the top of their agendas

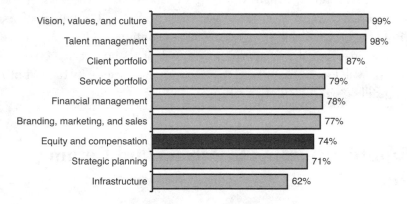

EXHIBIT 8.6   Almost all respondents believe they do a good job of managing equity and compensation

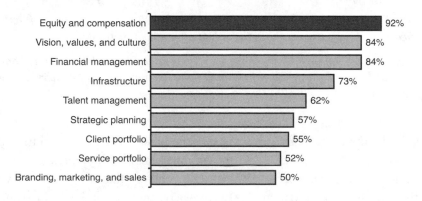

Over 90 percent of the firms studied have some form of equity-sharing program, as shown in Exhibit 8.7. These can include formal structural processes in which equity participation progresses in prescribed increments determined by well-articulated performance criteria. Or they can be more informal decisions by the partnership group to offer a piece of the ownership pie to a top performer or a new high-profile recruit.

EXHIBIT 8.7 The majority of PSFs have some form of equity sharing

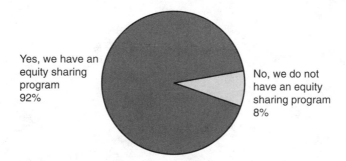

Yes, we have an equity sharing program 92%

No, we do not have an equity sharing program 8%

The firms we studied have an amazing variety of equity programs. Even firms in the same segment with identical ownership structures all have unique nuances to their programs. Although no two programs are exactly the same, some common characteristics emerged from our research that are fundamental to the best-run programs, as shown in Exhibit 8.8.

- *Equity participation requires a capital outlay.* The majority of firms studied (79 percent) require an initial investment into the equity-sharing program and periodic investments to increase the level of participation as professionals progress through the firm (see Exhibit 8.9). Leaders say that anteing up your own money creates a sense of ownership and management responsibility in the firm. As one CEO told us, "We used to give away ownership shares, but people didn't value it and didn't act like owners. Once we made them buy it, behavior changed, and they suddenly were very interested in making the firm profitable and successful." For many privately held firms, both small and large, partner investments are a major source of capital to fund operations and fuel growth.

EXHIBIT 8.8 Common Characteristics of Equity Programs by Ownership Type

	LLP	C Corporation Private	C Corporation Public
Promotion to Partner/ Principal	Buy-in is required for new partners. Most firms are on either a unit or point-based system valued at the firm's current book value at the time of purchase. Many firms arrange financing with a lender at a favorable rate and payback plan.	Varies. Sometimes a buy-in is required, financed by a loan from the firm or a pre-arranged lender. Sometimes shares are either awarded outright or given as stock options upon promotion to principal.	Typically, no buy-in requirement. Stock options or restricted shares are sometimes awarded.
Progression Through Firm	New partners start out with a preordained number of units or points and progress through a well-defined escalation process to move up the partnership seniority ladder. Each rung on the ladder represents a level or tier of partner (numbers vary from 5 to 15 levels) that meet specific performance requirements—usually a combination of quantitative and qualitative contributions. At each stage, partners may be asked to make a capital contribution to the firm to purchase additional units. This entitles them to a larger percentage share of the annual firm profits. Progression through the stages typically takes 12 to 15 years in most firms, and there is a cap on the total number of units/points you can own.	Stock and/or opportunities to buy stock are earned in a variety of ways as one progresses through the firm. Sometimes shares are given at recruitment, during promotions, or periodically for unusually large contributions to the firm. Some firms have mechanisms in place for employees to buy or sell shares internally at a certain time each year.	Restricted stock and/or stock options are usually reserved for the top ranks of the leadership team. Some public PSFs offer employee stock option plans to a larger percentage of the employee base.
Impact on Compensation	Annual partnership compensation is based on a percentage share of distributable income (net firm income after fixed compensation and expenses before taxes) determined by the number of units/points owned. For some firms this represents 100% of partner compensation. Others use a bonus component—typically 10 to 15%—determined by individual performance for that 12-month period. As partners move up the ranks, their level of risk and reward increases. For many firms, 90 to 100% of senior partner compensation is tied to firm performance and individual contribution.	Varies. In some firms stock is not tied directly to compensation. In other firms a portion of annual compensation—salary plus bonus—is paid in shares or options. The higher the bonus, the higher the percentage of equity.	Compensation includes a base salary; benefits package, and bonus plan. Bonus is a percentage of salary with a mix of ties to either financial or operational metrics. As in privately held C corporations, annual compensation may be a combination of base, bonus, and stock for the top management team.
Retire or Leave Firm	When partners leave the firm or retire, the capital investments that they have contributed to the firm over time are returned to them, and the firm reabsorbs their points or units. Sometimes capital is returned immediately, but often it is paid back over several years. Many firms also have retirement benefit plans that partners contribute to. This entitles them to a stream of income over a designated time period.	Most require that employees sell back their shares. When principals leave or retire, they are paid the cash value of their stock. This value is determined by a variety of formulas typically based on some combination of market and book value. Payout periods vary from 1 to 5 years.	There is no requirement to sell. Professionals typically have 90 days to exercise their vested stock options. Shares can be sold on the open market.

EXHIBIT 8.9   Most firms require a buy-in to equity sharing

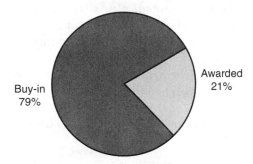

Buy-in
79%

Awarded
21%

- *Ownership progression is well defined.* The best equity programs have a well-defined escalation process through the stages of ownership, from beginning partners to the senior team. This is particularly true of LLPs adopted by most accounting and law firms, but many LLCs and privately held C corporations are strong advocates of a defined process as well. New partners start with a preordained number of units or points in LLPs and shares in C corps and progress through predetermined stages to move up the partnership seniority ladder. Each rung on the ladder represents a level or tier of partner (numbers vary from 5 to 15 levels) that meets specific performance requirements—usually a combination of quantitative and qualitative contributions. At each new level, partners may be asked to make a capital contribution to the firm to purchase additional units, points, or shares. Progression through the stages typically takes between 12 and 15 years in most firms, and there is a cap on the total number of units/points/shares one can own.

- *Risk and reward escalate with degree of ownership.* In some firms, the degree of risk and reward may steadily increase as partners move up the seniority ranks. Some report that 90 to 100 percent of senior partner compensation is tied to a combination of firm performance and individual contributions. These firms' leaders say that having some serious skin in the game drives both group and personal performance to make the business successful.

- *The business remains strong and viable when senior partners leave.* The majority of the firms in our study (83 percent) require that partners give back or sell their ownership rights to the firm when they retire or leave, as shown in Exhibit 8.10. Intuitively this seems like a good idea for continuity and growth. However, we heard several horror stories of equity programs that essentially brought down the firm when founders or high-equity-stake partners exited or retired. In LLCs and privately held C corporations, share price is determined annually—or whenever a buy/sell opportunity exists—through a predetermined valuation formula that typically is based on a mix of market and book value considerations. The danger is that sometimes the formula can overinflate the value of the business. In turn, this can increase the share price to the point where the firm can become overburdened by debt to pay off shareholders when they depart.

EXHIBIT 8.10   Most firms require that partners sell back shares when they leave or retire

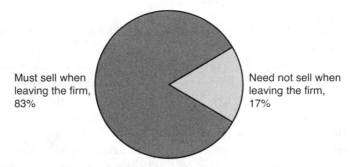

Must sell when leaving the firm, 83%

Need not sell when leaving the firm, 17%

Several leaders of the professional service corporations we studied complained that it was difficult to monetize the value of shares except when professionals leave or the firm is sold. As one CEO told us, "The way we do it actually incents high rollers to leave the firm—it's the only way they get their money." A few firms provide internal markets where once or twice a year employees can buy or sell shares to generate cash or increase investment in the firm. Dividends are another way to periodically provide a return on share value, but firms are reticent to offer them. They prefer a bonus system that rewards performance rather than pure ownership status and that can be taken out of pretax income to reduce the tax exposure.

We endorse the formula for distributing ownership and rewarding equity holders where new partners buy in to the firm at the current book value. They are required to buy additional units or points as they advance to each new level of seniority—also at book value, which entitles them to an increasingly larger percentage share in annual firm profits. When partners leave or retire, their capital investment is simply returned to them over a predetermined time period, and the firm reabsorbs their points or units. This model fosters a true ownership commitment and mentality, provides a tangible annual return on equity ownership, and does not break the bank when partners depart.

Rewarding the Partners: Dividing the Pie

This book states several times that professionals are motivated by much more than financial gain. However, the long, hard march up to seniority status in a PSF must offer both psychological and economic rewards. Firm leaders that we spoke with agreed that compensation is one of the most important ingredients to get right for the leadership team. Rick Dreher, Managing Partner at accounting firm Wipfli, described the impact of compensation, "If you start with the premise that you get what you reward, partner compensation is probably the single biggest item that you need to align with the vision and the culture." Compensation is an important tool to define and drive performance, reinforce values, and reward high-value professionals.

The size of the pie and how it is divided vary by firm and are dictated by the type of ownership structure, the size of the business, and the firm's values and culture. LLPs typically distribute 90 to 100 percent of the firm's net profits before taxes to the partnership. C corps vary in the amount of retained earnings, with some firms reporting an average of 15 to 20 percent annual reinvestment into the firm.

For most firms, partners' compensation is a combination of base, bonus, and some form of equity ownership—shares in C corporations and units or points in LLPs. As discussed, some firms ratchet up the risk/reward ratio as partners progress, reducing the base for senior partners—sometimes to zero—and increasing the percentage share in profits. In both private and public C corps, the compensation of the senior leaders is much more aligned to firm success. Up to one-third of the yearly base and bonus can be in the form of stock.

Distribution Models

The annual distribution of the spoils is a major event in most PSFs. The philosophies regarding how it should be done fall into three basic camps: the lockstep, reward-seniority system; the performance-based, reap-what-you-sow model; and a hybrid of the two, the modified lockstep compensation program. Leaders agree that whatever the reward structure and distribution philosophy, the process must be well understood by the partners, transparent, and perceived to be fair.

Our interviews revealed an enormous amount of passion around the pros and cons of the lockstep system. In this model, partners are rewarded equally based on the firm's performance and their level of seniority in the partnership. For example, all fifth-year, tier-two partners in the firm would receive the same percentage share of the bonus pool, regardless of their individual performance. Performance is baked into the system, because partners must meet specific performance criteria to move up to another level to increase their compensation. Proponents say that the lockstep reward system creates an extremely collaborative culture where the good of the firm outweighs personal gain. Partners are motivated to share clients and client work, business development, knowledge, and expertise. Getting the right people onboard who will support the system, together with a good performance evaluation and feedback program and a strong up-or-out philosophy to weed out weak contributors, are key to the success of this model. As Evan Chesler, Presiding Partner of Cravath, summed up, "If you don't have a consistency of quality and a consistency of commitment, the lockstep system becomes undermined over time. You need a very rigorous training and evaluation process."

Opponents to lockstep say that it tolerates mediocre performance and makes it difficult to attract top performers and get rid of noncontributors. The argument is that if you have a big franchise and brand name, you don't need as many stars, because the business comes to you. But at smaller firms you have to attract superior talent, and many believe that you can't do that with the lockstep model.

In performance-based systems, partners' percentage of the bonus pool is determined by their individual contributions and performance in relation to established criteria. In most firms compensation is based on a set of quantitative and qualitative metrics. Some have formulaic weighted-point systems to grade performance, but most rely on less-formal processes that combine formal measurements with subjective judgment.

Many firms utilize a combination of seniority and performance to compensate the partnership. At Latham & Watkins, 85 percent of compensation is distributed based on the unit level of partners, and 15 percent is based on annual performance. According to Bob Dell, the firm's Chairman and Managing Partner, the modified lockstep plan provides the best combination of incentives to "motivate performance without the trauma of eat what you kill." Dell says the biggest problem in performance-based systems is preventing hoarding of clients and leads. To counteract this tendency, firms must have a very objective merit-based credit system. At Latham, partners get credit for both originating the work as well as for generating new work for an existing client by referring business to other partners across the firm's global offices. Latham's compensation system places equal value on winning a new client as it does on building a client relationship, ultimately strengthening client service at the heart of the firm's practice. The system encourages collaboration and teamwork but requires a very tight reporting and monitoring system to manage effectively.

Evaluating Performance

"People don't always agree with the outcome, but they believe they have gotten their fair day in court."

"Keeping everybody happy is my biggest challenge."

In performance-based and modified lockstep models, compensation must be determined annually, whereas lockstep firms often have level-progression discussions every other year. The senior team typically spends an enormous amount of time making compensation decisions. Most midsized to larger firms have special compensation committees that are elected by the partners to assess partner performance, determine the distribution split, and mediate disputes. Evaluating partners and sharing rewards is a delicate and deliberate process. Getting it right motivates performance and instills loyalty; getting it wrong can result in an unmotivated partnership team and a potential exodus of top talent. The firms that best navigate the partner evaluation and financial distribution process share several characteristics:

- *A perception of fairness exists.* Not everyone will be pleased with the results of their evaluation and its impact on their paychecks, but the partners must all believe that the process itself is fair and that everyone is reviewed in exactly the same manner—with the same criteria and standards.
- *The process is transparent.* The steps in the process and the roles and responsibilities of everyone involved must be clearly established. Some firms advocate an open-book policy in which all partners know exactly where they stand in terms of seniority status and

annual compensation compared to their fellow partners. Other firms say that open systems are disruptive. As one CEO told us, "People are looking at three layers in determining whether they think they've been fairly compensated: One, they just have a visceral reaction to what they perceive they're worth; two, what they perceive their neighbor down the hall got; and three, what they perceive they could get at the competitor across the street."

- *The process is thorough.* The best firms have very structured evaluation processes that include multiple opinions, data sources, and points of contact. In many midsize to larger firms, every partner has an appraising partner who is responsible for gathering input from the partner being interviewed as well as from a sampling of peers, associates, and clients. The appraising partner then flows his or her report and recommendations upward through the appropriate layers in the organization, typically to the business unit heads, where the appraisals are further reviewed and refined, and then on to the compensation committee. The compensation committee thoroughly reviews each report, along with the financial stats for each partner—revenue originated, revenue managed, and profitability of clients—and makes a final recommendation on seniority status and annual compensation. Many firms assess a partner's contributions over a 2- to 3-year period to determine if performance is trending up or down.

  The compensation committee's recommendations are reviewed by the leadership team—either the board or the management committee, sometimes both—and ultimately by the CEO before receiving a final stamp of approval. Small firms that have a few partners and few management layers obviously don't need to follow this intricate of a path. However, regardless of firm size, it is very important that the partners believe that their individual contributions have been carefully assessed and acknowledged by whoever makes the compensation decision (see "Gensler's Principal Evaluation Process").

- *There is an opportunity to learn.* The best evaluation processes incorporate ongoing constructive feedback. This gives the partner being reviewed ample opportunity to participate in the review to tell his or her story and receive suggestions on areas to leverage and improve. The most effective performance review I ever experienced was at Booz Allen Hamilton in the 1980s. Every year, I worked with my assigned partner evaluator to create my own self-appraisal and suggest partners and peers to interview. My evaluator would summarize the feedback, present and discuss the results

Gensler's Principal Evaluation Process

Gensler has grown rapidly from a U.S. company to a global enterprise with 35 offices and 16 practice areas. "Our one-firm firm philosophy has remained a core value at Gensler," notes Co-CEO Andy Cohen. "It's been the basis of our growth, our partnership, and our global expansion. Our goal is to act as one seamless integrated organization."

In the early 1990s, Gensler set out to transform itself from a U.S.-based firm to a global firm. Consultants from McKinsey advised Gensler leadership to shift its principal promotions decision-making process away from local offices to a centralized function to facilitate decisions based on firm-wide core values and leadership along with local or practice-specific considerations.

Based on this concept, Gensler created its Principal Evaluation Committee (PERC), a nonpartisan group of senior Gensler leaders. Rotated annually, its members are drawn from the firm's board and management committee—and they represent all parts of the firm and all practices. PERC's mandate is to evaluate potential candidates from a firm-wide perspective to ensure that Gensler is promoting the best talent using a consistent and thoroughly understood set of leadership criteria. The result is a rigorous evaluation period spanning six months, from midyear through December.

While managing principals of local offices and firm-wide practice leaders nominate candidates for promotion, PERC brings a global perspective and sensibility to its mission. As a first step, nominating executives submit detailed analysis that evaluates candidates across many dimensions: growing and leading the firm; mentoring, coaching, and developing people; client service and trusted advisor role; developing new innovations; and community activities and outreach. Criteria in each category are clearly defined and communicated as professionals move through the ranks, ensuring a process that is fair and transparent.

As soon as PERC has the detailed nomination analysis, they conduct a 360-degree review of each person and his or her leadership attributes, soliciting as much feedback as possible about candidate performance, both internally and from clients. Ultimately, the committee makes recommendations to the board of directors, which approves the new promotions.

In analyzing the PERC approach as it has evolved, Cohen observes the following:

- If you're a global firm, make diversity in your partnership a priority. In the past few years, for example, Gensler has promoted new principals in Asia, the Middle East, and Europe.
- For a multilocation, multipractice firm, the basis for promotion has to be fostering a one-firm culture, and the process has to be nonpartisan. If you don't have this culture and vision, the whole evaluation process falls apart.
- Be ready to defend your rationale and "stick to your guns" when a decision not to promote a candidate is questioned by office or practice leaders.
- If candidates fall short the first time around, leaders need to be very candid about what needs to be improved. Let them know specifically the constructive leadership skills they need to hone. Then monitor their progress closely and give constant feedback.

with the evaluation committee, and then write a summary report to review with the managing partner and me. It was Booz Allen's policy at the time that everyone, regardless of rank, be given at least two solid recommendations on areas to improve over the next year. These recommendations had to be woven into my annual personal plan and would be measured the following year. The entire process was one of the most effective professional development and learning exercises in my career.

Partnership Performance Criteria

"There is the concept of 'Eat what you kill.' The belief is, in order to keep people and reward people, the money should go to the one who delivers the bacon."

"However you decide your compensation model will dictate what your talent looks like."

"Compensation is strategy in a professional service firm. How you reward people drives behavior with almost a perfect correlation."

Whatever the compensation model, partners are judged by a fairly universal set of performance standards (see "Compensation Criteria at Eversheds"):

- **Revenue**—As one COO told us, "Revenue contributions ultimately trumps everything." Like it or not, the partners are responsible for bringing in and managing client business. Chances are that few professionals make it to partnership level without exhibiting strong sales skills. In a large firm, the business can tolerate a combination of sellers to generate new work and doers to execute. Small, growing firms, however, do not have that luxury; partners must both find and do the work. To motivate the troops and generate revenue at ghSMART, principals are allowed to keep 60 percent of the revenue they personally produce and 25 percent of the revenue generated by principals who work on their client portfolio. This creates a tangible tie to revenue contributions and encourages collaboration.

- **Client relationships**—While the ability to generate revenue is top dog in the performance ratings, keeping and growing clients into long-term enduring relationships is a close second. Several firms award a substantial number of points to client asset building. The longer and more profitable the connection, the greater the reward. However, many noted the importance of rewarding partners who take on the challenges of starting up and growing a new relationship or market, often relinquishing a profitable client base to tackle the new assignment.

- **People building**—Partners who are skilled at recruiting, training, and mentoring the troops are highly valued. As discussed repeatedly throughout the book, people are the product in PSFs. In the apprenticeship-driven world of professional services, the senior team must be responsible for finding and developing the talent base.

- **Intellectual capital**—Particularly for the consulting-based segments of the industry, offering innovative and relevant ideas and services to the market is critical to survival. As Jim McTaggart, Founder and CEO of Marakon, summarized, "In today's marketplace, you've got to have something distinctive to say. You've got to invest in building intellectual property—that's the sine qua non in the consulting business." Many firms place high value on intellectual capital contributions and acknowledge and reward the partners who participate.

- **Firm leadership**—Running the firm is the responsibility of the senior team. Assuming a management position or leading an important initiative is viewed as an honor and a serious responsibility. The role is doubly difficult in a professional service firm, where the leadership team is expected to remain billable with

Compensation Criteria at Eversheds

One of the world's largest law firms, London-based Eversheds has 2,500 attorneys in 47 offices around the globe. According to Chairman Alan Jenkins, in 2004 the firm redesigned its compensation structure for its 350-plus partners. Moving away from its former lockstep approach, it created a more innovative and flexible profit-sharing system—one that was aligned with Eversheds' values, vision, and strategic goals.

Spearheaded by a small working group of partners, the firm's performance-based compensation system took almost a year to restructure. "The effort was intense," says Jenkins, "taking up a tremendous amount of management time." Ultimately, however, the new approach won the unanimous approval of the partnership. Key features include the following:

- **Five performance criteria**—To fully reflect the firm's values and growth strategy, partner profit sharing is based on five core principles:

    1. *Client impact*. Growing business from existing clients, developing new clients, effective client management, and ensuring the highest levels of service

    2. *People development*. Innovating, inspiring, and leading teams to high-quality performance

    3. *Supporting the firm's vision and values*. Sharing, teamwork, and business development for the benefit of the whole firm

    4. *Profit*. Partner contribution to firm growth and profitability

    5. *Strategic value*. The strategic importance of what is being done by or asked of the partner in question

- **Annual performance evaluations**—Every year, a 360-degree appraisal is conducted for each partner. The head of the group or industry team to which the partner belongs is required to discuss the performance of the partner against objectives previously agreed with that partner in the light of the 360-degree survey. Objectives are revised if appropriate. Progress towards those objectives has an impact on the partner's assessment for the biennial rebanding of the partner's compensation (see the next bullet point).

> • **Compensation strategy**—Every other year, the review process results in each partner's remuneration being adjusted. Each partner is asked to prepare a one-page summary of what that partner considers his or her contribution to be against the five criteria. The firm's senior management team undertakes an evaluation of each partner based on the self-assessment, the 360-degree reviews, and an assessment report prepared by the partner's practice group leader based on the annual appraisal exercise. The senior management team reaches provisional conclusions and conveys the results to the partners, who are free to comment on or challenge them. After each partner has had the chance to comment, the management team finalizes its decisions. Each partner is assigned a place on a 12-band system. Each band is valued at a certain number of points, and each point reflects a monetary value, depending on the firm's current profits.
>
> In Jenkins' view, the investment of time and energy made in restructuring partner profit sharing was well worth the results. "Any compensation system has to be consistent with a firm's culture and values," he notes. Since compensation strategy is a vital part of how any professional service firm operates, he believes it makes sense to put the effort into designing a system that is overwhelmingly, if not unanimously, supported by all the affected partners.

client work in addition to executing their management duties. Firms understand the complexity of these positions and add points for additional roles and responsibilities.

Partnership Selection: A Pivotal Decision

Partnership selection is one of the most critical decisions for PSFs, and the best firms devote considerable time and attention to the nomination and promotion process. Determining who will bring strength and value to the partnership, the clients, and the professionals in the firm is pivotal to the organization.

In PSFs, new partners come from two sources—lateral senior hires from competing firms or industry positions, and the homegrown pool of professionals who have risen through the ranks. Although a few of the large law firms we studied exclusively promote from within, most firms utilize a combination of sources. The selection criteria for each group varies. Lateral partner candidates are expected to bring seasoned expertise and experience, a leadership track record, and possibly a new book of built-in business. On the surface, it would seem that a lateral-hire decision would be easier than promoting a relatively untested associate in the firm. However, finding someone from the outside with the right cultural and work style fit and successfully launching that person into the firm can be quite challenging and disruptive to the organization.

Promoting from within provides the advantage of a long dating period in which both the professionals and the firm can decide over time if they are a match. But following this path takes considerable time and effort. As discussed in Chapter 3, "People," the best firms—both large and small—invest significant senior time to recruit, train, and groom talented professionals for advancement into the leadership ranks. For these firms, the criteria for partnership are carefully determined and clearly communicated to young professionals. As Damien O'Brien, CEO of Egon Zehnder International, put it, "We expect everybody we hire to become partner. Everyone, of course, doesn't make partner, but a very high percentage do. The feedback they get through their career and their progression in the firm is geared to that objective."

Criteria for Promotion to Partnership

The list of must-have qualities for a partner varies from firm to firm, depending on the culture and values, type of business, and growth and profitability goals. Most firms look at some combination of the following attributes:

- **Client skills**—Partner candidates must demonstrate their ability to identify and solve client problems and work effectively with client teams. Client relationship management abilities must be confirmed by both partner engagement leaders and the clients themselves.
- **Team building**—Candidates must rate highly on internal evaluations by partners, peers, and younger associates on team management, training, mentorship, and collaboration.
- **Business development**—Potential new partners must have played a significant role in growing a current client or must have participated in new-client acquisition and development.

- **Firm citizenship**—Firms are looking for partners who embody firm values and culture. Most look for a strong work ethic, professionalism, collaboration and team spirit, innovativeness, energy, and drive.
- **Future potential**—Partners must look into a crystal ball and subjectively estimate the candidates' potential to generate future revenue, contribute intellectual capital, and eventually take on a leadership position in the firm.

Partner Promotion Process

"You have to always have in mind who you're promoting to a partnership, because you are devaluing the value of the unit if you increase the number of units. This is very important."

"We have a full yearlong process to elect a partner, and it is absolutely rigorous."

Many firms in our study described highly collaborative and iterative nominating and selection processes (see "Making Partner at Egon Zehnder International"). Most mid-size and large PSFs have designated nominating committees of senior partners who are either a subcommittee of the board or specially elected by the partners. The committee is responsible for managing the often-rigorous and lengthy selection process. Participation on the committee is considered a prestigious position and responsibility in the firm. Most large firms field new-partner slates annually, although some admit new partners twice a year. For small firms, new-partner decisions are made much less frequently, when young professionals are deemed ready, and when the ownership group is prepared to share equity. A typical selection process follows four steps:

1. *The partner pool is determined.* The first step in the process is determining how many partners in total, and by practice and region, the firm can absorb. Unit leaders present their business and financial case for adding a partner, and management must decide which areas of the firm are growing, which are peaking, and which have gaps that need to be filled. Ultimately, leadership determines how many new partners are strategically and financially feasible. As one CEO told us, "Sorting reality from advocacy to identify the candidate pool is often a tough job."

2. *Candidates are identified.* After the number of new partners has been decided, business unit heads and the leadership team review

individual candidates and select the professionals to propose. Rarely do any surprises occur at this stage for either partners or candidates. Most professionals know well ahead of time when they are eligible for partnership consideration, and the leadership team has been carefully tracking high-potential candidates for many years prior to nomination. Most firms pride themselves on their "humane" progression process. As one managing partner told us, "We give people lots of early notice to tell them that we don't think they are ever going to make partner so they aren't humiliated when they don't make the cut."

3. *The committee reviews candidates.* After the candidates are identified, unit leaders prepare formal nomination packets for each person. Typically they include evaluation reports, recommendations from managers, and candidate self-assessments. The nominating committee then reviews each candidate in a process described nearly universally as rigorous and intense. In addition to scrutinizing the packets, committees often conduct several rounds of interviews with candidates, their managers, peers, and clients. Some firms bring in outside evaluators to provide a professional third-party perspective. Clifford Chance, for example, invites outside experts, including occupational psychologists and retired senior in-house counsel and members of the legal profession, to observe candidates at a final one and a half day course that all partner candidates who reach that last stage are required to attend.

4. *A final slate is selected for approval.* The committee debates each candidate and endorses a final slate to submit to the board or management committee for approval. The leadership team continues the debate and agrees on a new partner group. Some PSFs require a two-thirds majority vote from the firm partnership to approve each new partner.

Making Partner at Egon Zehnder International

"Making partner at international executive search firm Egon Zehnder International is not an easy process, but it's an open and equitable one," says firm Chairman Damien O'Brien. But, according to O'Brien, this was not always the case. At one time, the firm did not have a standardized nominating process. As the firm grew in complexity and size, many partners were concerned that the process was not sufficiently consistent for this global, equal partnership.

In response, the firm established the Partnership Candidate Evaluation Group (PCEG), which is elected directly by the partners and operates independently of the firm's management team. The group developed standardized performance criteria for new partners and mapped the steps in the nomination and approval process, which takes about 12 months from initial vetting to voting. Key aspects of the selection process are as follows:

- **Total transparency**—Candidate assessment is thorough and rigorous. Partner selection is based solely on merit and performance and is independent of the firm's economics. The annual appraisal process is aligned with the new-partner performance criteria established in the firm's Contribution and Performance Development Review system. It focuses on three key areas: firm values, client relationship building, and quality of execution. Consultants are evaluated against these qualifications annually. By the time candidates come up for partnership, they have gone through an intense 5-to-6-year review process and are well aware of the criteria they must satisfy to attain partnership.

- **Nomination**—Partner candidates are nominated by their office leaders with input from practice group leaders. After an initial vetting process, candidate evaluation begins.

- **Rigorous review**—After candidates are nominated, the PCEG launches a diligent review process, with members often flying around the world to spend several days with each candidate. They take references, discuss the candidate's career accomplishments and aspirations, review his or her work quality, and prepare a detailed document assessing the person's candidacy. The evaluation group then gets together, normalizes its evaluations, and forms its view of each person based on the selection criteria.

It then prepares detailed briefs on each candidate for consideration by the partnership.

- **Election**—After the PCEG briefs on nominees are prepared, they are distributed to the partnership at one of the twice-yearly global partners' meetings. Candidates are presented to the partners by their office leader for consideration and then election.

- **Ongoing evaluation**—As new partners gain experience, they continue to be evaluated using a different set of expectations embodied in a document called "What Good Looks Like." Senior partners, for example, are assessed based on their coaching and mentoring of junior colleagues, thought leadership, role in the business community, and impact as trusted advisors to CEOs and the chairmen of large companies.

Over the years, the firm has continued to fine-tune its partner and selection process. "The Partnership Evaluation Group has become a highly regarded committee within the firm, and our process runs smoothly and efficiently," says O'Brien. "We have created a strong, vibrant partner corps and leadership team. It has been well worth the effort."

CHAPTER SUMMARY

Partnership

- The concept of partnership is both an industry mind-set and a distinctive set of governance characteristics.

- Six characteristics are fundamental to creating an enduring partnership:
    1. Align around shared vision and values.
    2. Foster an environment of integration, teamwork, and collaboration.
    3. Treat the senior team as owners.
    4. Create an atmosphere of collegiality.
    5. Reward contributions appropriately.
    6. Cultivate stewardship.

- Professional service firms can be structured in a variety of ways. Limited liability partnerships (LLPs), C corporations, limited liability companies (LLCs), and S corporations are the most common choices. Each one has advantages and disadvantages.

- Over 90 percent of the firms studied have some form of equity-sharing program. Although specific aspects of the programs vary, the best-run programs have common characteristics:
    - Equity participation requires a capital outlay.
    - Ownership progression is well defined.
    - Risk and reward escalate with degree of ownership.
    - The firm remains strong and viable when senior partners leave.
- The three types of compensation models are lockstep, which rewards seniority; performance-based, which rewards individual contributions; and modified lockstep, which rewards both seniority and performance.
- Partner evaluations and annual compensation decisions are very important to get right in a PSF. The best processes are fair, transparent, thorough, and collaborative.
- Partnership selection is a highly collaborative and iterative nominating and selection process that typically follows four steps:
    1. The partner pool is determined.
    2. Candidates are identified.
    3. The committee reviews candidates.
    4. A final slate is selected for approval.

9

Strategy

Process, responsibility, and accountability

"We spend a lot of time, as a management team, just making sure we are aligned in our ambition."
—Steve Gunby, former Chairman, North and South America,
The Boston Consulting Group

"We don't really look at strategic planning in isolation. What we talk about is a continuous process throughout the year."
—Brett Marschke, COO, Duff & Phelps

"It is so simple to articulate the strategies. The question is whether you can in fact deliver on them."
—Rajat Gupta, former Managing Director, McKinsey

Some people view strategic planning as an art, some as a science—and some as an inspired combination of the two. Some define it in terms of vision and speak of shaping a future of potential and growth. Others describe planning as a tactical exercise—a game plan for deploying resources to capture maximum advantage in the marketplace. Respondents described their strategic planning processes as everything from intensive brainstorming marathons over weeks or even months to routine annual budget exercises.

Regardless of how they define or execute their strategic planning, leaders agree that engaging in this process is vital to achieving alignment around a firm's vision and building internal momentum. A robust strategy focuses resources, clarifies decisions and intent, energizes execution, and unleashes potential.

More than 70 percent of respondents agreed that strategic planning belongs on management's priority list, as shown in Exhibit 9.1. However, this topic sparked less passion and energy than many others we explored. Even though 57 percent gave themselves fairly high marks for execution, as shown in Exhibit 9.2, many admitted that that they are working to improve performance in this area.

EXHIBIT 9.1   More than two thirds of respondents place strategic planning high on the management agenda

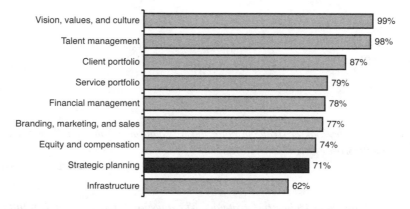

EXHIBIT 9.2   Performance on strategic planning is mixed

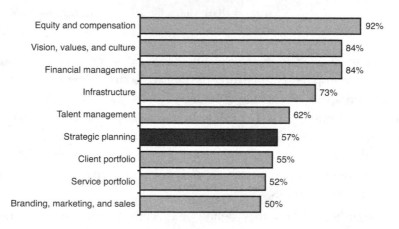

"You know the phrase—the cobbler's children have no shoes. We're great at putting together and evaluating and analyzing a strategic plan for Domino's Pizza, but not so good at doing it for ourselves."

"The challenges to planning well are the very traditional ones that we hear from our clients. 'I don't have time to do this' on the one hand or 'I already know the answer' on the other hand."

Why Strategic Planning Matters

"Vision without a plan is nothing."

"There is a certain discipline that comes from forcing the exercise to anticipate what the future will bring and how to respond to it which provides great value to the firm."

"It doesn't matter much what the strategy is; it's about the process you go through to get to the strategy."

Many leaders say they have a hard time applying the same rigor and resources to strategic planning for their own enterprise that they exhibit on behalf of their clients. As one CEO admitted, "It is challenging to treat ourselves as a client and put our strategic minds in service of our own business." Strategic planning takes nonbillable time, and it is a battle for leaders to get professionals to focus on what many see as a time-consuming distraction from client service and billable hours. And when it comes to implementation, finding the right levers to pull, whether formal or informal, to incent professionals to execute against plan can be a delicate task.

Despite the challenges, planning in PSFs is growing in both importance and sophistication. Fully seven out of ten of our respondents (71 percent) indicated that they have a formalized institutional planning, review, and measurement process that ties results to compensation, as shown in Exhibit 9.3.

EXHIBIT 9.3   The majority of firms have a formal planning process

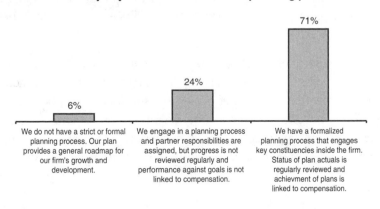

6%	24%	71%
We do not have a strict or formal planning process. Our plan provides a general roadmap for our firm's growth and development.	We engage in a planning process and partner responsibilities are assigned, but progress is not reviewed regularly and performance against goals is not linked to compensation.	We have a formalized planning process that engages key constituencies inside the firm. Status of plan actuals is regularly reviewed and achievment of plans is linked to compensation.

Many valuable benefits flow from engaging in a thoughtful, construc-
tively debated planning process:

- **Focus**—The most obvious benefit of strategic planning is its role in
  keeping a company firmly aligned with, and focused on, its organizational vision. A carefully conceived and designed plan translates a
  firm's vision into a clear road map so that professionals at all levels
  know where the firm is going and how it intends to get there. In
  contrast, a strategic vision without a strong execution plan creates
  confusion rather than clarity.

- **Discipline**—Engaging in a strategic planning process forces a
  firm's leadership team to put aside daily concerns and client work
  and ask themselves tough questions about the future. It also encourages top management to reevaluate previous decisions in light of
  new circumstances and to refresh firm direction. The rigorous
  analysis that results from stepping back and assessing how to best
  respond to different conditions or contingencies can be immensely
  valuable. Many see strategic planning as a core top-management
  responsibility. In their view, adopting a long-term perspective,
  assessing potential obstacles and opportunities, and evaluating firm
  positioning with the goal of capturing maximum competitive advantage are all central to a leadership role.

- **Motivation**—The psychological benefits of planning are among
  the most important for professional services and are one of the key
  reasons to engage in a broad-based, inclusive strategic planning
  process. Planning is a tool to stimulate collaboration, rally the
  troops, and create a sense of renewal and mission around organizational goals. A coherent plan provides the opportunity to generate
  excitement and buy-in by reenergizing professionals about the
  firm's potential for growth and profitability—and their role in bringing a strategy to fruition.

Many leaders believe the journey is more important than the destination. The process that a firm engages in to arrive at a strategy is actually
more valuable than the strategy itself. A substantial number of those
interviewed pointed out the strong link between a vibrant planning
process and effective execution. The process builds trust, commitment,
and enthusiasm among the leadership team, which is vital to successful
implementation.

Five Essentials for Successful Strategic Planning

"It doesn't matter what your job in the organization is; you should be able to figure out how it leads to the firm's strategic imperatives and its success."

"I just spent four hours with a whole group of people going through a scenario planning process, looking at different possibilities and timelines for when the economy will either get better or worse. I highly recommend it for other firms."

Five common characteristics emerged from our interviews that are fundamental to successful strategic planning:

1. *Integrate long-term strategic planning with annual plans.* Many firms favor a comprehensive approach to strategy formulation that combines periodic long-term visionary planning events with annual operational and financial planning exercises and goal-setting. In general, the issues dealt with at the highest strategic planning level have to do with decisions that have major implications for firm direction, service delivery, internal investment, and resource deployment. Such far-reaching concerns range from geographic expansion and investments in intellectual capital to adding new services or restructuring from a country-centric operating model to one based on practice areas. In contrast to broad issues such as these, annual operational and financial planning exercises tend to be more tactical in nature, mapping out short-term goals and revenue targets.

2. *View strategic planning as a continuous cycle, not a one-time event.* Given the volatility of global markets, many leaders stress the importance of not viewing planning as an isolated, finite event or exercise, but rather a fluid, ongoing cycle of review and adjustment. To accommodate rapid market shifts, new opportunities, and unexpected threats, strategic planning needs to be adaptive and responsive. It should be treated as a creative, nonlinear process, and the plan should be revisited periodically.

   Sometimes a lightning-rod event or external environmental issue surfaces with the potential to transform the firm's business in some fundamental way. When this happens, it's inevitable that long-term plans will be affected; in certain situations, the firm may even be forced to rethink its current operating model. At times like these, flexibility is essential. A firm has to be willing to take stock, regroup, go back with a blank piece of paper, and really challenge the entire plan. In anticipating circumstances like these, scenario planning—an underutilized tool in the professional service business—can be especially helpful.

3. *Incorporate external as well as internal analyses into strategic planning.* It is vitally important that service firms avoid organizational navel gazing. They must look beyond their own windows and walls to identify long-term trends and market forces that could affect their businesses or point the way to unmet client needs and new service offerings.

    Savvy firms are constantly taking the pulse of their clients and the industries they serve. Planning is never done in a vacuum, with a group of leaders sitting in a room talking to themselves. Incorporating solid external data into a realistic assessment of internal strengths and weaknesses is the foundation for successful business planning and decision making. Some professionals we have worked with have been adamant that they don't need to talk to the market, because "we know our business." Although this is largely true, surprises almost always come up when the firm conducts a bit of research. The market perception of the brand is weak or spotty, clients are not interested in buying some of the services the firm is selling, or, as discussed in Chapter 5, "Services," opportunities to expand into a new service or market have not been explored.

4. *To ensure buy-in, collaborate with stakeholders to develop plans.* Generating support at all levels for the strategic plan is as critical for professional service firms as it is for the clients they counsel. As many of the leaders we spoke to noted, in a partnership, collaboration is the touchstone of strategic planning. If partners don't feel they've been heard and don't own a plan's objectives, they feel no obligation to embrace them or measure their performance against them. However, as many respondents stressed, achieving total consensus on goals and directions is rarely possible. After feedback is solicited and processed, it is up to the firm's leadership team to move forward decisively, usually without unanimous support.

    Knowing when to discuss, debate, and, finally, decide on a clear strategic direction is a sensitive timing issue. Firms charting strategies on a global scale face a further challenge in orchestrating inclusive planning and review processes. CEOs at the helm of enterprises with global footprints find it immensely demanding, but critical, to ensure that major stakeholders at country and regional levels are actively involved in planning. It's also vital that any strategy

Planning at Peppercom

"Understanding what's next from a client's standpoint is the engine that drives the firm," says Steve Cody, Managing Partner and Cofounder of strategic communication and public relations agency, Peppercom. "The marketing communications world is a living organism," he adds. "A month in our industry is probably like a year in manufacturing." Taking the pulse of the marketplace is key to Peppercom's success. The firm combines a formal strategic planning process with constant monitoring and refreshing to stay attuned to its markets.

Using a dynamic approach to planning, Peppercom gathers and evaluates real-time data and adjusts its strategy on an ongoing basis. It generates input in a variety of creative ways: through weekly meetings with an independent strategist; monthly service-line refresher courses; offsite brainstorming; and an annual firm-wide brainstorming event.

The heart of Peppercom's planning process is its war room, which features a chart mapping the firm's existing and prospective clients and market events. The chart provides an at-a-glance overview of which accounts are growing and which might be in jeopardy. The firm uses this data to align its short-term actions with its long-term plan, which focuses on five core segments: professional services, finance, high tech, B2B, and consumer home goods. "Our goal," says Cody, "is to be the best in class in each of these segments." Along with monitoring account status, the firm is always doing primary research—delving deeply into its clients' business needs, analyzing their main points, and coming up with relevant new service offerings.

Peppercom often looks outside its industry to gain a broader perspective and spark nontraditional thinking. It works closely with an independent strategist, taps external sources for input, and hires from outside the industry; recent hires include an MIT professor and a managing editor from the *Wall Street Journal*.

Once a month, a member of one of the firm's service lines meets with management to give an update on new developments in their world. The high priority area is scrutinized with the goal of answering critical questions, such as: What's new in digital? What's new in sustainability? What's happening in licensing? Peppercom holds strategy meetings offsite every 6 months with its management team and strategic consultant.

"At these sessions," says Cody, "the firm looks at who we are representing today, who we would love to represent 12 months from today, and what clients don't make sense for us long-term."

Another innovative planning tool—and one which has resulted in some very exciting strategic outcomes—is Peppercom's annual Dream Day. Every December, the firm closes it offices and brings all its employees together to take a blue-sky approach to envisioning the firm's future. Typically, the firm emerges from Dream Day right before the holidays with a broad blueprint that it combines with its end-of-year offsite input to create a working plan for the coming year. Not only has this empowering approach helped the firm win new business, it has also become a branding tool that attracts great new talent.

envisioned is tested—not just in current markets, but in emerging ones as well.

5. *Communicate constantly, and regularly review progress against goals*. Once key stakeholders are onboard, it's equally important to keep them fully engaged and in the loop during the execution phase. Many leaders also strongly advocate driving the key elements of a strategic plan down to the staff level so that employees in support positions have a clear view of the direction the firm is taking and recognize the importance of their own roles in helping the firm stay on track.

Orchestrating the Planning Process

The majority of firms are committed to a dynamic, inclusive process that embraces a multiyear time horizon, annual execution initiatives and objectives, quarterly or monthly reviews, and ongoing review and adjustments. Most firms collaborate across the planning process, with the leadership team setting multiyear goals for strategy and growth and partners providing substantial feedback.

The planning process generally unfolds in four broad stages, as shown in Exhibit 9.4. It progresses from long-range planning through the updating and fine-tuning of both long-term and annual plans.

EXHIBIT 9.4   The PSF planning process

Long-term plan	Annual plan	Review and monitor	Update and refresh
Every 3–5 years	12-month cycle	Quarterly/monthly	Ongoing
Leadership team requests external market analysis to spot trends, identify service needs, and test competitive strengths	Leadership team sets preliminary goals	Leadership team meets with business leaders on a regular basis to review status of annual plans, offer feedback, and agree to adjustments	Leadership and partnership are continuously reviewing plans, markets, and competitive position, and adjusting both long-term and annual plans as needed
Leadership reviews market analysis, shares aspirations for firm, and sets preliminary goals for strategy and growth	CFO or COO requests plans from the matrix leadership: heads of services, geographies, industries, and key clients	Leadership provides partners regular reports on status of plan to actual	
Leadership uses a collaborative process to gather ideas and comments on the preliminary plan	Leadership rolls up plans, adjusts appropriately to align with long-term goals, and creates firm-wide business plan	Unit heads and leadership are held accountable for achievement of plans	
Leadership synthesizes all input and finalizes plan	CFO develops budget based on plan		
Leadership submits plan to partnership for approval, if governance model requires	Leadership and business unit leaders review and revise business plan and budget		
	Leadership team and business unit leaders agree to master plan		

Long-Term Planning

"I've never figured out how to execute against a 5- or 10-year plan. Three years looks like a long time."

"The strategic plan animates the vision."

"Some firms have gotten a long way by just putting one foot in front of the other. It's going to take a lot more planning than that to survive going forward."

For many firms, the long-term planning process is launched with an external analysis aimed at identifying high-impact trends, pinpointing service needs and gaps, and testing competitive positioning within global markets. This analysis often includes in-depth discussions with clients as well as secondary research on the market and the competitive landscape.

After the research has been conducted and analyzed, the leadership team incorporates the data into their discussions of firm goals and direction and develops a preliminary strategy and plan for the firm. Although long-term planning typically is a top-down process, most firms incorporate a collaborative partner review process that can include one or more rounds of partner feedback, via either individual responses, practice or partner meetings, or focus group settings.

After feedback is received, the leadership team spearheading the planning initiative generally revisits its original plan, digesting and incorporating suggested changes. Then it makes another set of recommendations that are again reviewed and revised collaboratively before the plan is submitted for final approval and approved by either the full partnership or the leadership team, depending on the firm's proxy policy (see "Hewitt's Planning Process").

Some firms routinely factor long-term strategizing into their planning processes. Other firms are motivated to engage in long-term strategic thinking by a pivotal internal or external event, such as a leadership change, a merger, or a seismic market shift.

Like most firms in the advertising segment, BBH was faced with a fundamental shift in the market—from conventional to digital advertising. The firm adopted a formal long-term planning strategy and process to rethink its entire service approach and shape a new operating model that reflects a world dominated by interactive media. Building this model over the long term requires substantial commitment to new capabilities and analytical tools. According to Chairman Steve Harty, rethinking both the firm's long-term strategic direction and its fundamental operating dynamic was essential, because "failure to change—getting stuck in the old model—means financial death."

Most firms (60 percent) that engage in some form of long-term planning employ a rolling 3-to-5-year time frame, as shown in Exhibit 9.5. The idea is to plan far enough ahead to allow for incremental steps in achieving significant changes, such as expansion into new markets, while remaining flexible enough to respond opportunistically to market shifts, resource changes, and external events.

Hewitt's Planning Process

Human resources consulting and outsourcing firm, Hewitt Associates, has created a multilayered ongoing strategic planning process that stresses heavy partner involvement and ownership at every stage. According to Matt Levin, Senior Vice President, Corporate Development and Strategy, the firm's planning approach is characterized by the dynamic interplay of broad strategic initiatives and annual planning exercises.

The process kicks off in April, leading to a presentation of the strategic plan to the board in June. Once the firm-wide planning process is completed, corporate comes up with financial targets and, over the next 2 months, operating plans are designed and put into motion. Overall, the firm's strategic planning process has four primary elements:

- **External analysis**—During the early stages of planning, the firm looks at its market share, industry trends, the growth rates of core products, and competitive positioning.

- **Internal growth analysis**—The team zeroes in on the firm's divisions and their ongoing business activities and current product portfolios. The natural trajectories and growth rates of the businesses are analyzed; and pricing strategies, organic product extensions, speed to market, and selling processes are examined. Hewitt provides business units with a planning template covering both long- and short-term goals and projections.

- **Long-term planning**—Long-term planning occurs in a very cross-functional way. People are encouraged to bring new ideas, products, or services they've developed at the practice level—or anything else that promises to drive meaningful revenue improvements and boost the firm's overall growth rate. Leaders across the firm are encouraged to step back from the paths they've been on, take stock of their business, and gather their thoughts on future direction. The company incorporates perspectives from its "high potentials" (individuals identified as future stars) by assigning them to small teams to identify and explore new initiatives. Levin believes that involving younger consultants in the strategic planning process has been beneficial to both Hewitt and the professionals. "If you look at some of the initiatives we launched as a result of the strategic planning process, there are young leaders who can say that they've had major career inflection points as a result of the process."

> • **Regular reviews**—There are two levels of monthly review of performance against the business plan: a monthly leadership financial review at the Hewitt-wide executive level, and a separate monthly review where the P&L owners around the world report on their business and explain their financial results.
>
> The planning process is taken very seriously at Hewitt. Results against plan are considered in performance evaluations and, ultimately, in compensation decisions. "The firm is committed to growth with intention," says Levin. "Strategic planning is an important process to keep us on track and aligned with our organizational goals."

EXHIBIT 9.5   Most firms use a 3-to-5-year, long-term planning cycle

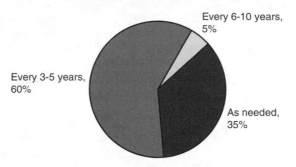

Every 6-10 years, 5%

Every 3-5 years, 60%

As needed, 35%

CSC frames its long-term planning approach as a rolling 3-year outlook designed to assess market trends and map internal capabilities to service options. It makes decisions based on a classic demand-based analysis about where the firm will place its bets and where it won't in terms of deploying its resources. The ongoing review and fine-tuning of the CSC plan kicks off at the end of July, builds momentum in September and October, and is completed in November and December.

A majority of the firms engaged in long-term planning use the 3-to-5-year time frame, but a handful of companies work with even longer time horizons. McKinsey has adopted a longer perspective than most firms when it comes to shaping its internal strategy. According to former Managing Director Rajat Gupta, the firm undertakes a major examination of its strategy once a decade. The process is a multimonth, if not multiyear, effort in which the firm looks at different major strategic questions and directions. The process is largely driven by client needs and comparative positioning and is often "more aspirational than anything else." In the early

'90s, it led to the firm's decisions to establish a full global footprint and to adopt industry groups as its organizing principle. The firm did not develop a strategic planning document. As Gupta explained, "As we like to say in our own strategy practice, 'Strategy is a portfolio of initiatives,' and we have a portfolio of initiatives that is ever-evolving."

In general, the firms that engage in long-range planning view it primarily as a leadership responsibility. The CEO usually drives the process, most often with the active involvement of the firm's leadership team and/or board. A few firms have created a strategic planning function and recruited seasoned professionals to spearhead strategy development and monitor progress against objectives. Some PSFs have turned to outside advisors to design and implement their long-term strategic plans or to act as facilitators to help the firm manage the process internally. Typically, these advisors are independent consultants or business school professors who work directly with top management but who also interact at some stage with a firm's partner corps. Freshfields, for example, has a strategic advisory group that includes both in-house talent and outside experts who are responsible for outlining the parameters of the firm's strategic vision.

Annual Planning

All firms have some sort of annual business plan, ranging from an operational plan flowing from their long-range strategic plan to a tactical plan for deploying resources for the next 12 months. Most commonly, the plan is a combination of strategic objectives and specific, operational, short-term implementation tactics.

While long-term planning is driven from the top, annual plans are a more collaborative top-down/bottom-up process driven by all layers of management and the primary functions. They typically involve more people, including business unit heads, practice group and service line leaders, and office and region heads. One CEO explained, "The planning process must be a partnership between the people who manage the firm in the center and those who manage it locally."

Annual planning begins with the leadership team setting preliminary goals for the firm overall. Then, typically, the COO or CFO is charged with reaching out to the matrix leadership—the practice or service line, geography, or industry leaders—to develop individual plans, often using a template format. The operating unit leaders work with their partner groups to determine what they can reasonably accomplish based on the key accounts in their area, a competitive environment assessment, and local practice initiatives, among other factors.

The leadership team rolls up the plans and makes adjustments to align unit goals with the firm's long-term objectives. As one COO in charge of his firm's process said, "We stare at the merged plans and ask, does that make sense?" The leaders will push back if revenue projections are too low, or costs too high, but most agree that it's the frontline partners who have the best idea of what the potential is in their geography or practice area.

The CFO then develops the firm budget based on the plan, and both the leadership and the unit heads review and agree on the final plan. The plan is an amalgamation of group plans combined with an overarching plan covering any white-space programs and initiatives not owned by any practice group or region (see "Annual Planning at Ernst & Young").

Review, Monitor, and Update

"The issue is the environment is changing so rapidly that the planning process needs to be very adaptive and be able to flex and bend."

Most firms with formal annual planning processes in place are fairly rigorous at monitoring progress against plan. A representative of the firm leadership—it could be the COO, CFO, CEO, or a partner on the executive committee assigned to monitor a unit—meets with business unit heads on a regular basis—typically quarterly or monthly. They assess performance against plan and offer direction and feedback to unit leaders. These meetings help leadership keep a pulse on the direction of the business, surface potential problems early on, and gather current market information from the frontline leaders. The review process often results in adjustments to the plan to reflect the dynamics of the business, keeping the plan flexible and fluid, or, as one CEO said, "a living, breathing document, rather than a binder on the shelf that nobody looks at."

Many firms provide monthly updates on progress against plans to the firm partnership and administrative leadership. The most technically savvy firms provide real-time dashboards, allowing leaders to monitor progress 24/7. For most, annual plans are reviewed and updated if needed quarterly

Annual Planning at Ernst & Young

Annual planning at Ernst & Young is a disciplined and methodical process. According to Mark Gaumond, America's Senior Vice Chair, Markets, all partners throughout the organization participate. "It's a very comprehensive process," says Gaumond, "but it gets everyone to buy into and execute on the goals we set." There are two components to the planning process that run in parallel each year:

- **Financial planning**—The financial plan deals with the operational side of the business. Assumptions on existing and future headcount, utilization, production, and rates-per-hour expected from the various markets are calibrated into annual revenue, cost, and earnings targets.

- **Revenue planning**—The revenue plan is top-line focused and aspirational. It starts with the individual partners coming forward with their views of what they may be able to achieve and deliver in the marketplace. Partners are encouraged to think broadly about client needs that might be addressed by Ernst & Young's four service lines: Assurance, Tax, Advisory, and Transactions. The plans roll up to a revenue target that is typically higher than the financial plan target.

The process of developing the plans is transparent, collaborative, and iterative, beginning 4 or 5 months before the start of the fiscal year. Using a standardized template and toolset, individual partners prepare plans that are rolled up by client, office, subarea, and area, and are ultimately approved by an area operating committee and board. All geographies and service lines have input into the plans, and assumptions and goals of each unit are shared openly.

Once plans are approved, results are monitored monthly and are reported quarterly. At midyear, a comprehensive review is conducted, and plans are updated as necessary. On an individual partner level, adherence to plans is built into partners' individual goals, and results are considered in compensation decisions.

Gaumond says Ernst & Young essentially runs the business off the financial plan and "pushes hard to make the revenue plan." He describes a healthy tension between the two plans, "If you are not careful, excessive focus on operations—or the bottom line—can limit

> topline growth. On the other hand, you cannot be out generating business for new business' sake without any financial discipline. You have to keep it in balance."

and long-term plans annually. However, many firms constantly monitor market and competitive trends that impact the business and adjust plans to reflect changing conditions and opportunities.

Accountability

"Trying to get people to understand, number one, that looking at the financial performance is important and then, number two, that it can lead to consequences has been quite a long-term process."

"The only reason we're not a 10 on your continuum is we don't have the exact linkage to compensation yet."

Tying performance against plan directly to compensation is a controversial topic in professional services. Some do it rigorously, others say it is culturally inappropriate for their firms, and many claim it is only one of many variables considered in compensation decisions. As discussed in Chapter 8, "Partnership," many firms use a combination of quantitative and qualitative metrics, often with a good deal of subjectivity, to determine partner compensation.

Carl Roehling, President and CEO of architectural firm SmithGroup, explained that metrics are very carefully reviewed in quarterly meetings where office directors report on progress against their business plans. According to Roehling, the firm deploys a host of metrics to track the director's performance, including a substantial number of intangibles. Co-CEO of Gensler, Andy Cohen, agreed that it's not just about the numbers: "At the end of the day, it's about doing world class design, bringing value to our clients, and hiring and nurturing the industry's best talent." Gensler grades people on many "soft" metrics as well as on financial results. As Cohen said, "Someone might have had a phenomenal year on the numbers, but didn't do well with clients or didn't mentor and coach people and didn't bring in great talent. And they're not getting that great a bonus."

For many firms, the process of review and accountability is extremely thorough and strictly adhered to. Several firms described weekly, monthly, and quarterly reviews of financials, tactics, and strategies that can be brutal if performance is off target. Compensation is all about performance against targets. In the publicly traded companies we studied, the scrutiny and level of accountability are even more intense, and much discipline is involved in the process.

CHAPTER SUMMARY

Strategy

- Firm leaders agreed that defining and executing against an organization-wide strategy is essential for success. Two-thirds place strategic planning high on the management agenda.
- Strategic planning offers several important benefits:
  - **Focus**—Planning keeps the firm aligned with and focused on its organizational vision. A carefully conceived plan translates the vision into a clear road map so that everyone knows where the firm is going and how it intends to get there.
  - **Discipline**—Engaging in a strategic planning process forces leadership to put aside day-to-day management and client responsibilities, take stock of the market and their businesses, and reevaluate and refresh firm direction.
  - **Motivation**—Planning is a tool to stimulate collaboration, rally the troops, and create a sense of renewal and mission around firm goals.
- Successful planning processes have five common characteristics:
  1. Integrate long-term strategic planning with annual plans.
  2. View strategic planning as a continuous cycle, not a one-time event.
  3. Incorporate external as well as internal analyses into strategic planning.
  4. To ensure buy-in, collaborate with stakeholders to develop plans.
  5. Communicate constantly, and regularly review progress against goals.
- The planning process unfolds in four broad stages, progressing from long-term planning exercises to annual execution initiatives and continuing with ongoing reviewing, monitoring, and updating (see Exhibit 9.4).

10

Structure

Design, governance, and style

"No matter which structure you land on, it's always the clarity of definition around roles and responsibilities—and communication, communication, communication—that will determine the success of your matrix model."
— Phil Rohrbaugh, Vice Chair of the U.S. firm and
Managing Partner of the Chicago office, KPMG

"You need to have a governance system in which the authority and the responsibility to make certain decisions is assigned to a set group of people so the aircraft carrier of a law firm can navigate the seas."
— Ralph Baxter, Chairman and CEO, Orrick

"We really hate bureaucracy. That is why we are pretty flat and there is not a lot of politics happening here."
— Donna Imperato, President and CEO, Cohn & Wolfe

The choice of organizational structure and governance model has critical implications for professional service firms. Together they form a firm's internal architecture—the invisible scaffolding that supports everything, from day-to-day operations to strategic planning and effective execution. The structure delineates the organizational layers and management reporting hierarchies within the firm. Governance is the leadership style—collaborative, dictatorial, or corporate—and the policies, systems, and procedures that underpin the enterprise. Organization design choices can reinforce or undermine culture, endanger or enhance performance and service quality, and enable or diminish profitability.

Talking about organizational charts, management layers, policies and procedures—the nuts and bolts of how a firm organizes to conduct business and make decisions—wasn't a particularly passionate topic for our interviewees. Organization structure and governance ranked lowest on the leadership agenda. However, it still was very much on the list of priorities, with 62 percent of the interviewees giving it top marks, as shown in Exhibit 10.1.

EXHIBIT 10.1   Infrastructure and governance ranked last in order of importance

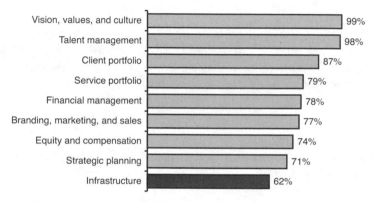

Firm leaders agreed that, although not as sexy as values or culture, decisions related to structure and governance are a vital component to success and long-term viability and an essential piece of the management mosaic. In fact, interviewees rated their performance fairly high in this area, with 73 percent giving themselves good or excellent reviews for having an effective organizational structure and governance model, as shown in Exhibit 10.2.

EXHIBIT 10.2   Three-quarters believe they do a good job managing infrastructure

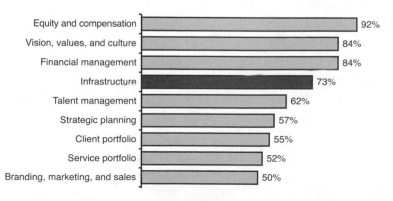

Why Getting It Right Is So Challenging

"The challenge is how to find the right structure to make sure that you execute effectively on your strategy."

"I don't think a year passes that we don't make some changes to the organizational model to better address the complex needs and dynamic nature of the firm."

"One of the problems with scale is that unmanaged autonomy can be catastrophic."

In traditional command-and-control environments, the distinction between leaders and followers is clearly defined, and hierarchical decision making predominates. The opposite is true in a partner/owner enterprise, where the prevailing model is a network of peers, and major decisions must always involve a high degree of consensus. Professionals need and demand generous doses of freedom and flexibility in practicing their skills and serving clients. If they believe their firm's structure and/or governance approach undermine rather than support their independence, even the most disciplined and loyal of professionals is likely to ignore or bypass them.

Like traditional corporations, professional service firms need an effective structure to support and coordinate the business of serving clients in a profitable manner. For firm leaders, the toughest challenge is crafting an organizational model that gives professionals independence to operate creatively within a stable, efficient infrastructure. Many firms find that there is a fine line between too much freedom and too much bureaucracy.

To further complicate the decision process, there is no one-size-fits-all approach to structuring a professional service business. Just as there is no ideal strategy or execution model, there is no perfect organizational structure. The real key is alignment with a firm's values, culture, and strategic direction. As one firm leader noted, "I think that the vision, the values, and the culture drive the organization more than its structure. You can succeed with multiple variations of infrastructure and governance."

Organization design is not a rigid process, but an evolutionary one. Structures must evolve over time to adapt to changes in firm direction and growth. Many of the firms that participated in the study have changed structures several times during the course of their life cycle. Firm leaders agree that structure is a useful lever to employ to keep the business running smoothly and to stimulate growth and change the firm's direction. However, adeptly managing the structure lever is an art in itself.

Seven Essentials for a Successful Infrastructure and Governance Model

"I really believe if you want to improve an organization, you need to change it. An organization that is going to be sustaining and is going to succeed in the long run is an organization that's able to adapt to the constant flux and the constant change that the environment creates."

When it comes to operating efficiently and having a well-oiled governance mechanism in place for top-level decision making, the best-run firms share seven defining characteristics. Specifically, these high-performing enterprises do the following:

1. *Embrace a one-firm concept.* Successful firms strive to cultivate a one-firm mind-set by developing organization structures that foster a collaborative, rather than siloed, operating environment. While aggressively pursuing global expansion via organic growth and/or acquisitions, they work hard to ensure that increased scale does not erode their one-firm spirit of collegiality and service.

2. *Operate transparently.* Closed-door decision making by a single leader or small leadership cadre is not a recipe for success in a consensus-driven culture. For the partner/owner model to work, everyone must feel that they've been heard and have participated in debating and resolving key issues. At the very least, they must completely understand and approve of the decision-making process. The most effective leaders are those who provide both access and action. They are adept at walking the line between ensuring that professionals feel they have a participative role in setting a firm's direction and making the hard choices required to move forward.

3. *Train professionals in business skills.* Star performers rise to the top of their firms based on their professional acumen, not their business skills. As a result, the fundamentals of running a business efficiently and profitably are often well outside their knowledge base. And yet, as firms grow larger and more complex, a blend of professional expertise and business savvy is becoming essential. PSFs operate most effectively when they can tap into a strong team of professionals who are proven client relationship builders with a strong grasp of business practices and bottom-line realities. More and more firms are seeing the benefits of adding executive skills to their professional development mix. Increasingly, firms are providing MBA-type

training to senior professionals to better prepare them for the multi-faceted responsibilities they face as they rise to leadership positions.

4. *Use professional nonbillable support teams.* Although they want professionals to be exposed to business basics, successful service firms stick to their knitting. When it comes to managing operations, they hire sophisticated administrative executives and give them wide latitude within their areas of responsibility. Over the years, noncore functions—finance, marketing, information services, and human resources—have grown increasingly professionalized. Across all industry segments, professional service businesses are cautiously adding new slots to their organization charts by bringing onboard COOs, CFOs, CMOs, CIOs, and CHROs. As firms seek to build strong administrative teams, many are acknowledging the importance of these roles by putting the executives who hold these positions on their management committees.

5. *Emphasize process efficiency.* The best-run firms strive to ensure that their revenue-producing professionals focus the lion's share of their time and talent on client work and relationship building. These firms invest substantially in systems and support mechanisms to boost internal efficiency and speed service delivery. To streamline their operations, they take aggressive advantage of technology to build cost-effective back-office operations. To enhance efficiency and reduce costs, leading-edge firms are using global integration tools employed by traditional multinationals, from shared services to outsourcing and offshoring (see "Clifford Chance Offshoring Program").

6. *Clearly define roles and responsibilities, policies and procedures.* Reporting relationships can be particularly confusing in a multi-service, multiproject professional service firm. At any given point in time, professionals—even senior partners—report to multiple people and have multiple people reporting to them. The lines of who is doing what and for whom are often blurred and change regularly as client projects come and go. The best-run firms map roles with care so that whatever hat or hats a professional is wearing—engagement manager, business unit leader, practice group head, trainer, or mentor—the responsibilities are well defined. Performance against expectations are monitored and measured to determine progression in the firm as well as annual compensation.

In addition to defining roles, the day-to-day business of running the firm is well established and documented. Policies and guidelines from quality assurance to client and engagement management standards, performance reviews and reporting, and billing

Clifford Chance Offshoring Program

With 3,600 lawyers in 29 offices across 20 countries, Clifford Chance is one of the world's leading law firms. In 2006, the firm began to explore the pros and cons of centralizing and offshoring some of its business services. According to David Childs, Global Managing Partner, the shared service concept provided an attractive opportunity to reduce costs, improve efficiency, and standardize service quality and consistency.

The firm established its Shared Services Center outside New Delhi in 2007. The Center's 300-plus people manage about 10 percent of the firm's business service functions including human resources, finance, IT, business development, and administration. In addition, the firm established a separate program called Knowledge Center India, which engages in paralegal-level activities such as research, due diligence, and document drafting for Clifford Chance offices. Amanda Burton, Chief Operating Officer, who led the development of the Center and now oversees its operations, offers the following advice to firms considering an offshoring option:

- *Do what's right for your firm.* Given the investment involved, scale is key to making this option work. It's important to weigh offshore pros and cons carefully in light of your firm's size, growth strategy, and centralizing capabilities.

- *Investigate other industries.* Look beyond your own industry to identify innovative approaches and new ideas. When the firm began to explore offshoring, Burton talked to many clients in financial services, who offered valuable do's and don'ts—and also reaffirmed their own decisions to pursue this option.

- *Choose the right location.* Clifford Chance selected New Delhi for several reasons: English language capability, a strong talent base which included several good law schools, 24/7 coverage, and cost.

- *Treat offshoring as a major project.* If you pursue an offshore strategy, have a strong business case, project plan, and launch, timetable to roll out, and the people capable of delivering the desired results: The firm imported a Clifford Chance lawyer to set up the Knowledge Center and sends an attorney every 6 months to train and oversee the paralegal team. "Offshoring is a big commitment," says Burton. "People worry about their jobs and how shifting administrative and/or knowledge-based activities offshore

> will affect their ability to function effectively. Don't underestimate the importance of change management."
>
> - *Invest in cultural training.* This is especially critical if you plan to locate your offshore program in a country that you don't currently operate in. It can help you hit the ground running and attract the talent that will best serve your needs.
>
> While the investment in time and energy in setting up its offshore shared services program has been substantial, the savings that Clifford Chance has begun to reap have proven impressive. The firm now has one team performing a range of business functions versus 29 teams in 29 offices, and the project is on track on its business case goal to deliver 8 million pounds in annual savings. As Childs sums up, "By reaching out to clients for advice, building a strong business case, committing to change management, and investing in cultural training, the firm mitigated the risks involved and set the stage for greater operational efficiency."

and collection processes are clearly defined for all levels of professionals.

7. *Adapt structure and governance when appropriate.* PSFs are fluid organizations operating in fluid environments. The best firms keep an eye on their structures and governance models and periodically review their effectiveness. Whether it's a tweak or a major change, firms remain agile and adapt as necessary.

Organizational Structure: The Scaffolding That Supports the Firm

"In a professional service firm, a conventional linear diagram doesn't really represent power or the reality of how organizations work. People-based organizations have a delicate balance of responsibility and commitment."

"We value being as flat as possible. The premise is we believe the best decisions can be made as close to the client as possible."

While many variations emerged, the organization charts of the firms surveyed proved to be remarkably similar in their basic configuration, as shown in Exhibit 10.3.

EXHIBIT 10.3   Common elements in a PSF organization chart

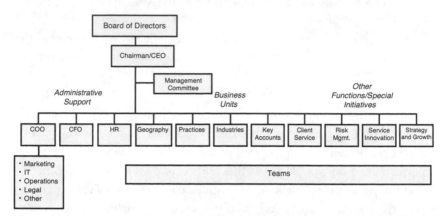

At the upper layer of the chart is the firm's top leadership team, often consisting of one or two oversight groups: a board of directors and/or a management committee, and a chairman and/or CEO. Directly below this level is a second layer that includes the leaders of various business units, typically heads of regions, practices or industries depending on how the firm is organized; the heads of key administrative support functions; and senior professionals who manage special functions and high-profile initiatives of importance to the firm. Underpinning the entire organization is a fluid network of cross-functional, often cross-border teams that are attached to clients, services, and geographies, and a host of specialized activities such as intellectual capital development, training, and growth initiatives.

Variations on structure are driven primarily by differences in size, geographic reach, practice diversity, and culture. We found an overwhelming preference among the best-run firms interviewed for lean organizational structures that keep both hierarchical reporting and bureaucracy to a minimum. The following sections describe each organizational layer in a typical PSF structure.

Board of Directors: Composition and Selection

"We've got a number of categories for board members. We're looking for practice mix: gender, age, and, really, any other unique attributes that appropriately represent the full partnership."

"Our board is elected by the firm, and their allegiance is to the firm as a whole, not to their narrow section of interest."

As shown in Exhibit 10.4, nearly three-quarters (73 percent) of the firms studied indicated that they have a board of directors in addition to a management committee.

EXHIBIT 10.4   Most firms have a board of directors

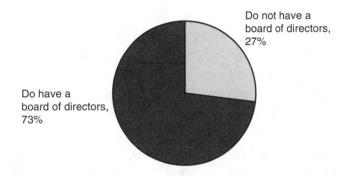

Do not have a board of directors, 27%

Do have a board of directors, 73%

Typically, a board of directors is not involved in day-to-day decision making or firm operations. Instead, most frequently, the board provides corporate governance oversight, monitors shareholder value concerns, and provides impact analysis and final approval of top-level strategic decisions and investments. Some CEOs and management committees use board members as sounding boards. In this consultative capacity, board members help the CEO think through ideas, assess marketplace threats and opportunities, and arrive at decisions concerning long-term vision and strategic direction.

Most boards have standing subcommittees. A nominating committee, for example, may be charged with overseeing succession planning and identifying people for key roles. Other common standing groups include a compensation committee, which monitors partner revenue distribution, and an admissions committee, which oversees the promotion of new partners. Board members may also serve on ad hoc committees created to investigate special projects or urgent issues. Typically such ad hoc groups consist of selected board members and partners at large with expertise in the area being addressed.

In the vast majority of privately held firms, the board of directors is composed of senior partners. Typically, board membership mirrors a firm's broad demographics and includes a mix of professionals representative of the firm's practice areas, geographic footprint, and, in some cases (although not many), age and gender. In some firms, key functional positions may also be represented on the board. For example, to ensure that its board reflects a diversity of backgrounds and viewpoints, Smith-Group has adopted a 9/9 board structure, with nine members who represent practices and disciplines and nine management executives focused on business and operations.

Boards vary dramatically in size, with smaller firms having as few as 5 to 10 members and larger firms typically 15 to 20. McKinsey is run by a board of members who serve 3-year terms and act as the firm's ultimate policy makers. These board members are distributed among four permanent committees that handle all major decisions related to their area of expertise: a client committee, a people committee, a knowledge committee, and a finance committee.

A few privately held firms have appointed outside directors, but this is rare. Dewberry, for instance, is a family business and balances the family members on its board with an equal number of outside directors. Gensler's ten-member board consists of the firm's founder, practicing partners, and an outside board member—a strategist who offers expert counsel on key issues. DLA Piper has a global board consisting of members drawn in equal numbers from its U.S. and non-U.S. operations, along with two independent outside directors.

As required by federal regulatory agencies or dictated by investors, firms that are either public companies or partially owned by third-party investors have boards that include outside members—much like that of a public company. For Booz Allen Hamilton, which is partially owned by the Carlyle Group, Ralph Shrader, the firm's CEO, serves as chairman of a board that consists of two of the firm's senior partners, three senior executives from Carlyle, and two outside directors.

The majority of firms (69 percent) elect their board members, as shown in Exhibit 10.5. Most members serve for a predetermined period, typically 2 to 3 years, and are eligible for election to a second term. Elections typically are staggered so that no more than one-third of board members are replaced in any given year.

EXHIBIT 10.5   Most firms elect rather than appoint board members

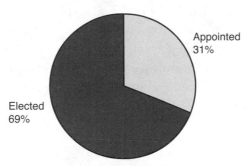

Nominating policies differ widely. In many firms, any full-equity part-ner can run for the board of directors. In some firms, any partner can sim-ply throw his or her hat in the ring. In still others, a candidate must be nominated by another partner. When it comes to electing members, gen-erally every partner has an equal vote, and the majority rules. In some firms, however, more experienced partners have accumulated more units of partnership and therefore have more votes. In firms where board mem-bers are appointed, new members may be chosen by the CEO with input from others on the board, or a slate of potential candidates may be nomi-nated by the board chair and then voted on by the board.

Chairman: Selection and Role

Overall, the position of chairman wins mixed reviews across the indus-try. Among the firms in our survey, 52 percent indicated that they did not have both a chairman and a CEO, and 48 percent said they did, as shown in Exhibit 10.6.

EXHIBIT 10.6   About half the firms surveyed have both a chairman and CEO role

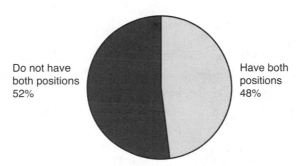

In firms that have both a chairman and a CEO, 64 percent elect the chairman, as shown in Exhibit 10.7. The scope of the chairman's role varies widely, but typically it does not involve oversight of day-to-day operations. In isolated cases, this position is purely that of a figurehead. More often, however, the chairman primarily performs one of two functions: serving as guardian of the firm's vision and values, or acting as the firm's ambassador—the face of the firm to major clients and the public.

EXHIBIT 10.7   Most firms elect the chairman

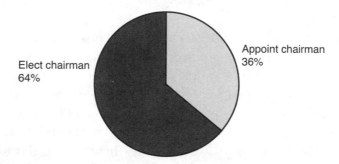

Elect chairman
64%

Appoint chairman
36%

In the guardian role, the chairman's chief function is to ensure that a firm is staying on track in its progress toward attaining its long-term strategic goals. Some chairmen see this role in broad brushstrokes: building a great company, maintaining the integrity of the firm's vision, and nurturing its culture. In an ambassadorial role, a chairman generally plays a more active part in helping orchestrate the firm's long-term growth and profitability by offering advisory input on engagements, mobilizing contacts, and identifying promising strategic initiatives. Some chairmen who serve as the public face of their firm may also interact with major clients, represent their firms at high-level industry forums, and be involved in business development.

CEO: Selection, Role, and Succession

In contrast to the big-picture, hands-off role of the chairman, the CEO is charged with the day-to-day, year-to-year responsibilities of running the organization. The flat, lean organization structures of most PSFs mean that the CEO often has an amazing number of direct reports. This pulls the CEO into all areas of the business, from operations, finance, marketing, and human resources to business unit management and frontline client work. It is, as discussed in Chapter 11, "Style of Leadership," a very demanding job.

Selection

The process of selecting the firm's CEO varies dramatically across firms—ranging from informal to elaborate nominating and vetting procedures. Overall, the approaches to candidate identification and selection fall into three broad categories:

- *The current leader selects a successor.* In this selection model, the current leader chooses the new head of the firm. Many of the interviewees said that an important part of their job as the senior leader in the firm is to ensure that their organization has a legitimate candidate or candidates who could potentially succeed them. Most say that their choices are not handpicked exclusively by them, but are individuals who have demonstrated skills, experiences, and the aptitude to continue to learn, grow, and develop. It is the leader's responsibility to make sure that these individuals get the right kind of experience so they can eventually take the helm. Even in firms where the leader chooses a successor, the partnership always has a say in the decision.

- *A hybrid selection/election process.* In the hybrid model, the outgoing leader and the management team (or board) appoint the new CEO after input from the firm's partners. This input process can be extensive and time-consuming in a professional service partnership environment where everyone has a voice and collaboration is key. In some firms, partners ultimately vote on a slate of nominees, and in others the board makes the final decision (see "Election Process at Skadden, Arps").

- *The partners elect.* In some firms, leadership selection resembles a presidential election. The multistep election process starts with a solicitation of nominations from all firm partners. The firm leadership committee selects the top group of candidates—typically around ten—who must present position papers that are distributed to all partners. The partners then cast another vote, and the list is narrowed to the top two candidates. These candidates must publicly debate the issues before the partners. The partnership then casts a final vote, and the candidate with the most votes is elected.

Election Process at Skadden, Arps

In 2009, law firm Skadden, Arps selected its third Executive Partner in the firm's 61-year history. Executive Partner Eric Friedman reports that the firm was proud of the "open and transparent" selection process it completed. Friedman's predecessor, Bob Sheehan, who was finishing a third 5-year term, initiated the selection process 2 years earlier when he told the Policy Committee that it needed to identify a successor.

The Policy Committee appointed a Succession Committee, made up of nine partners from around the firm. Led by Mike Rogan, cohead of the firm's Global Transaction Practice, the Succession Committee included partners from Skadden's major practices and geographic regions. The committee developed a questionnaire that was sent to all partners, asking them to discuss any concerns they had about the firm, their vision for the future, the characteristics they would like to see in a new Executive Partner, and any suggested changes to the management structure, such as whether the firm should have comanaging partners. In an initial "first pass" to gauge sentiment, the partners were asked to submit suggestions on whom they might recommend for the position.

The Succession Committee reviewed the feedback and then fanned out across the firm to meet one on one with each of Skadden's then-450 partners to gather opinions and recommendations. The committee developed an initial list of 19 candidates. It was reduced to five based on a synthesis of the information derived from the meetings with partners and another review of the responses to the questionnaires. The five top candidates were asked to submit in writing their vision and goals for the firm and answer questions such as "Why are you the right person for the position?", "How do you see this role?", and "What major challenges does the firm face?" Each candidate was interviewed by the Succession Committee over a 2-day period.

The committee agreed on one candidate to recommend to the Policy Committee, which unanimously approved his recommendation. Then they submitted the nominee to the partnership for a confidential electronic vote. Under firm governance provisions, the partnership was required to vote by secret ballot to be tabulated by an independent third party. The candidate, Eric Friedman, was elected as the firm's next Executive Partner in May 2008 and formally assumed the role in April 2009. The entire process took less than four months.

Friedman says, "In retrospect, the selection process was especially useful to me because it provided the opportunity to think about how the firm needed to position itself in a more competitive legal environment. My partners have been extremely supportive as we work to reinforce our position as the premier law firm providing services to major corporations and financial institutions on their most difficult financial and governance issues. Also, the transition itself was very smooth. We gradually morphed over a 12-month period from Bob, to Bob and Eric, to Eric."

Friedman notes that the move from leading day-to-day client engagements to a more strategic client advisory role required a significant adjustment in how he ran his practice. "Bottom line, the transition afforded everyone—myself, my clients, and my partners—an opportunity to recalibrate how it might work going forward."

Term Limits for the CEO

"I think that changing the leadership is just a way of sort of shaking the carpet out in the wind and getting it nice and fresh as you bring it back in."

Term limits for the CEO/managing partner position proved to be a lightning-rod issue that provoked lively discussion. As with the to-bill-or-not-to-bill question discussed in Chapter 11, most leaders fell firmly into one of two camps. Either they felt strongly that changing leaders on a regular basis helps keep a firm fresh and attuned to markets needs, or they believed that frequent leadership changes disrupt operations and can endanger a firm's brand or credibility in the marketplace.

One of the main arguments in favor of term limits is that operating within an established time frame pushes a CEO to aspire to a higher level of performance. "I actually think the 4-year term is a good thing," observed Jerry Leamon, Global Managing Partner, Services, Deloitte Touche Tohmatsu Limited. "You get people coming in who have huge ambitions about what they want to accomplish, and they do extraordinary things to get it all done during their tenure."

Despite the intensity of views pro and con on this issue, the majority of firms have chosen to give their leaders open-ended mandates. In fact, four out of five of the firms surveyed do not impose term limits on their CEO/managing partner, as shown in Exhibit 10.8.

EXHIBIT 10.8   Most place no term limits on CEOs

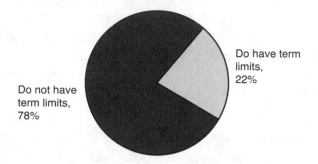

Succession Planning

"I think organizations are making a big mistake if they rely on just, 'Oh, the next leader will come.'"

"There's no succession planning because anybody can be nominated. We have a very open and free process for leadership. It should be a distributed leadership model, not a tight sort of hierarchical management model."

Given the rich crop of potential leaders, how do professional service firms choose one for the top slot? Our interviews revealed the surprising finding that many firms have no succession plan or process in place. Of the firms that said they do have a plan, a significant number outlined what could more accurately be called an approach. Overall, only 54 percent of our interviewees say their firms have a program in place to identify future leaders, as shown in Exhibit 10.9.

EXHIBIT 10.9   Slightly more than half have a succession plan

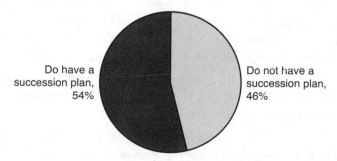

Among the 46 percent who said they have no succession plan, the reasons given varied. Some interviewees say that succession planning is culturally inappropriate for their organization. As one former CEO said, "We have an abundance of very smart people who are capable of running this organization. Leaders rise to the top on their own." For this firm and for several others in our study, firm leaders emerge naturally and are chosen through a general election process when needed. Others noted that they are still too new or too small to require a formal plan. Quite a few others expressed concern about their lack of a planning process and are debating how to develop a program.

For the firms that do have some form of plan, the degree of structure and formality varied widely. Several firms have nominating committees in place that are responsible for formal succession planning for all key roles—looking at the next generation of leaders and maintaining a short list of potential candidates.

Some firms have a leadership development group that identifies and grooms professionals for all the firm's top leadership positions across regions, practices, and industries. Each firm leader is required to look several layers down into the organization to identify candidates for his or her role and for the subroles in his or her area of responsibility. As one partner explained, "Every year I am required to identify or reconfirm my successor and answer a few basic questions: Are they ready now? If not, when, and what skills do they need to get there?"

For other firms, thoughts about the successor to the firm leader are just that—thoughts with little solid action. Plans for replacing the leader are ignited only when the current leader announces his or her plan to retire or step down.

Management Committee: Composition and Selection

In most professional service firms, the management committee—also called the operations, executive, or policy committee—is responsible for overseeing day-to-day operations and working with the CEO to manage the business and monitor financial performance.

Executives who report directly to the CEO usually comprise the management committee. Depending on how a firm configures its management committee, members may include the leaders of business units, the heads of key administrative functions, and senior professionals overseeing special projects or initiatives. Many firms have designated committee slots for these positions in the organization structure, and professionals automatically become committee members when they are appointed to those roles. Depending on firm size, these committees typically have from 5 to 12 members, with some committees having as many as 20 to 30, although this is unusual. Most committee members do not have term limits; they continue to serve as members of the committee as long as they retain their role in the firm's leadership structure. Overwhelmingly, these committee members are appointed rather than elected, as shown in Exhibit 10.10.

EXHIBIT 10.10   Most firms appoint rather than elect management committees

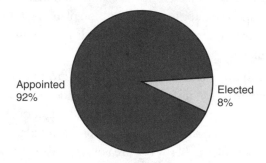

Appointed
92%

Elected
8%

Business Units: Structure and Seat of Power

"The optimal organization has a balance between geographies, functions or practices, and industries."

"I think what you need is a tension in the matrix. If you drive it down one dimension in the matrix at the expense of all the others, you suboptimize somewhere else."

Business units in professional service firms are organized across two, three, and sometimes four dimensions—regions/offices, practices/service lines, industries, and, in the case of advertising and public relations firms, key accounts. This complex matrix organizational model with its multiple cross-organizational reporting requirements is routinely panned by most business gurus and has been proven to be notoriously difficult to manage. Why, then, do PSFs tenaciously embrace this model, and why does it seem to work so well in the professional service industry? There are several reasons why a matrix structure is well suited for PSFs:

- *It supports a consensus culture.* As a network of peers, a professional service firm can thrive only if it fosters a consensus-driven environment. The matrix model provides multiple leadership opportunities for senior professionals to play an active participatory role in firm management.

- *It provides maximum flexibility.* PSFs are fluid organizations. In serving clients, professionals operate in multiple teams, practices, and geographies. A matrix structure offers the flexibility needed to run a multiclient, multiproject-driven business. It also enables firms to optimize and share talent and resources across geographies, functions, and clients.

- *It accommodates growth.* Even the smallest PSFs offer multiple skills and service capabilities. As firms grow, they tend to bring in more specialized professionals to expand service offerings and move into new geographic regions. Eventually, they channel their growth by breaking their organization into more manageable units. Well suited to facilitating expansion, the matrix model allows firms to retain the lean, flat operating structure that best supports a consensus culture.

Inevitably, as a firm grows, one dimension of the matrix model predominates. It becomes the seat of power that controls the business unit P&L and drives planning, performance, reviews, and compensation decisions. Which dimension of the business units becomes the dominant driver in a firm depends on a complex interplay of factors: culture, markets, client needs, and geographic reach. Structuring internally by either practice area or geographic region are the two approaches that most firms opt for as their enterprises expand. For the firms studied, geography was the dominant driver, followed by practice/service lines, as shown in Exhibit 10.11.

EXHIBIT 10.11 Geographies and services are primary seats of power in most firms

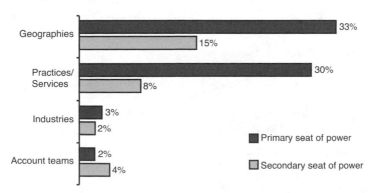

Geographies — 33%, 15%
Practices/Services — 30%, 8%
Industries — 3%, 2%
Account teams — 2%, 4%

■ Primary seat of power
☐ Secondary seat of power

The business unit organizational map in a firm where geography dominates looks different from that of a practice-driven firm, as shown in Exhibit 10.12. But the same matrix principle of multiple reporting relationship and cross-functional teaming applies.

EXHIBIT 10.12   Business unit structures

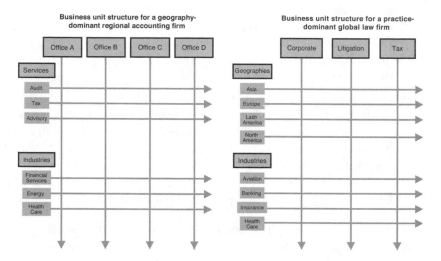

Distinct advantages and disadvantages are inherent in each organizational choice. Organizing by geography tends to result in a stronger, tighter operating model, whereas organizing by industry tends to result in more robust go-to-market capabilities. In general, using practice/service lines as a firm's dominant organizing vehicle leads to more consistent execution.

Historically, geographies have tended to be the dominant seat of power for many firms. However, as many people have experienced, this model can all too easily promote competition rather than collaboration, which can result in damaging bottlenecks and fiefdoms to the detriment of the organization as a whole. One firm's performance, for example, was dangerously compromised, according to a senior executive, because its regions were "absolutely Napoleonic" in their single-minded focus on serving only their own geographies.

As firms grow more global, the practice/service model is likely to become more dominant. Increasingly, firms are gravitating toward this approach because they find that practices are the most efficient organizing vehicle for building an operating system that can deliver client value on an integrated global basis. A practice-driven infrastructure facilitates cross-border team building, knowledge management, and resource deployment. It also enables firms of varying sizes to fully leverage the matrix model and its network of professionals so that they can deliver just-in-time expertise anywhere in the world. Many firm leaders contend that having practice groups predominate is essential for successful global integration.

When it comes to creating a high-performance operating model, whether it is driven primarily by industry, service line, or geography, the secret to success is striking the right balance among dimensions so that while one predominates, the others remain robust and well tended. If a firm pushes too hard in one direction at the expense of the others, it risks suboptimal performance. Creating tension in the matrix—just the right amount of push and pull among the units—is critical to keeping the model dynamic and effective.

Other Functions/Special Initiatives

Many firms identify areas of focus that they believe are important enough to warrant an elevated spot on their organization chart and a seat at the management committee table. These can be areas that a leadership team views as vital to preserving firm culture or critical to the management of their business. Client service, quality control, innovation, thought leadership, talent development, and risk management are all examples of issues that have a huge impact on growth and profitability and that may be accorded special attention. Several of the largest firms included in our study have added a new global integration role to their leadership ranks with the mandate to consolidate multiple geographies into fewer, more unified units.

Administrative Support

"You simply can't do this job well without a good COO."

"You can mitigate a lot of headaches by having strong leadership on the administrative side."

For many professional service firms, the administrative side of their organization chart continues to evolve. Many firm leaders expressed an interest in upgrading the sophistication and performance levels of their support infrastructures. At the same time, there is a persistent reluctance to invest substantially in upgrading the nonrevenue-producing side of the house.

This hesitancy is rooted in several concerns. First, star performers tend to believe that they can do it all—including mastering and running the business aspect of their firms. Second, many enterprises are justifiably concerned about the cost of bringing onboard high-level executives who are not revenue producers. Small and midsize firms are especially sensitive to the revenue impact of nonbillable support positions. Finally, there is a well-founded fear that business management executives recruited from the corporate world may be unable to function optimally in a nontraditional matrix environment. War stories abound of senior people recruited from outside the industry who quickly became frustrated with the consensus culture and bolted.

Despite these caveats, nonbillable executives are on the rise. Although administrative responsibilities vary from segment to segment and firm to firm, this side of the organization chart has some consistency. In general, the top spots—those who have a seat at the management committee table—tend to include the COO (if the firm has one), the CFO, and the CHRO. Nearly half of our respondents have a COO role, and virtually all have a CFO, although this position varies dramatically from a pure financial controller to a respected partner-level executive.

The COO role is evolving across the professional service industry. Many firms are finding that a strong COO can have a transformative effect on operations, improving efficiency by effectively deploying and managing resources and technology. Having a trusted executive manage the administrative functions and operating issues reduces the CEO's number of direct reports and allows him or her to pay more attention to strategy and market-facing issues. In fact, some CEOs today insist on having a strong COO onboard as a precondition of their service.

Changing the Structure

At critical junctures in their growth, firms find themselves facing internal and/or external pressures to change the organizational structure or governance policies and procedures. In some cases, rapid expansion forces them to break into smaller units; in others, evolving client needs drive a shift in focus and operating structure. Whatever the trigger, at some point in time, firms find that their organization structure is becoming an impediment rather than an asset to the organization. When this occurs, successful enterprises regroup, take stock, and reconfigure.

Several common signs indicate that it may be time to reevaluate the structure and governance model:

- *Clients start complaining*. When clients become concerned about the quality and consistency of the work across geographies, or are frustrated with the complexity of the firm's hierarchy and siloed practice areas, it's time to change.

- *Partners don't know each other anymore*. Size is the major factor that drives change to structure and governance. Up to a certain size, the firm can rely on the fact that everyone knows each other and works well together. At some point the firm becomes too large to work effectively as a single unit.

- *It takes too long to make important decisions*. This is a sign that either the wrong leaders are in place or the structure or operating procedures are getting in the way.

- *Communication among the partners seems to go awry too frequently*. A sense that communication isn't working well often happens as organizations grow geographically. Old ways of communicating don't work in an increasingly dispersed environment.

- *Professionals regularly don't follow the rules*. Professionals like to do things their own way. However, when both the professional and the support team consistently refuse to conform to the operating policies and procedures, it is time to regroup. Instead of trying to force everyone to take certain paths, as set forth in the "rule book," maybe the rules need to change to conform to how people work, communicate, and get things done.

- *Some start to feel like second-class citizens*. A them-versus-us scenario can develop as a firm adds new geographic locations, often called satellite offices. It becomes harder to retain talent as professionals become disenfranchised and feel like they are on the outskirts.

Governance Style

"Our partners generally accept that management must be allowed to manage—as long as they have a fair opportunity to have their voices heard."

In the professional service industry, governance style ranges from monarch-like dictatorial decision making to a totally inclusive emphasis on consensus building and partner involvement (see Exhibit 10.13).

EXHIBIT 10.13   Governance style ranges from dictatorship to total consensus

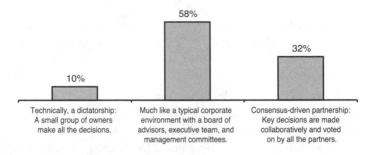

As partnerships by their very nature, PSFs require some degree of consensus on key governance issues. Nearly a third (32 percent) of the firms surveyed placed themselves in the high range of our scale in terms of their consensus-driven governance style. Another 58 percent claim they are somewhere in the middle, and a minority (10 percent), typically smaller firms with the original founders in place, keep the decision-making reins tightly controlled by a small leadership team. One firm leader in this category saw himself as a "benevolent dictator."

Although they are committed to navigating between consensus and decision, a number of leaders interviewed stressed that a collaborative firm isn't the same as a democratic one. The governance style that most firms embrace involves a leadership team that operates fairly autonomously in a number of key areas while remaining participative and transparent enough to keep partners engaged and supportive. Clearly, operating with a relatively pure consensus model is easier in a smaller firm. As firms scale up, gaining agreement around key decisions becomes far more challenging. In the largest high-performance firms, the partnership as a whole rarely or only selectively votes on issues. Partner vote-worthy matters generally include electing a new partner slate, partner expulsion, and/or opening new offices. In larger firms, maintaining a governance style firmly rooted in consensus decision making requires constant work and an enormous amount of communication with partners (see "A.T. Kearney Revamps Structure and Governance").

A.T. Kearney Revamps Structure and Governance

In 1996, the partners of management consulting firm A.T. Kearney voted to sell their firm to global business and technology services company, EDS, and become an operating division of the publically traded organization. Ten years later, the partners negotiated a management buyout to repurchase the firm and, in 2006, A.T. Kearney became what Managing Officer and Chairman of the Board Paul Laudicina calls "an 80-year-old start-up." The 170 partners that participated in the MBO essentially had the opportunity to recreate the firm. "We had a young group of aggressive, ambitious partners all anxious to roll up their sleeves and make a success of this new firm that they owned," says Laudicina.

A team of partners was selected to negotiate the terms of the buyback and prepare for a "constitutional convention" held in Atlanta, Georgia, to align the partnership around key governance, ownership, and structural issues that would become part of the new shareholders' agreement and Articles of Association. "It was all about entrepreneurship, accountability, and responsibility," says Laudicina. "Ten years of public company corporate mentality had created an employee–employer mentality, and we needed to return to an owner–partner psychology and ethos." Specific decisions included:

- **Ownership and equity**—The firm became a privately held corporation. Each new officer is required to make an investment to become a shareholding partner. Shares are bought based on the book value determined annually by the board, and shares must be sold when partners leave the firm. Partner compensation is performance-driven and based on quantitative and qualitative metrics.

- **Governance**—There was a strong bias post-MBO that the firm have a very open and free process for leadership. "There was a sense that the leadership of the organization should be a broad, diverse group of partners," notes Laudicina. "We wanted a transparent, distributed leadership model, not a tight hierarchical management model. The partners agreed to a one-partner, one-vote system, with a partnership elected Board of Directors and Managing Officer who serve a maximum of two consecutive 3-year terms if reelected. The board and managing officer positions are elected though an open nominating process, and every voting partner is an eligible nominee. Nominees are required to post position papers on their platform that are reviewed by the partners; whoever receives the highest number of votes is elected to the position.

- **Structure**—Laudicina formed a senior leadership team consisting of himself, the Chief Operating Officer, the regional leaders and administrative heads—CFO, CHRO, General Counsel, and the Chief Communications Director—all of whom had to be newly hired and their departments reestablished post the separation. Like most PSFs, the firm operates in a matrix structure with geographic units, ten industries, and eleven service practices. Unit leaders report to the COO and are appointed by the Managing Officer after input from partners. Immediately post-MBO, most of the leadership authority within the firm, along with P&L responsibility, were endowed in the geographies. "We needed to jumpstart the new organization quickly and establish cohesiveness with clear lines of authority without ambiguity among the local partners," says Laudicina. "However, the firm is determined to create a more balanced distribution of power and is moving in that direction."

The firm has tried to incorporate lessons learned from the EDS corporate experience, particularly the value of clearly established processes. "A very rigorous and strong central series of process capabilities supports and ensures key initiatives such as the integrity of the code of conduct, the uniformity of training and human resource policies, consistency around brand development and projection, and financial stability," says Laudicina. "The challenge is maintaining disciplined processes within an entrepreneurial partnership structure—if you can balance the two, you've got the best of both worlds."

CHAPTER SUMMARY

Structure

- There is widespread agreement that a firm's infrastructure and governance model has a major impact on its overall performance, service delivery, and strategic execution. The key is to align structure with strategy and culture.

- Choosing the right operating structure for the firm presents three major challenges:
    1. Finding the right balance between freedom and bureaucracy is difficult.
    2. There is no ideal "one-size-fits-all" model.
    3. Structures must continually evolve to adapt to changes in firm growth and direction.

- The best-run firms share seven defining characteristics. These enterprises do the following:
    1. Embrace a one firm mind-set.
    2. Operate transparently.
    3. Train professionals in business skills.
    4. Use professional nonbillable support teams.
    5. Emphasize process efficiency.
    6. Clearly define roles and responsibilities, policies and procedures.
    7. Adapt structure and governance when appropriate.

- Governance styles range from dictatorial to consensus-driven, with most well-run firms committed to striking a healthy balance between participatory decision making and efficient execution.

- PSF organizations are flat and lean, keeping bureaucracy to a minimum. Although variations emerged, PSF organizational models have many similarities (see Exhibit 10.3).

11

Style of Leadership
Characteristics, grooming, and advice

"The challenge is really how to take this very, very talented, high-strung group and mold them into a confident, cohesive team. It would be easier if they were less talented and more malleable."
—Ralph Shrader, Chairman and CEO, Booz Allen Hamilton

"You've got to convince people with whom you are working that they want to follow your vision."
—Ben Fisher, Principal and COO, Perkins+Will

"A good leader is someone who uses their mind for a sense of direction and analysis, their heart to manage the people, and their guts to have clear values and vision."
—David Dotlich, Founder and Chairman, Pivot Leadership

As stated at the beginning of this book—and as our research has amply demonstrated—leading a professional service firm isn't for the faint of heart. A successful leader of professionals wears an impressive array of hats: visionary, values watchdog, motivational coach, consensus builder, and, in many cases, rainmaker and revenue generator as well. Throughout this journey we were continually amazed at the candor, humor, and humility of these very impressive leaders of the world's top firms. They all clearly enjoy their jobs and were delighted to share their insights into the art and science of leading a complex professional service firm. But what makes them tick? What are the key characteristics of a successful leader, and how do firms find and groom future leaders?

Without a doubt, the alchemy of successful leadership is a seductive topic. Everyone wants to crack the code. Of all the ingredients in the professional service mix, leadership is probably the most essential to success—and often the most elusive. In most industries the person in the corner office calls the shots. Operating within a traditional command-and-control environment is relatively straightforward: the divisions between leading, managing, and following are clearly defined and widely understood. In contrast, the matrix structure that most professional service firms have embraced is a far more dynamic business model; it's flat, fluid, fragmented, and often unruly. "In a partnership," observed one CEO, "everyone's an owner, so you have to make sure that everyone's interest is heard and dealt with."

The core missions of a leader—to build the long-term value of a business and to protect and promote its brand—are goals that professional service leaders share with their counterparts in other industries. However, how those objectives are achieved differs dramatically in the professional service arena, where creating a cohesive, collaborative, and efficient environment is essential to success. Professional service firms are totally dependent on the productive capacity of the firm's professionals—the engine that drives performance and generates growth. One of a leader's primary jobs is to keep that engine humming and on track. As one CEO noted, "When you're running a professional service firm, you can't hide behind a gigantic portfolio of assets or a significant manufacturing capacity that's going to produce physical goods."

In a professional service setting, influence trumps control. Leadership requires powerful motivational skills and adroit maneuvering, coupled with the willingness to make tough calls and to take the heat for them. It also requires a consummate communicator to manage a partnership of equals in which everyone is an owner and entrepreneur.

Essential Characteristics of a Successful Leader: Emotional Intelligence and People Skills

"When I think of the former leaders in our organization, they have all had a restless nature, a sense of excitement and ambition to make our organization better, and an enthusiasm that was contagious."

"My job is to be the custodian of a great institution—to leave it better than I found it. I try to lead by consensus. I try to do it by listening carefully to the views of all those who want to express them, but it's never unanimous. And there are always going to be people who disagree. It's very easy to lose heart and lose your way."

We asked interviewees to describe the most important characteristics of a successful service firm leader, as shown in Exhibit 11.1. By a wide margin, the traits they believe define successful leadership fall under the umbrella of strong interpersonal skills and emotional intelligence. In fact, of the 12 success characteristics identified in our interviews, only one, "Understands the business," involves technical expertise. The other 11 qualities considered essential for effective leadership can accurately be described as soft skills necessary to effectively navigate the interpersonal dynamics of a partnership enterprise.

EXHIBIT 11.1 **Characteristics of a successful leader in a professional service firm**

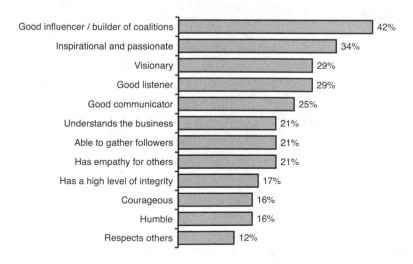

Good influencer / builder of coalitions	42%
Inspirational and passionate	34%
Visionary	29%
Good listener	29%
Good communicator	25%
Understands the business	21%
Able to gather followers	21%
Has empathy for others	21%
Has a high level of integrity	17%
Courageous	16%
Humble	16%
Respects others	12%

Good Influencer/Builder of Coalitions

When everyone in an organization is an owner, intellectually intense, and has a view of what should be done and how it should be accomplished, getting the buy-in necessary to make decisions can be an arduous process for those at the helm. Add a healthy dose of skepticism—one of the defining characteristics of a high-performing professional—and, according to our study respondents, you have a mix of traits that makes building a cohesive team immensely challenging. Yet achieving alignment among these high performers is critical to a leader's success in a professional service enterprise, according to many of the executives interviewed. Without it, strategic focus dissipates, a silo mentality predominates, and fragmentation occurs. Building consensus in an entrepreneurial environment requires a gifted facilitator. This person must command respect, inspire confidence, and reinforce cultural values within a firm's partner corps, while also reassuring individual performers that their experience and expertise will be recognized and rewarded. Shifting between mobilizing a partnership around pivotal decisions and managing the needs and expectations of what one CEO called "anxious overachievers" requires enormous patience and mental agility.

Inspirational and Passionate

The ability to inspire and excite people around ideas, strategies, and opportunities is one of the most compelling traits of a leader in virtually every industry. But when the business is dependent on strong individual performance, the ability to inspire people to operate at optimal levels and consistently provide excellent client service is of paramount importance. Passion, energy, and enthusiasm are the currency leaders use to obtain buy-in from their colleagues. As one managing partner told us, "If you don't passionately care about the business and the service you provide and the value you are bringing to clients, you should find something else to do."

Visionary

Our respondents placed high value on a leader's ability to create, clearly articulate, and align a partnership around a vision and then sustain that vision in the face of external and internal pressures. Time and again in our interviews, we heard that professional service leadership isn't just about the power of ideas; it's about emotionally engaging people around a shared vision. That vision must be both compelling and attainable in order to mobilize people to pursue it and to keep them on course. Respondents caution that leadership without followership does not work. Paul Reilly, CEO of financial services firm Raymond James, explained the concept, "The problem with leaders is that sometimes they convince themselves they've earned the right to lead, and they charge the next hill, and they turn around and there are no troops behind them. You can't be way out in front, and you can't be way out in back." Marcia Silverman, Chair of Ogilvy PR, has had the enviable opportunity of leading her firm through an unprecedented period of growth and renewal. She knows firsthand the importance of collaboration and communication as the firm progresses through change (see "Ogilvy Public Relations Worldwide: Leading Growth").

Good Listener

Almost one-third of respondents identified strong listening skills as one of the key requirements for successfully guiding a professional service firm. Here again, many interviewees raised the issue of striking a balance between listening long enough and well enough to gather input from the right people without being overwhelmed by the force of their positions or paralyzed by the diversity of their opinions. The appetite for debate in a professional service firm can be almost insatiable.

A good listener leaves his or her ego at the door while skillfully managing the egos of others. As one firm leader told us, "Strong leadership is grounded in the ability to listen and to be able to incorporate a lot of partner voices into a cohesive course of action—a program and a plan for how to move the company forward." The best firm leaders carefully consider the views of various internal constituencies before fully and firmly committing to a course of action, even in the face of powerful and vocal skepticism. As one firm chairman told us, "It's much more important that your partners believe that what you're going to do is the product of an inclusive open discussion rather than they believe it's the right thing to do."

Ogilvy Public Relations Worldwide: Leading Growth

During her 9-year tenure as CEO of Ogilvy PR, Marcia Silverman has led her firm's expansion into one of the communication industry's outstanding agencies worldwide. After 29 years in the business, she now serves as firm chair focused on building the firm's intellectual capital and providing strategic counsel to a select group of major clients.

Silverman presided over a situation that most leaders would envy: helping to chart her firm's future during a period of unprecedented global growth and change in the industry. In Silverman's view, overseeing growth on a global scale requires an activist manager—one who's both attuned to client needs and intensely involved in finding, developing, and retaining talent. Reflecting on her CEO role, she identified a number of critical leadership success factors:

- *Foster a nurturing culture.* "Culture is a very important word at Ogilvy PR," says Silverman. "One of the reasons for our success is our nurturing and collaborative culture." Culture emanates from the top and is reflected in how a firm's senior management team operates. Silverman built a team of people who respect one another, work well with each other, and model collaboration.

- *Value people's strengths.* In contrast to a "command-and-control" management style, Silverman adopted a "Let 1,000 flowers bloom" approach in leading Ogilvy PR. Instead of dictating policy, she focused heavily on building a strong management team—and on finding new talent and helping people discover and develop what they are best at. "You have to develop people from the very beginning," observes Silverman. "We've been most successful when we've cultivated future leadership from within."

- *Break down geographical barriers.* In her role as CEO, Silverman continually stressed the importance of breaking down regional barriers and promoting knowledge sharing and collaboration on a global level. As she puts it, "We want our practices to be global: We want to have Beijing work with Washington as well as Brussels." Moving in this direction is challenging, but Silverman believes it's vital to better serve the firm's global clients. Her successor as CEO is intent on continuing to build the firm's global presence and capabilities.

- *Respect intuition.* Silverman believes that intuition has played an important role in her development and that it's a critical, but undervalued, aspect of leadership in business. She recently taught a course at Georgetown University and found that while it is possible to teach the technical aspects of leading—such as how to delegate and develop a strategy—when it comes to building a welcoming culture, knowing how to inspire people, and fostering enduring client relationships, it's intuition, not formal training, that makes the difference.

Silverman says it is a mistake for women aspiring to leadership to act like the stereotypical authoritative figure. "People respect women leaders who teach, share, and collaboratively involve their people," says Silverman. "Women must honor and leverage their natural intuitive and nurturing natures."

Good Communicator

Effective leaders stay connected. They visit the trenches to identify issues and problems that need handling, they stay attuned to shifting levels of client and partner satisfaction, and they know the key internal stakeholders and regularly reach out to them. Bruce Boulware, retired COO of law firm O'Melveny & Myers, explained the dynamics, "Communication involves connection, constructive candor, and listening. It also involves curiosity—seeking contrasting views. That's how you get creativity and innovation and create forward thinking in a structured environment." Communication in normal times is important, but in a time of crisis it becomes imperative. Tim Flynn, Chairman of KPMG International, was thrust into the top position in the firm in a time of major turbulence. "Communication," said Flynn, "was perhaps my most important leadership lesson" (see "KPMG: Leading Through a Crisis").

KPMG: Leading Through a Crisis

KPMG International Chairman, Tim Flynn, knows a great deal about leadership in a time of crisis. Flynn assumed the role of Chairman of KPMG's U.S. member firm in June 2005 in the midst of two major firm events. In May KPMG learned that it faced government charges over tax shelters it had sold at an earlier time to individuals. And one month later the firm's much-loved Chairman, Eugene O'Kelly, was diagnosed with a brain tumor that gave him months to live.

O'Kelly quickly stepped down, and the leadership appointed Flynn. According to Flynn, "There was no time for a 100-day plan or an orderly transition; I had to jump in with both feet." The new Chairman faced four daunting tasks: confront the charges, calm and retain the firm's partners and employees, prevent an exodus of clients, and restore the firm's credibility.

- *Act decisively; communicate openly.* "When crises arise, leaders have only a short window of opportunity to make the right decisions, aggressively communicate what needs to be done, and then execute with little room for error," says Flynn.

  Within days of becoming Chairman, Flynn addressed the charges head-on, admitting wrongdoing and working with his new team over the summer to reach an agreement with the government that allowed the firm to move forward. He also quickly went to the partners to explain his plan. He asked them to give the new leadership team 90 days to sort through the issues and presented a set of guiding principles that the firm's leadership team would follow as they brought the matter to resolution. He repeated these guiding principles every time he spoke with the partners over the summer.

  Flynn personally contacted hundreds of partners individually to solicit feedback. Eight days after settling the case, Flynn called all partners to a face-to-face meeting in Dallas for an open-microphone Q&A session to frankly discuss the matter and respond directly to questions. He and his team set forth the significant changes they would put in place to ensure that something like this would never happen again. This was part of a broader strategy designed to engage partners and employees through consistent, direct communication with leadership.

The firm also worked hard to communicate with clients. Flynn, John Veihmeyer (who was elected KPMG Deputy Chairman the same time Flynn became Chairman of the U.S. firm), KPMG partner Sven Holmes (a former federal judge), and Executive Vice Chair of Operations, Jack Taylor, visited more than 100 audit clients to answer questions and aggressively address any lingering concerns.

Reflecting on the experience, Flynn says, "One of the chief lessons I learned is the importance of open and honest communications. You must be willing to put yourself out in front and acknowledge when you don't know everything. Don't overpromise, be realistic, and present a process to deal with the crisis and then execute against it."

Flynn, who was elected Chairman of KPMG International in 2007, adds, "In situations like these, you cannot predict exactly how things will turn out. But people are concerned; they have a strong need to understand how events may impact them directly. It is very important to clearly communicate the key elements of any resolution. We set forth very early on a set of guiding principles that would be the basis for any final decision. These guiding principles allowed the partners to understand what the firm would look like upon resolution and how it would impact them and their teams."

• *Ethics and integrity are key.* "For any organization to establish or restore credibility, it starts with having the right corporate culture," says Flynn. "Are people incentivized to do the right thing? Does the culture value and reward integrity? Is long-term growth valued over short-term gain?"

Flynn and his team quickly made changes to the firm's governance structure and launched a rigorous ethics and compliance program to embed and enforce an ethical culture into the organization. He believes such initiatives are crucial for all organizations.

"When people ask me what it takes to be successful, I used to answer hard work, skills, and a little bit of luck. I don't discount any of those attributes, but these days I emphasize what I used to take for granted—that *the* most important way to be successful is to act with integrity," adds Flynn.

Understands the Business

Understanding the business is a given for leaders of professional service firms. Virtually all the leaders we interviewed grew up in their respective professions and are highly skilled and respected in their areas of expertise. Many have spent their entire careers in the organizations they now lead. All have managed some of their firm's most valued client relationships and have generated significant revenue over time.

Some leaders acknowledge that the best client service professionals are sometimes not the best firm leaders. Leading a firm and leading a client engagement require very different sets of skills. However, no one we interviewed contested the importance of having hands-on knowledge of the business. David Childs, Global Partner of Clifford Chance, gave up his title as leader of the firm's Corporate M&A practice, a role he truly enjoyed, and made the difficult decision to forgo billable work to focus on firm management (see "Clifford Chance: Leading Through Transition").

To Bill or Not to Bill

"The idea that the managing partner needs to be billable in order to have credibility with partners is just baffling. You get your credibility with partners by doing a good job at whatever you're doing. If you're a client-facing partner, you do it by doing a great client job. If you're a managing partner, you do it by doing a great job of managing the firm, not by giving a load of tax advice."

"A lot of partners would say that was part of why we are successful: We have somebody who eats, sleeps, and wakes up thinking about the firm and not about a client."

Should leaders also be revenue producers, or should they focus solely on running the business? To bill or not to bill emerged as one of the most hotly debated issues in our research, with respondents registering strong opinions on both sides.

Overall, retaining a producer role clearly outstripped the pure-leadership position. Sixty percent of respondents said they are billable, and 40 percent described themselves as nonbillable, as shown in Exhibit 11.2.

Clifford Chance: Leading Through Transition

In 2003, David Childs became COO of Clifford Chance, one of the world's largest law firms; in 2006, he was elected Global Managing Partner. In assuming his management positions, Childs gave up his title as practice leader of the firm's Corporate M&A practice, a role he relished. He also decided to "put the firm first" and forgo billable work, although he continues to spend time with clients.

During his tenure, Childs has led Clifford Chance through a major transition: reducing its partnership ranks by 15 percent, relocating many of its support staff functions to India (see "Clifford Chance Offshoring Program" in Chapter 10, "Structure"), and maintaining its strategic direction in the face of global financial turmoil. In describing his straightforward style, Childs observes, "I think a lot of people in management roles overcomplicate it all. People like clarity. I try and keep messages very simple, very clear, and, if necessary, very aspirational—setting high targets."

- *Choose your goals carefully, and execute consistently.* According- ing to Childs, the best advice he received on management was to stay focused. When he started his new job, someone told him, "The very first thing to do is write a list of five or six things you want to achieve during your 4-year term. Stick to that list, and prioritize your time by doing things that will lead to its achievement." Building on his background, Childs says, "I really apply M&A techniques. If I need to get from A to H, I systematically go from A to H and don't let my team deviate from that goal."

- *Don't spin bad news.* Sugarcoating tough messages can be misleading and counterproductive. In people businesses, notes Childs, managers tend to shy away from delivering bad news or confronting underperformance. In his experience, it's best to be "open and very honest and not spin things." After gaining consensus for the decision to reduce the firm's partnership, Childs delivered the tough news to some of his colleagues in a caring but straightforward and businesslike way.

- *Invite questions in times of uncertainty.* As a leader, it's impor- tant that you appear upbeat and confident about the future. The best way to allay anxiety in uncertain times is to commu- nicate often and through face-to-face meetings as much as possible. In periods of turmoil, Childs encourages people to ask him whatever they want; nothing is off-limits. If people hesitate to raise issues publicly, he urges them to ask questions privately via e-mail.

- *Don't let external events derail your strategy.* When faced with a crisis—the financial meltdown of 2008, for example—reacting to short-term events, however traumatic, can endanger your strategy. If you believe that your direction remains the right one over the long term, don't deviate from it. In spite of the financial crisis and its impact on major clients, Clifford Chance continued investing and pursuing its growth objectives. Keeping its management team intact in the face of major disruption was one of the keys to maintaining a steady course.

- *Consider coaching as a management tool.* Clifford Chance as a firm views expert coaching as a valuable resource. From a management perspective, coaching is very useful in reinforcing strengths and addressing gaps. Childs has used coaches to sharpen his communication skills and as sounding boards.

Elected in 2010 to a second 4-year term and lauded by his partners for his efforts, Childs feels honored to have been entrusted with the job of steering his firm through a difficult period in its history. Even so, he readily admits that "I'm never satisfied by how the firm performs. We can always do better."

EXHIBIT 11.2   Producer-manager versus full-time leadership

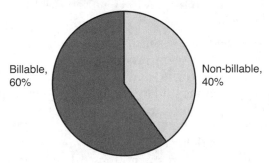

Billable, 60%

Non-billable, 40%

Although the majority of our interview base is firmly in the billable category, the degree of individual billability varies dramatically. Some leaders indicated that they spend 10 percent of their time on revenue-generating client work, and others said they devote up to 80 percent of their time to clients. We hypothesized that the larger the firm in size and revenues, the smaller the percentage of time a leader bills. But, somewhat surprisingly, even in the firms surveyed that had revenues of more than $10 billion, we found leaders with varying degrees of client responsibilities.

Those who advocate a producer-manager model cited three major reasons for their stance. Many leaders feel strongly that they must remain engaged in the firm's mainline activity—which is, of course, working with clients. Actively working with clients, solving client problems, and identifying opportunities raises the leader's stature and enhances his or her ability to lead in a professional service firm. As one CEO explained, "The principle is that if you are going to lead a group of people like our firm of professional succeeders, you need to have established your credentials outside the building."

Along with maintaining credibility, billable leaders cited the importance of staying in touch with their profession, clients, and markets. Without billable activities to anchor a leader to the professionals and the marketplace, it is all too easy to become disconnected from both partner priorities and client needs. The marketplace can be very fluid for professional services, and active client work can help leaders stay on top of market needs and trends.

Finally, the majority of leaders who remain billable clearly enjoy working with clients and choose not to sacrifice the satisfaction it gives them to the administrative demands that leadership imposes. They find it personally rewarding to develop their professional discipline during a peak period in their careers, and they see client work as an invigorating antidote to the responsibilities of leading a diverse, often fractious, partner corps.

On the other hand, the two out of five respondents who reject the producer-manager model believe that growing a business and direct client work can and should be mutually exclusive. Those firmly entrenched in the nonbillable camp offered two primary reasons for their position. First, they contend, it is incredibly difficult to function as a revenue producer on major client engagements while adequately addressing the myriad issues associated with building a business based on a participatory matrix model. Far from helping leaders stay connected to clients and markets, according to this view, the demands of billable work can be a dangerous distraction which can divert a leader's energy and focus from both short-term threats and long-term strategic planning.

Second, those who believe that the producer-manager model isn't conducive to successful leadership dispute the idea that revenue generating is required to keep a finger on the pulse of the market. They contend that a leader doesn't need to be immersed in billable client work to preserve active, productive relationships with key clients and/or to stay attuned to marketplace realities. In their view, a leader can successfully maintain and energize client-and-market connections by serving as a sounding board for partners on high-profile client engagements or by meeting with project teams and clients on a regular basis. Several CEOs say they have adopted a nonbillable advisory role with major firm clients. This role allows them to interact with clients and firm partners on high-impact projects while freeing them from the accountability and time constraints of project management.

One CEO said neither end of the spectrum works that well. As he summed it up, "Heavily-focused client people don't have the vision and breadth to lead and deliver change. People who don't spend time with clients get out of touch with the business and lose traction with the partners." The key, according to most firm leaders, is to find the proper balance that works most effectively in your own organization.

Grooming a Global Leadership Corps: Finding and Nurturing Future Leaders

"You can tell very quickly whether someone's got the spark that will inspire other people and can transmit electricity to the rest of the organization."

"We try to identify future stars and be sure they are given a good mentor really early on. If you ask every one of our senior people, they will name someone who mentored them."

In successful professional service firms, as elsewhere, leadership is not confined to the top; it cascades throughout the organization. Along with recruiting new talent, building a robust, self-renewing leadership corps is one of the major preoccupations of the senior executives charged with guiding their firms' futures. Are leaders born, or can leadership be taught? No clear consensus emerged. Some CEOs asserted that there is an undeniable "leadership spark"—a natural ability that's inherent; some people have it, and some people don't. Other respondents asserted that leaders are "made rather than born" and that grooming them is more a matter of development than destiny.

But wherever they land on the "born versus made" spectrum, we found strong agreement on the critical importance of developing leadership talent. The approaches that leaders and their firms have adopted for identifying and developing potential leaders run the gamut from ad hoc, "let talent bubble up" approaches to formal programs. We did find broad consensus on two issues. Most believe that identifying and cultivating fledgling leaders very early in their careers is key, and most feel that their firms could benefit from a more systematic leadership development strategy.

The leadership development approaches fall into four not mutually exclusive categories:

- **Informally providing exposure and opportunities for growth**—A significant number of respondents believe that leaders are groomed most effectively by allowing them to progress naturally through the organization. Most leaders we spoke with advanced through the ranks by taking on a rich mix of assignments with progressively increasing management responsibilities. Supporters of this approach believe that leaders develop experientially by observing and learning from others—absorbing knowledge about the business and about their strengths, weaknesses, and management styles.

- **Internal exchange programs/management rotations**—Quite a few firm leaders say they effectively use internal exchange programs to move promising young professionals around the organization to experience and learn the geographic and skill dimensions of the business. As one managing partner told us, "We grow up in the practice and office silos in our organizations, and it is very difficult to capture the big picture of the business for most professionals."

  At HOK, for example, the firm has made a concerted effort to identify leadership qualities it wants to foster: personal character and integrity, financial ability, and professional excellence.

The firm has put in place an internal exchange program in which promising young performers are relocated for 6 months at a time and exposed to different kinds of work in a different part of the world. According to HOK Vice Chairman Clark Davis, outstanding performers are invited to participate in leadership initiatives such as special boards or task groups.

Similarly, the international law firm Cuatrecasas, Gonçalves Pereira has designed a fast-track career program for academically gifted professionals. Every 6 months for a period of two and a half years, these lawyers are rotated from practice to practice and office to office, gaining invaluable exposure to the firm's clients in major economic centers, including New York, London, Madrid, and Paris.

- **Mentoring**—One-on-one coaching is one of the tools that many professional service firms use to give promising performers an up-close and personal look at team building, decision making, and practice management. Having a seasoned professional offer guidance on client problems, internal growth opportunities, and interpersonal issues can be a huge benefit to a young, ambitious professional—and help put him or her on the fast track to a leadership position, according to many respondents. Although formal mentoring programs are often challenging to manage in professional service firms, we found some good examples of mentoring and "buddy programs." These are discussed in detail in Chapter 3, "People."

- **Formal development programs**—We uncovered some impressive formal leadership development programs in several of the firms studied. The common elements of our top-rated programs include early identification of future leaders—typically in the first 3 to 5 years, ongoing training modules that progress over several years, formal mentoring and review by senior partners, and special task force assignments for the team in training. The investment these firms make in leadership development is significant, but the payoff, they say, is worth it. As one CEO told us, "Recruits love it, clients appreciate it and see the benefits, and the firm has a steady pipeline of capable future leaders to take us forward."

A growing number of firms have committed major resources to either intensive or ongoing leadership training for gifted professionals who have the potential to assume top management positions. O'Melveny & Myers has teamed with the Kellogg School of Management in Illinois to develop a customized executive education program for the firm's leadership team (see "Cultivating Leadership at O'Melveny & Myers").

Ketchum created the Ketchum Leadership Institute to help developing leaders understand the firm values and behaviors, and explore the characteristics of their leadership and how those characteristics resonate with the firm's values. Dewberry annually targets 15 to 20 outstanding performers for a special leadership program (see "Emerging Leaders Program at Dewberry").

Cultivating Leadership at O'Melveny & Myers

Founded in the late 1800s, the law firm of O'Melveny & Myers has grown into a far-flung global enterprise with 1,000 lawyers in 14 offices around the world. In an effort to unify the firm in the face of fast-paced expansion over the past decade, the firm's partners developed a values statement around a set of core principles—excellence, leadership, and citizenship. As the firm grew in size and diversity, effective leadership emerged as one of the key attributes that it wanted to cultivate in order to promote camaraderie, transcend cultural differences among its global partnership, and effectively connect strategy and people.

With this in mind, in 2006, the firm's Chair, A.B. Culvahouse, Jr., commissioned a task force that led to the establishment of the O'Melveny & Myers Leadership Institute, a customized executive education program. To help design and run the Institute, the firm teamed up with the prestigious Kellogg School of Management in Illinois. The Institute's overarching objective was to provide partners and senior managers with leadership training that is relevant to their markets, sensitive to cultural issues, and responsive to fundamental changes in the global economy.

Collaboration between O'Melveny and Kellogg has been close and intense. The law firm appointed a team of partners and staff led by then-Chief Operating Officer Bruce Boulware and Michelle Egan, its Managing Director of Talent Development. This team joined forces with Kellogg faculty members and Joe Hannigan, Kellogg's Academic Director, to tailor the program to O'Melveny's goals and global leadership structure. The result is a high-impact, transformational program that is bringing a new level of cohesiveness to the firm's worldwide partnership.

Since the program's launch, almost 200 O'Melveny partners and senior business managers have traveled to Kellogg's Allen Center from each of its 14 offices for intensive weeklong leadership development sessions. The topics on their agendas range from strategic planning, building client relationships, and fostering innovation to team dynamics and values-based decision making. According to Boulware, "It has been an exceptional relationship, providing our partners and senior managers with leadership learning in the context of our markets and other issues."

The development approach is stimulating and hands-on. Small groups focus on bringing fresh ideas and insights to real-life challenges and opportunities facing O'Melveny & Myers. One of the biggest benefits is the chance to meet and interact with far-flung colleagues on relevant projects that contribute to the firm's future success. Ultimately, O'Melveny intends to have all 250 partners, as well as selected managers, take part in the Leadership Institute program.

Given the volatility of the global marketplace and the increasingly complex needs of its clients, O'Melveny & Myers sees the training that the Institute provides as essential to its growth. As Culvahouse puts it, "Effective leadership and teamwork are more important now than at any time in our firm's history. This is an effort from which we will benefit for many years to come."

Emerging Leaders Program at Dewberry

Architectural and engineering firm Dewberry launched an Emerging Leaders Program in 2006 to groom future leaders. According to former CEO Ron Ewing, "The firm just wasn't seeing a big enough pool of internal candidates to move into leadership positions."

The program is a year-long development program for a class of 15 to 20 staff who have been with the firm for a minimum of 2 years and have from 5 to 10 years of experience. The program is open to both architectural and engineering staff as well as to marketing, legal, and HR employees. As Ewing explains, "We are looking for a mix of technical and support staff backgrounds. We're hopeful that each team member will move into a project management role and then aspire to leading a larger group—maybe a department or ultimately an office."

At the beginning of each year, each office manager or business unit manager is invited to write a letter of recommendation nominating one or more staff members to attend the program. A steering committee including the CEO, COO, Training and Development (T&D) Director, and selected regional and division managers reviews the list of recommendations, along with each candidate's performance reviews and salary history for the last 3 years. The committee short-lists about 20 to 30 nominees, who are asked to write a one- or two-page self-assessment and narrative of how they think the program will benefit them. "We're looking for insight, self-awareness, an interest in self-improvement, and either a career or professional goal that will be advanced by their participation in the program," says Ewing. The committee discusses each candidate in detail and selects the finalists. Each candidate, whether chosen for the program or not, receives a debriefing from his or her manager or the T&D Director.

The program involves a development workshop each month. The team is responsible for a special group project as well as an individual development project that must be completed at year's end. Once a year the firm hosts an alumni event at firm headquarters for all program participants to meet and network. According to

Ewing, the program has really caught on. Over one-third of the staff has asked their managers to be considered for the program. "I think it's very important that our people understand that we are investing in them as individuals," says Ewing. "And, of course, if they are successful as individuals, they tend to stay with the company, and the company will be successful, but it's more important that they know we care about them as a person."

Dewberry tracks program participants to determine how many are actually promoted, and it tracks the group's turnover rate in comparison to the larger population. "We see a marked improvement in the people that come out of the program," says Ewing. "They are better employees, better project managers, and better communicators. We really do have a cadre of individuals with a very broad understanding of the company."

Some Parting Advice for Leaders

"Be sure you want to do it."

"There is an under appreciation for the skill it takes to lead one of these kinds of businesses."

"Be honest. If you erode trust, the entire organization can collapse like a house of cards. Walk the walk, own fault, admit mistakes."

We asked interviewees to give us a few words of parting advice for other firm leaders. We got some wonderful one-liners, such as "Don't drink your own bathwater," and quite a few cautionary thoughts, including "Be very careful out there," "Don't forget to breathe," and "Stay healthy." Following are a few common themes that emerged from these discussions:

- *Adopt a leadership mind-set.* Recognize that you are now a leader. See this as a new phase of your career that requires an entirely new set of skills and priorities, and allocate your time and energy accordingly.
- *Stay open and curious.* Being a leader is a continual learning process. Being open to new ideas is vital. Stay fresh and

engaged by asking questions, talking to people, reading, and keeping abreast of new technology and its impact on your business. Always try to learn something new every day.

- *Invest in your own development.* Professional service leaders tend to focus on everyone else's development and neglect their own. Many high-level leadership programs are available. Stimulate your creativity and stoke your passion by choosing one that gives you insights into the leadership styles of successful people in other industries.

- *Reflect; don't just react.* The day-to-day demands of running a partnership can be incredibly demanding and time-consuming; firefighting is part of the job description. It's important to step back periodically and take time to reflect on the big picture: emerging client issues, long-term strategic imperatives, and global market trends.

- *Keep your nerve.* Remember that no one is as smart as they'd like to be, and no one can see the future. Listen before you act, but don't let listening immobilize you. Ultimately, you must make a decision, live with it, and do the best you can. Never be afraid to make a mistake. Admit it if you're wrong, and then try something else.

Author's Note ──────────────

I believe this book presents a very good picture of the professional service industry, and I feel privileged to have had the opportunity to interview the impressive firm leaders who participated in our study.

But as I step back to review the manuscript, I realize that we've really only scratched the surface of this fascinating business. There are so many more firms to study, topics to examine, and examples to present. About six months before finishing the initial draft, I told anyone who made the mistake of asking how it was going that I would never write another book. But just like childbirth, the pain fades, and my next book on the industry is brewing in my head.

In the meantime, let's keep the dialogue going. We have created a tremendous network of senior leaders across segments who have much to share. Repeatedly during our conversations we uncovered wish lists of topics—from strategic to tactical—that our interviewees asked us to explore with other leaders.

Broderick & Company will be launching a series of activities—webcasts, e-newsletters, and an ongoing survey program—to continue to take the pulse of the industry and share knowledge. Please send me your wish list of areas and issues to investigate, and we will incorporate your ideas into our continued studies. I hope you found many valuable takeaways in this book, and I look forward to our continued conversation.

Maureen Broderick
mbroderick@broderickco.com
www.broderickco.com

INDEX

 Wharton School Publishing

In the face of accelerating turbulence and change, business leaders and policy makers need new ways of thinking to sustain performance and growth.

Wharton School Publishing offers a trusted source for stimulating ideas from thought leaders who provide new mental models to address changes in strategy, management, and finance. We seek out authors from diverse disciplines with a profound understanding of change and its implications. We offer books and tools that help executives respond to the challenge of change.

Every book and management tool we publish meets quality standards set by The Wharton School of the University of Pennsylvania. Each title is reviewed by the Wharton School Publishing Editorial Board before being given Wharton's seal of approval. This ensures that Wharton publications are timely, relevant, important, conceptually sound or empirically based, and implementable.

To fit our readers' learning preferences, Wharton publications are available in multiple formats, including books, audio, and electronic.

To find out more about our books and management tools, visit us at whartonsp.com and Wharton's executive education site, exceed.wharton.upenn.edu.

 Wharton
UNIVERSITY *of* PENNSYLVANIA

 Pearson
Education